# inspired
# 3D MODELING AND TEXTURE MAPPING

**TOM CAPIZZI**

**Publisher:** Stacy L. Hiquet

**Marketing Manager:** Heather Buzzingham

**Managing Editor:** Sandy Doell

**Acquisitions Editor:** Kevin Harreld

**Project Editor:** Amy Pettinella

**Marketing Coordinator:** Kelly Poffenbarger

**Technical Reviewer:** Rick Grandy

**Development Editor:** Kevin Harreld

**Copy Editor:** Laura Gabler

**Interior Layout:** Bill Hartman

**Cover Design:** Michael Ford

**Indexer:** Sharon Shock

ISBN: 1-931841-50-0

Library of Congress Catalog Card Number: 2001098235

Printed in the United States of America

02 03 04 05 SP 10 9 8 7 6 5 4 3 2 1

*To My Sons, Chris and Nelson*

# Foreword

By Douglas Smith

Visual Effects Supervisor

Working in the field of visual effects, I think about my contribution to the world. There is so much apparent imbalance in the human condition. How does the importance of what I do for a living compare to that of a doctor, a politician, or a fast food worker?

When I think about how my work contributes to society as a whole, I feel there are two ways to measure the value: one is pure entertainment, which has some value, and the other more important way is inspiring imagination.

Imagination is probably the most important factor in problem solving and literally creating the future that we will all inhabit. Right now the visual effects world occupies a unique place in the global culture as a way of presenting new ideas through the storytelling process. At the same time the visual effects world seems to parallel other areas of creative work.

One day while I was watching television, I thought of a way that imagination was enhanced through visual effects. The sound was off on the show I was watching, but I saw a shot of a person drawing pencil lines around a two-dimensional geometric shape. This shot on the television dissolved into a shot of a 3-D wireframe object rotating on the screen of a monitor. As the camera pulled back, I recognized Frank Gehry, the architect viewing the rotating digital form. Even without any audio, I understood instantly that he was "previsualizing" a new building design with the help of a digital model.

The fact that I could so quickly understand the 3-D form made me think of how today's world of architecture is related to visual effects. Then it occurred to me that medicine, engineering, vehicle design (auto to aeronautical), publishing, computer games, advertising, and the Internet are all areas where visual effects is changing the way that objects are being visualized.

The common thread seems to be the use of the computer and the problem-solving thought process. It is an interesting type of "convergence" because it would seem to indicate the processes are developing a common language. Twenty years ago the ability to model and texture an object in 3-D on the computer was essentially non-existent, except in the crudest forms with the most expensive computers. Today, it is staggering what can be done with fairly inexpensive software and hardware. This process is opening up the ability to let imaginations flow on an individual level regardless of where one lives and increasing creativity on a global scale.

Also, twenty years ago a "blue screen shot" seemed like magic to most people even in the movie industry. Today, the concept behind a "blue screen shot" is readily understandable for anyone who has played around with digital photos or attempted to put together a presentation using a computer.

In a parallel situation, today, the concept behind a medical research simulation would probably be understood quickly by someone who is doing simulations for car design, airplane design, city planning, and especially 3-D visual effects.

The visual effects industry has built tools that attempt to simulate and alter what we understand to be visual reality. These tools are not limited by the rules of physics. This means one can "fake" reality if it achieves the desired result.

The truth is, faking reality is what visual effects is all about. Digital effects, like traditional miniature effects, demand that only what appears in the final shot is built and animated for the camera. There is no reason to build a model of a car complete with working mechanics, just to get a shot of a car traveling down a road. Unlike traditional miniature effects, however, digital models do not require wires or armatures to create animation. Digital models defy the bounds of the physical world.

Areas within visual effects have many more man hours applied to them than in other disciplines. There is a daily quest to represent nature and the world around us as seamlessly as possible while still having the ability to control the action and tell the story. Because the digital world is still in its relative infancy, the tools of modeling and texturing are changing at a dramatic rate. These tools are constantly being optimized and refined.

Innovation starts with imagination. Visual effects people problem-solve all day long. Their job is to use their imaginations and to help create the future. I hope the projects we work on help create a better future.

DS

## About Douglas Smith:

*Douglas Smith, a visual effects supervisor living in Los Angeles, worked on* Star Wars *at the beginning of his career. His visual effects work continued when he worked as a partner at Apogee. He has worked on such films like* Star Trek: The Motion Picture, Never Say Never Again, Coming to America, Firefox, *and* My Stepmother is an Alien.

*In 1996, Doug shared the Academy Award® for his special effects supervision on* Independence Day. *More recently, Doug has been heavily involved with digital production, supervising the digital effects work on* Dr. Dolittle 2, Flintstones in Viva Rock Vegas, *and some computer animation sequences in Tim Burton's* Planet of the Apes.

# Acknowledgments

I would like to thank my family for their time and understanding, which made this book possible.

I would also like to thank the folks at Premier Press for helped me more than they know. Thanks to Kevin Harreld and Amy Pettinella who helped create this book, and taught me the process of writing a book, for which I will always be grateful. Thanks to Laura Gabler for making my text readable.

Thanks to Rick Grandy, a smart guy who held my feet to the fire. I am truly grateful for his contribution.

Thanks to the folks at Rhythm & Hues who made this book possible. I would like to thank John Hughes, Randy Roberts, Pauline Tso, Bill Kroyer, Richard Hollander, Doug Smith, Scot Byrd, Stacy Burstin, Dan Quarnstrom, and all of the other folks who personally provided some of the best material that appears in this book. I would also like to extend special thanks to Eileen Jensen, and the lighting supervisors on *Scooby-Doo* for their patience during the time it took to create this book. Creating a talking dog is hard work; it is even harder while writing a book.

I would also like to thank the other authors in the "Inspired" series, because this was truly a group project. Thanks to Mike Ford for being there, even at 2:00 in the morning, to make these books better. Thanks to Kyle Clark and Dave Parrish for making sure that we stayed on the same page.

Also, special thanks to the people who made contributions to this book: Lopsie Schwartz, Travis Price, Jef Shears, Dane Shears, Max Ancar, Tom Dickens, Ken Brilliant, Jay Johnson, Ian Hulbert, Yeen-Shi Chen, Chien-Hsiung Wang, Allison Yerxa, Paul Giacoppo, and all of the other folks who provided their valuable time and work.

# About the Author

Tom Capizzi, currently a technical director at Rhythm & Hues Studios, has been involved with many aspects of computer graphics for over 13 years. During that time, he has also accumulated over 11 years of teaching experience at such respected schools as Center for Creative Studies in Detroit, Academy of Art in San Francisco, and Art Center College of Design in Pasadena.

His teaching awards include the bestowment of the Art Center Digital Research Project Grant for the year 2000 (DRP 2000), where Tom researched the use of acquired 3-D data to create models and texture maps for film and video production.

Tom spent several years in the Detroit area working on engineering visualization at Ford Motor Company and computer aided industrial design (CAID) at Sundberg-Ferar, an industrial design firm that has been in business for over 65 years.

He was also manager of the animation department at Atari Games in Milpitas, California, where he managed over 40 digital artists and art-directed the arcade game *San Francisco Rush*.

Tom is currently working in the field of feature film production. Working at Rhythm & Hues since 1996, he has worked as a modeling and lighting technical director on many feature productions. His credit list includes *Dr. Dolittle 2, The Flintstones in Viva Rock Vegas, Spawn, Stuart Little, Mystery Men, Babe 2: Pig in the City, Mouse Hunt,* and *Scooby-Doo*.

# Contents at a Glance

# Contents

# Introduction to *Inspired 3D Modeling*

This book is intended to be an overview of a very broad and complex area of specialization. It is intended to be the book that I wanted to read while I was starting out in the field of modeling and texture mapping. There were many things I wanted to know. How did computers start being used for commercials and film? Who was there when the first flying logo was animated in a feature film opening? Why are there so many ways to model one thing? And which way is the best for which situation?

This book is written from the view of the inside of the production environment. I cannot say I know all of the answers, but I am very fortunate to have access to many people who do know the answers, and when I didn't know, I went out of my way to find out. I did this because I wanted to write a book that I would want to buy.

There is material in this book that cannot be found in any other book. It is geared toward the individuals who are serious about getting involved with production quality modeling and texture mapping. This book is not a software manual. The procedures in this book are illustrated using Maya, a high quality 3-D software package. But, Maya is a tool. This is not an owner's manual; it is a book about a trade. This book is not about a single tool in the toolbox.

I try to introduce the reader to principles and practices that can be applied to any quality 3-D software package. As anyone who has been in the 3-D digital production business will tell you, all 3-D packages have basically the same tools, the buttons are just in different places. This book will focus on the modeling practices that tie these different packages together, the geometric entity types common to all 3-D software packages, the practices to get 2-D texture maps on models, the insights from people who invented the computer graphic business, and advice from the people who are working in the business.

I feel very passionate about this technology. I began working with computers as a logical extension of the markers and airbrushes I used to create realistic renderings by hand. An airbrush artist can work 40 hours on one image just to try to achieve realism. Computers today can display images in real-time that can fool the eye into believing that the image is real. The key to this realism lies with the models and the texture maps. 3-D geometry, in the computer, is real. The highlights running across the edges of the objects are the same highlights we see on real objects, the sheen passing across the digital character's skin is the same specular sheen we have on our skin. These practices of modeling and texture mapping are based on reality. Is it any wonder that we are getting to the point where we cannot trust our own eyes when we see computer-generated images?

Once the artist understands these practices, he or she can begin to use these tools to create his or her own realities. This is not just what we do for a living, it is a way of looking at the world.

Recently I was fortunate enough to visit the Aquarium of the Pacific in Long Beach. The creatures that inhabit these environments are excellent examples of a different view of the world. The majority of the people who passed by these fantastic creatures felt that they just saw a "real cool fish." This book is for the people who saw more than that. This book is for the visionaries. For those individuals who can sit in front of a tank of aluminum-colored fish and industrial-looking giant crabs and create a story where these creatures inhabit a world in which the sounds of an off-planet mining colony are churning in the background, this book is for you.

*Inspired 3D Modeling and Texture Mapping* was written to give you the tools you need to create your visions.

# Computer Graphics Primer

This primer is a short description of some technical aspects surrounding the world of computer graphics. The concepts discussed are the backbone for how 3D software works. A basic understanding of these elements will be crucial to navigating the CG environment.

## The Basics

The structure of the worlds that we create within 3D are complex systems that can be a little overwhelming. Whether you are new to 3D or need a quick guide to refresh your memory, use this primer as a reference to the basic elements of computer graphics. By understanding the basics of your 3D software, you can take your first steps toward developing your skills in the fascinating world of computer graphics.

### Cartesian Coordinate System

The three-dimensional (3D) world in computer graphics applications is visualized using the Cartesian Coordinate System.

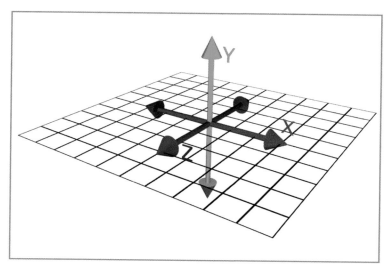

**Figure I.1**
The three components of the CCS system are X (width), Y (height), and Z (depth). The center of the 3D world (0, 0, 0) is referred to as the "origin."

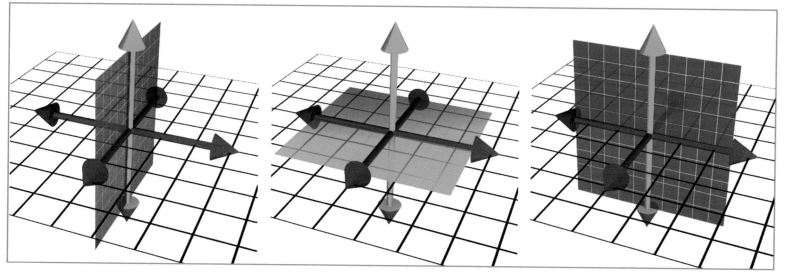

**Figure I.2**
The three major planes about the origin are the XY, XZ, and YZ.

### Right- and Left-Handed Systems

The "hand" is a way to determine which direction of any component (x, y, or z) is positive or negative in relation to the others. To determine positive versus negative in either system, hold up the appropriate hand, palm toward your face. Stick your thumb out to the side; this represents positive X. Point your index finger straight up; this shows positive Y. Extend the middle finger toward your face; it's pointing out positive Z.

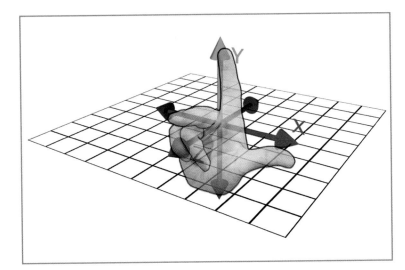

**Figure I.3**
Maya is a right-handed system.

### Hierarchy

A hierarchy is a relationship of nodes to other nodes described in terms of parent, child, and sibling. By default, a child node will inherit what is done to its parent node, transforming along with it and maintaining the same spatial relationship.

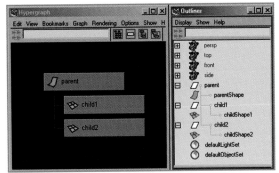

**Figure I.4**
A parent/child hierarchy.

### Transformations (World, Local, Object, Gimbal)

The transform mode determines how you interactively manipulate nodes by changing what relationship you modify. **World space** manipulates an object with an axis of the same orientation as the world, regardless of the hierarchy. **Local space** is an alignment of the transform axis to the parent of the object. The transform channels of a node (rotate, translate, scale) are all stored in local space. **Object space** is the result of an object's transform in addition to the hierarchy above it.

**Gimbal space** is a breakdown of local space rotations. It displays each axis separately, showing you each rotation channel's actual orientation, rather than the accumulation of them as is shown in local space. Object rotation occurs one axis at a time. The **rotation order** (by default: x, y, z) specifies which axis rotates first, second, and third. Similar to a hierarchy built with the first axis on the bottom and last axis on top, the first axis inherits the rotation of the second and third. The second axis inherits the rotation of the third; the third axis inherits the rotations of the parent.

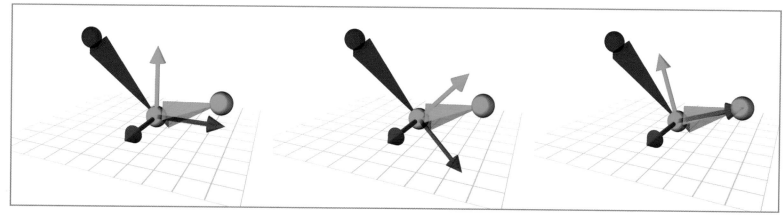

**Figure I.5**
World space, Local space, and Object space (from left to right).

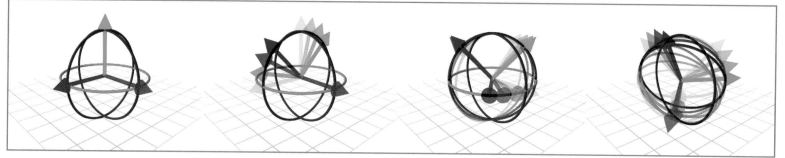

**Figure I.6**
Displaying Gimbal: no rotations, x rotation; adding y rotation; adding z rotations.

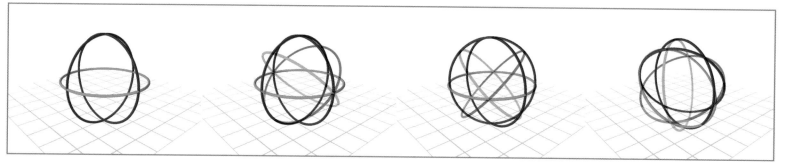

**Figure I.7**
The resulting local rotation rings over the Gimbal rings.

# 3D MODELING AND TEXTURE MAPPING

# PART I

# CG Overview

# chapter 1
# Industry Background

This book guides you through the intricacies of 3-D modeling and texture mapping. You should understand that these things are a small part of a larger industry that includes discrete disciplines (lighting, setup, and animation). Other parts of this profession include different studios, economic factors, and other influences that will affect your work in this field as profoundly as any new modeling or painting feature in your favorite software. Because modeling 3-D models and texture mapping these models are varied disciplines that are directly tied to computer graphics in general, it is appropriate to examine the scope of computer graphics to understand modeling and texture mapping.

Computer graphics for entertainment is a specialized area of computer graphics. Entertainment graphics has become a huge industry by itself. This relatively new business has allowed people equipped with training, talent, and interest in creating beautiful images an opportunity to participate in high-profile film and video game projects. People entering the computer graphics industry with modeling and texture mapping skills can take advantage of opportunities in film, television, and games. No other time in the history of entertainment have so many opportunities been available to so many people. It must be made clear, however, that these opportunities are business opportunities. No industry exists without a flow of money in and out of the hands of the people involved with the business aspect of the industry. A brief overview of the business side of the industry is explained in this chapter.

No industry, including computer modeling, is born in a vacuum. Special effects created with real explosions and traditional photography gave way to digital means of creating the same kind of images. Animation created using cels and hand-drawn characters now had the technology to dramatically increase productivity and tell the same stories in new ways with an incredible new look. Designers who were responsible for directing these first digital images also played an important part in creating the images that defined the industry. These issues will be discussed in this chapter, and some of the people who were involved with these issues will be introduced.

## Business Overview

Throughout the lifetime of any industry, computer graphics being no exception, are high points and low points in the amount of work available and the amount of money that can be made in that industry. The trend over the last few years indicates that the computer graphics industry is restructuring itself. The industry is becoming more focused on project-based hiring and task-based education for simply accomplishing the job at hand. This quick-in, quick-out treatment of employees mirrors the way the traditional film industry has been structured for many years.

Today the computer graphics industry is becoming an increasingly unfriendly place for artists seeking full-time employment. Recently an enormous number of studios have been closing their doors. Warner Digital opened its doors in the digital marketplace in 1995; two years later, it closed down. This was a bleak message to the industry of things to come. Since then, other studios have closed and downsized, and now only a handful of players remain.

It is ironic that so few computer graphics studios remain because the film industry in general is continuing to break records in box office returns. Computer-generated films generally do exceptionally well financially. Of course, there are exceptions to this rule. For every movie like *Shrek*, which made more than $260 million in box office returns in 2001, there are the tragedies, like the visually stunning *Final Fantasy*, which did not even earn enough to cover the advertising budget for the same year.

The game industry is also doing a booming business. In 1998, the game industry's gross income outperformed the domestic gross income of films released in the United States. With the release of Microsoft's X-Box and Sony's Playstation 2, it is expected that the gross income for video games will outperform the gross income for the film industry as a whole in the very near future. The game industry makes billions of dollars annually. But those huge profits are generally shared among the top 10 to 20 titles per year, leaving hundreds of titles per year gasping for air.

By understanding the history of this profession and the reasons why it became what it is today, it is possible to navigate the pitfalls of this business with less uncertainty. To understand this evolution, you must examine the way that the computer graphics industry originated and get acquainted with the players and the projects that are part of the history of computer graphics.

Mainframes gave way to minicomputers, and microcomputers were introduced as were their expensive cousins, the workstations. Each new chip enhancement and media format enabled digital artists to move closer and closer to their goal of having creative horsepower at their fingertips.

The difference between what the studios were paying for computer hardware then and what they are paying now is even more dramatic. Here are some examples:

**1975:** Cray computer with in-house software

- ◆ Price of computer is $3.5 million plus salaries of programmers and artists.
- ◆ Production time is six months for a 30-second commercial.

**1980:** Development of the minicomputer with in-house programs

- ◆ Price of computer drops to $250,000.
- ◆ Number of workstations increases; production time drops to three months per commercial.

**1984:** Wavefront offers first off-the-shelf software

- ◆ Cost of software is $100,000.
- ◆ Production costs drop as studios reduce the need for programmers and digital artists.

**1990:** Unix workstations with off-the-shelf software

- ◆ Price of computer is $100,000; price of software is $100,000.
- ◆ Production costs and time drop as more stations become more affordable.

**1995:** Personal computers running Microsoft operating system with inexpensive software

- ◆ Price of computer is $10,000; price of software is $10,000.
- ◆ Production costs drop because of competition.

**2001:** Personal computers running Microsoft, Linux, and Mac operating systems with inexpensive software

- ◆ Price of computer is $2,000; price of software is $1,500 to $7,500.
- ◆ Smaller shops make prices more competitive.

Salaries, on the other hand, have increased overall. The cost of living and inflation only account for a part of what has become a fairly lucrative career choice for many digital artists and technicians. Without getting too involved with this controversial discussion, salaries are the single largest expense related to digital content creation. Today more than ever, this remains an undisputed fact.

## Early Influences of Computer Graphics

During the birth of computer graphics, there was a stage of technology that can be seen as a bridge between what was considered traditional special effects and the digital realities that are seen on the screen in films that are released today. These influences include the attempt to create digital images to replace images created using traditional methods for special effects and animation. The effect of design and innovation also play a role in the progress of digital imagery; this will be examined as well.

### Designing the Look of Computer Graphics

The challenge that most computer graphics artists face in the current production environment is to create images that perfectly match photography. Sometimes this is to seamlessly integrate a synthetic object into a photographic background, and sometimes this is to simply make a digital object look real. The urgent need to make most computer graphic images photo-real was not always the goal. The first computer graphics images were created with a specific look to them. One reason these images looked so stylized is because the technology was limited, and the resultant look was stylized to compensate for the lack of resolution and detail. Another reason was because the designers had a specific vision in mind when designing the images, and that vision steered the way computer-generated images were expected to appear for several years.

## The Psychedelic Roots of Digital Imagery

Generally, the look of the images created in traditional cameras could be seen as a foreshadowing of the era of digital effects. Two photographic techniques that allowed designers and directors to create imaginative images within the camera were slit-scan photography and backlit graphics.

*Slit-scan photography* allowed dramatic effects created using mechanical means. The process of creating slit-scan photography is an informative and interesting discussion. But for the purposes of this book, it is simply important to note that this is the technology used to create the time-warping effect toward the end of *2001: A Space Odyssey* (1968). The look created by this camera technique is mind-bending.

*Backlit graphics* are sets created using colored paper or fabric with light or slides projected in back of them, which creates a graphic look for live-action photography. The look achieved using this technique is sometimes referred to as *candy-apple neon*. This technology was originally invented for live stage shows. By using slides and bright lights projected in back of backdrops, many effects could be created during a live performance.

Slit-scan photography and backlit graphics provided a certain psychedelic look. The designers who created the first computer graphics images were raised in the era of psychedelic stage shows. A specific example of this is the work of Richard Taylor, the visual effects designer who created the effects for *Star Trek: The Motion Picture* (1979) and co-supervised the special effects for the film *Tron* (1982). Richard worked at a production facility in Los Angeles called Robert Abel and Associates. This studio was responsible for many cutting-edge images during the late 1970s and 1980s. The pivotal work created at that studio, and the talented people who were involved with those productions, spawned a major part of what is considered to be the beginnings of all computer graphics.

Before Richard became involved with visual effects at Robert Abel and Associates, he co-founded a company called Rainbow Jam, which created the light shows for the Grateful Dead. These stage shows that were performed by the Grateful Dead were legendary, used 32 slide projectors to project images onto a huge wall in back of the band. This use of animated light paved the way for the brightly colored graphics that later appeared in commercials and short films that used computer graphics in the early 1980s.

## Vector Graphics and Flying Logos

Some of the first computer-generated images seen by the public used vector graphics. This way of rendering images does not appear on the screen like the shaded images that we see today. Vector graphics look like bright lines that define the outline of a shape. Early examples of vector graphics can be seen in video games, such as the arcade titles *Asteroids* and the original *Star Wars* arcade game. The first productions that used vector graphics were created by displaying a single image on the screen, photographing the image off the monitor, advancing the frame on the monitor, then taking another photograph. This painstaking process was as unforgiving as it was slow.

In 1979, Disney contracted the opening shot for the film *The Black Hole* to be produced using vector graphics. John Hughes, who was then a technical director, produced this shot for Disney. The model of the title was created using 3-D polygonal geometry, which was displayed on a computer screen in wire frame display. This animation is possibly one of the first flying logo animations, certainly one of the first that appeared on film. Flying logo animations became the first widespread use of computer graphics. The models for these logos usually required some kind of logo or font to be exported as a spline into a 3-D modeling program where it could be turned into a 3-D model. Flying logos became so popular that the use of computer graphics logos became overused. By the late 1980s, simply moving a model of text around on a computer screen became boring.

## Early Digital Character Models

Creating digital characters was a goal for computer artists since the very first images began to appear on computer screens. Some of the first character models developed for digital production were put together so they would move as separate elements. Some characters lend themselves to this design very readily. One design is the stained glass knight that appeared in the movie *Young Sherlock Holmes* in 1985. This character used separately modeled pieces of glass that were suspended in midair, but when seen as a whole they appeared to be a character.

This film debut of a digital character was preceded by a landmark character design that appeared on television earlier that same year. In November 1984, Robert Abel and Associates produced the first computer-generated 30-second commercial, which aired during the Super Bowl in 1985. This commercial, produced for the Council for Canned Foods, was called "Brilliance" but is more commonly referred to as "Sexy Robot" and remains a milestone for the entire computer graphics industry. Creative Director Randy Roberts developed the look for this commercial, and the staff at Robert Abel and Associates created the animation and rendering pipeline to create the finished product.

The "Brilliance" commercial was a groundbreaking project in several ways. This commercial has the distinction of being what became the first application of live-action reference in computer character animation. It also is a historic modeling

**Figure 1.1**
The robot used for the "Brilliance" commercial. Images courtesy of Randy Roberts.

task, creating one of the first complex articulated characters for a television commercial. Figure 1.1 shows the body of the robot model used for this commercial. When a character has to be animated using separate pieces of geometry, robots are a natural design choice.

The process for creating this model started with detailed drawings of the robot, which were translated into a sculpture. The sculpture was then cast in plaster to create a mold, then filled with flexible foam. When the foam model of the robot was pulled from the mold, the foam model was sliced into thin layers. Each of

these layers was placed on a digitizing table, and the profile of each slice was digitized using a 2-D digitizing system. These digitized lines were loaded into the computer as polylines and were arranged vertically to create a wire frame model of the robot. Once these lines were arranged correctly, the line could be linked with polygonal faces to create the model. Figure 1.2 shows the head of the robot, which was created using the technique of surfacing thin cross-sections. The figure on the left shows lines on the robot's head representing the slices of data used to create the model; the figure on the right shows the rendered robot head.

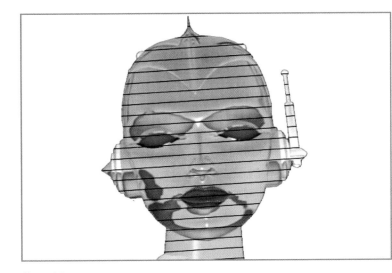
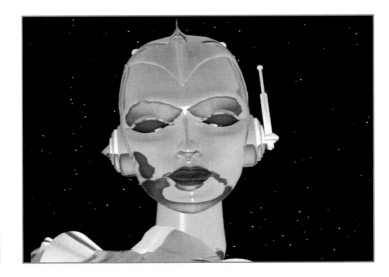

**Figure 1.2**
The robot's head for "Brilliance." Images courtesy of Randy Roberts.

1985 was huge for the field of digital imagery. In addition to the birth of digital imagery, several other landmark projects were created during this year. The animated film *Tony De Peltrie* premiered in 1985, introducing the concept of deforming facial animation using separate models. The model for the character Tony De Peltrie was created by digitizing a sculpture with a 3-D digitizer. Additional face shapes were digitized from the expressions on the face of a real person. An interpolation algorithm was used to establish a correlation between the points on the digitized sculpture and the points created from digitizing the human face.

Different face shapes were used as key frames to create animation. A *key frame* is a point in time during an animated sequence where the animation of an object changes in some way. The process of creating face shapes for different expressions is still used today to make facial animation.

Another impressive animation created in 1985, *Hi-Fidelity*, was not particularly noteworthy from a modeling standpoint but was an expression of design and style through color and texture mapping techniques. The animated short was created as a showcase to illustrate how computer graphics can be used to make art as well as entertain. This project, designed and directed by Randy Roberts, is a whimsical look at the love affair between two geometric characters. The music, animation, and design of the piece work together to establish a mood and a look. Figure 1.3 shows the style of the characters, which are expressed by the colors and texture maps that are applied to their simple geometric forms.

In 1986, Del Monte approached Robert Abel and Associates to create a commercial with a bold concept and high production values. This kind of project is called *blue sky* because it allows a lot of freedom to the director to create a truly original commercial. The commercial, which was for Hawaiian Punch, would be the last project that Robert Abel and Associates would do as a company. Again, Randy Roberts directed. But this time a designer named Dan Quarnstrom was called upon to create some designs for the memorable characters used in the commercial. This commercial was a tour-de-force in modeling and texture mapping digital characters and sets. The commercial is called "Chain Reaction." Figure 1.4 shows the variety of imagery that was seen in this commercial. The stylized character designs give a lighter tone to this realistically rendered factory scene. These models are segmented to make animation easier, but the logistical complexity of the commercial is multiplied many times because of the sheer numbers of robots that are in the commercial.

**Figure 1.3**
A character in the short animation *Hi-Fidelity*. Images courtesy of Randy Roberts.

**1. Industry Background**

7

**Figure 1.4**
The Hawaiian Punch "Chain Reaction" commercial. Images courtesy of Randy Roberts.

## Next-Generation Character Models

Advanced character modeling requires that the models comprise a single surface that bends at the joints and are not separated as discrete parts that animate separately. Most 3-D characters seen today have a continuous skin. Even some Internet game characters will have a continuous skin instead of separate limbs that animate like marionette puppet limbs. There are many examples of characters like this. In 1991 the film *Terminator 2: Judgment Day* had a character whose single continuous surface had a shiny chromelike appearance. This character made extensive use of models created as animation shapes, or morph targets.

**Figure 1.5**
Character designs created for *Eggs of Steel*. Images courtesy of Dan Quarnstrom.

## Modeling a World

Video game design, modeling, and texture mapping enable a rare opportunity to create an entire world, complete with multiple environments and characters. For the game *Eggs of Steel*, several full-motion video segments were produced and were played as short movies that appeared throughout the game.

The design of these environments and characters in these short animations determined the amount of detail required for the modeling and texture mapping. Dan Quarnstrom's stylistic designs lend themselves to a realistic rendering style but with a cartoon sensibility. Figure 1.5 shows the designs Dan created for several characters, and Figure 1.6 shows these characters in a frame from one of the animated segments.

Environments are a separate challenge in a video game. They are complex and large and can be difficult to manage and render. The environments created for *Eggs of Steel* were certainly no exception. These complex designs create 3-D worlds rich in detail. Figures 1.7 and 1.8 show a typical concept for the game environment and the way the environment looked in the final game.

**Figure 1.6**
The final rendered characters from *Eggs of Steel*. Image courtesy of Dan Quarnstrom.

**Figure 1.7**
Environment design for *Eggs of Steel*. Image
courtesy of Dan Quarnstrom.

**Figure 1.8**
The final rendered environment in *Eggs of Steel*.
Image courtesy of Dan Quarnstrom.

## Effects

*Special effects* can refer to many things. Some films use special effects to create explosions and tidal waves. Some special effects films use traditional film cameras to shoot images of flying miniature spaceships. This technology is known as *motion control*. Use of this technology made possible the complex effects for films, such as *Star Wars*, *Blade Runner*, and many others. Motion-controlled cameras were used to photograph small replicas of objects, such as spaceships, boats, and buildings. The camera would fly by the small model in a beauty pass filming the images of the model with correct lighting. Another camera pass would film the model with no lighting at all, but with a brightly lit blue screen placed behind it, creating an image that could be used as a mask. This image would be used to composite the miniature into another scene. Different shots of different miniatures could be layered many times using the same camera movement. In the film *Star Wars: Episode VI—Return of the Jedi* (1983), there was one shot that used more than 100 different ships composited in the scene, all using the same camera movement.

More recently, some film producers have originally planned to have all the effects in the film created using traditional methods, and then throughout the course of production they realized that digital effects are much more flexible and cost-effective in the long run. Some of the most famous examples of this are *Jurassic Park*, *End of Days*, and *Independence Day*.

### Analog Motion Control in *Star Wars* versus Digital Motion Control in *Blade Runner*

Motion control of cameras for the purpose of creating composited images was the first practical application of computers to create images for film. Motion bases that had cameras mounted to them would use stepper motors to make identical multiple passes of something like a miniature spaceship against a blue screen. The cameras were moved in specific directions for every frame, which allowed the miniature model to be photographed.

*Star Wars* was a pivotal film in the development of this technology, but the cameras that were creating these images in 1977 were not computer controlled—not yet. The stepper motors that controlled the cameras in *Star Wars* were controlled using an analog device that recorded the movements of the camera operator on magnetic tape. These movements could be repeated over and over to create the multiple camera passes required for the special effects. The technical expertise of Richard Edlund and the creative expertise of Dennis Muren helped create these effects. These men are still considered to be some of the premier names in the visual effects industry.

In 1979, Douglas Trumbull created the effects for the film *Star Trek: The Motion Picture*. Douglas hired Richard Hollander to help create a motion control system for the camera effects work. Richard created a computer-controlled system called COMPSY, for "computer multiplying system." Richard designed and programmed the device that took a camera controlled by stepper motors and moved it along a motion path using a truly computer-controlled device.

In 1982, David Dreyer was the visual effects supervisor for *Blade Runner*. Richard Hollander was hired for this film to use his camera control system to create a flying highway system. Richard used his system to make hundreds of camera passes for ships flying through a futuristic Los Angeles.

These traditional film cameras were being animated using computer animation. They were real, physical cameras, but the algorithms used to animate the cameras are identical to the algorithms used to create computer animation of computer-generated images. The data that drives these cameras can be imported into a computer-generated scene to animate the digital camera and vice versa.

Movies, such as *Blade Runner*, used traditional film cameras to create new kinds of images with the help of computers. These did not appear to be digital projects at all. But because of the electronic wizardry involved with the programming of the cameras to capture multiple passes for compositing, they laid the groundwork for what has become an industry dominated by the computer.

### Stop-Motion Animation versus Computer Animation in *Jurassic Park*

In *Jurassic Park* (1993), the traditional stop-motion puppets that were intended to be used for the dinosaurs gave way to state-of-the-art puppeteering techniques. Phil Tippett, a famous stop-motion animator and visual effects supervisor, worked on the previous *Star Wars* movies and developed new technology, *go-motion*, that made stop-motion puppetry look seamless. Go-motion enabled a programmable robot to move the puppet frame by frame, supplying the "motion blur" needed to make the dinosaurs look real. But something was still missing. Stop-motion photography had been pushed as far as it would go.

Industrial Light and Magic was the digital effects house that was working to integrate the go-motion dinosaur animation created by Phil Tippett into the movie. There was a strong desire for this film to push the envelope for the look of the dinosaurs, and the digital crew at Industrial Light and Magic stepped up to the plate. The digital crew provided a test of some dinosaurs running and jumping, composited over a photographic background plate. When director Steven Spielberg saw this test, he was sure that this was the way to go for the dinosaurs that would be seen from head to toe. This is a legendary turn of events that is used to illustrate how, in the throes of production, digital effects have proven themselves to look more believable than traditional effects.

Figures 1.9–1.11 show the groundbreaking and amazing work done on *Jurassic Park*. The professional look of these images raised the bar for the entire industry—

these images are still considered to be a yardstick by which the look of digital creatures can be measured. The models created for this film used surfaces that allowed the creatures to remain flexible throughout many extreme movements. The flexibility of these models is attributed to the curve-based surfaces that were used in the modeling process. The realism of the texture maps used to define the detail of the skin makes the viewer believe that the dinosaurs in this film could be real.

**Figure 1.9**
The digital dinosaurs created for *Jurassic Park* set the standard for creature modeling in 1993. Copyright © 2002 by Universal Studios. Courtesy of Universal Studios Publishing Rights, a Division of Universal Studios Licensing, Inc. All rights reserved.

**Figure 1.10**
Jurassic Park. Copyright © 2002 by Universal Studios. Courtesy of Universal Studios Publishing Rights, a Division of Universal Studios Licensing, Inc. All rights reserved.

**1. Industry Background**

13

**Figure 1.11**
Jurassic Park. Copyright © 2002 by Universal Studios. Courtesy of Universal Studios Publishing Rights, a Division of Universal Studios Licensing, Inc. All rights reserved.

## Motion Control versus Digital Aircraft in *Independence Day*

*Independence Day* (1996) is another example of a film that started out having the effects slated to be nearly 100 percent traditional. The director of the film, Roland Emmerich, stated that *ID4* was going to be "the biggest miniature shoot ever." Using the motion-controlled cameras previously used in *Star Trek: The Motion Picture* and *Blade Runner*, the process of shooting miniature photography entailed multiple camera passes, and although this process was much easier than the technology used before the 1980s, it was still cumbersome and painfully slow compared to digital imaging.

On their previous film, *Stargate* (1994), Emmerich and Dean Devlin (who worked with Emmerich on *ID4*) experienced some problems with digital effects, and consequently, claiming to be "old fashioned filmmakers," they wanted to avoid digital filmmaking on *ID4*.

Twentieth Century Fox set up a digital production facility at Pacific Ocean Post, which was involved with compositing and postproduction of *ID4*. A small group of 3-D digital artists began doing animation tests on the film. One of the artists who worked in this facility was Art Jeppe. Jeppe began doing a test of a fighter jet chasing an alien spacecraft through a canyon. The shot seems pretty simple by today's standards. The camera was positioned overhead, and the jet flew in from below and then shot off screen.

When the director and producer saw the shot, they realized that this method had a lot of potential. While reviewing the shot, the director would say things, such as "That's great. Now have the jet take a little dip, then zoom off screen right." If the shot was created using miniatures, the reply would be, "Sorry, that's a miniature, we cannot do that." If the shot was digital, the animator would say, "Sure, no problem."

Devlin and Emmerich, who were publicly denouncing the use of digital effects at the beginning of production of *ID4*, bought a digital studio of their own called Centropolis, where they made the movie *Godzilla* (1998). They continue to produce many computer-driven effects films there today.

## Latex Creature versus Digital Creature in *End of Days*

A more recent example of this kind of turnabout is the movie *End of Days* (1999). In this film was a sequence where a giant, monstrous version of Satan rose up out of the floor of a cathedral. The original plan was to have Stan Winston Studios create a giant puppet for the creature and animate it using puppeteers. The puppet was created, and filming commenced.

However, from the very beginning, the production crew knew that they would need to use a digital character for the shot of the creature coming through the floor. The digital effects crew already had modeled and set up the creature for the floor shot. And as production continued, the puppet shots were proving to be less than satisfactory. John (D.J.) DesJardin, the digital effects supervisor for *End of Days*, did test shots where the puppet was intended to appear. When the director was shown these tests, the number of puppet shots began to decrease until there were no puppet shots at all in the final film. Despite the fact that Stan Winston Studios did an excellent job crafting a puppet that could create a performance, it looked like a puppet. Physical puppets need to be operated in the physical world where gravity must be considered a factor. Computer graphics have much more flexibility. A digital creature does not have to deal with the laws of physics. No sluggish performance can be attributed to the massive size of an object with a digital creature.

## *Animation*

Traditional animation is one of the most time-consuming and laborious endeavors in the film industry today. Aside from the limitations in animation due to the vast amount of work required to get one or two seconds of animation on the screen, these drawings need to be created by individuals who possess unique illustration skills. In the field of traditional animation, computer animation has become firmly entrenched and is used in almost all animated features being released today. Since the very first animated feature that used computer imagery, *The Great Mouse Detective* (1986) from Disney, animated features have used computer graphics to create difficult-to-illustrate mechanical objects. With a single computer model, the animator can pick an object, rotate it, and move it through perspective with ease. This task was once an overwhelming drafting challenge for the animator.

Recently, animated features have used more and more 3-D models to aid in storytelling. Examples range from the beautiful chandelier and ballroom in *Beauty and the Beast* (1991), the animated lion cave in *Aladdin* (1992), and the amazing performance of *The Iron Giant* (1999). The animation of hard geometric forms, such as trains, cars, buildings, machines, and other man-made objects, are the best candidates for replacing hand-drawn objects with 3-D models in an animated feature. These man-made objects are difficult to correctly draw in perspective over a series of hundreds of frames. The computer can do this automatically and easily.

The magic carpet in *Aladdin* is a good example of how texture mapping can replace hand-drawn animation. This carpet, with its complex colors and patterns, appeared correct in every frame because the texture map used on the 3-D model rendered perfectly. This kind of increase in productivity allows animators and directors to create much more satisfying work and better films overall.

**1. Industry Background**

15

More and more organic 3-D models, such as trees, mountains, and even people, are being replaced in traditional animation for many reasons. One example is the crowd sequences in *Prince of Egypt* (1998). The flocks of 3-D human characters can be multiplied and animated easier than drawing hundreds of characters moving through the entire sequence.

New modeling processes developed for animation are making it easier for modelers to create more organic models faster and easier. In the short film *Geri's Game* (1997), Pixar Animation Studios, a premier computer animation facility, used a method to smooth the surface of a coarse, simple 3-D model. This process created a natural appearance to what originally looked like a low-resolution model. Figure 1.12 shows a frame from this short film.

The computer graphics feature film industry began with Walt Disney Pictures in partnership with Pixar Animation Studios when they released *Toy Story* (1995).

Since then, many other features have been introduced as well. The response by the public toward computer-generated feature films has spawned many new computer graphics feature film projects to be approved by major studios. Traditional animation has fallen to second-class status compared to the huge successes of recent computer-generated features.

When the Academy of Motion Picture Arts and Sciences finally introduced an animated feature category for its yearly awards for the year 2001, computer-generated features were nominated for all three top slots. This is just one indication of the overwhelming influence computer-generated images have on the public at large. It will be increasingly difficult for traditional animation to compete with computer-generated imagery. The tools and techniques for generating 3-D digital worlds and characters are becoming very efficient, and the quality of the images is getting better and better. No significant advances in technology have been made in 2-D animation for years.

©Pixar Animation Studios

**Figure 1.12**
The character Geri from *Geri's Game*. © Pixar Animation Studios

**Figure 2.7**
The Cray computer at Digital Productions cost thousands of dollars just to keep it running.

operate the Cray. Yet the people that put together this conglomerate made these outlandish estimates as to what they could do in the way of revenue volume. It just wasn't sustainable. They couldn't do nearly that volume or generate near that amount of revenue. So without the revenue to sustain it, it just collapsed. They had to lay off large numbers of people.

Before any of that happened, Randy Roberts approached me and asked me if I would start a new company with him. He was thinking that we would own it, and he would be the director. I said, "Sure, we can do that." That was in the fall of 1986. Omnibus purchased Robert Abel and Associates in the summer of 1986, right before SIGGRAPH. So we started putting together a team. I asked Charlie Gibson if he would join, then Charlie asked Keith Goldfarb, Frank Wuts, and Pauline Ts'o. We figured we needed another director, so we invited Cliff Boule. We also had a relationship at that time with Steve Beck.

So we put the company together, but we needed a name. We came up with hundreds of names. Nobody could agree on any of them. Then one day we were working on the Hawaiian Punch robot commercial. I was working next to Neil Escuri. He said, "I know you guys are forming a company, and I know you're having trouble finding a name. I got this name. I was going to use it for my company but I'm not going to form a company anymore, so if you want the name you can have it. The name is Rhythm & Hues." We accepted the gift from Neil.

We formed Rhythm & Hues, and Omnibus was laying off the people that we had talked to when we were originally going to form our company. Pauline, Keith, and Charlie joined at that time. Omnibus basically shut down the software division of Robert Abel and Associates, so there was pressure on us to really get Rhythm & Hues running.

I had a studio over on Larchmont Boulevard, and a couple of doors down there is a guy that lived there that was apparently involved with some kind of love triangle. On New Year's Eve, 1986, somebody firebombed his studio, and the fire swept north and engulfed my studio where I had my computer. I had one of the first Silicon Graphics computers made, and it was essentially destroyed by the fire. At the time, I didn't think I had any insurance because a few months before I got notice from the insurance company that they had canceled my insurance. They canceled it because of a leak in the roof and a stain on the wall. A month or two after the fire, my insurance agent called. I told him that was too bad that they canceled my insurance because I just had a fire. He said that he only canceled the property insurance; he didn't cancel the computer insurance. The insurance was replacement value, and I originally purchased that computer in 1984. Bill Kovaks and Jim Keating were using it to write the Wavefront software. So they used had already it for a couple years.(Figure 2.8 shows the Wavefront Logo.)

At the beginning of 1987, I had the replacement value insurance, which got us a brand new Silicon Graphics computer instead of the old obsolete one I owned before. That was really quite fortuitous. I didn't get any money out of the settlement but got a brand-new computer. The computers were very expensive back then. My first computer cost over $80,000. So getting the latest Silicon Graphics computer was really quite a coup.

Our studio had one state-of-the-art computer and a graphics workstation. And I had about $70,000 saved up, so we got started on that. We paid ourselves less than we were making at Robert Abel and Associates by far. Everyone even went on half salary, from our already nominal salaries.

Then in early April 1987, Omnibus disappeared, and everybody was laid off; they closed it down. One day, people came back to work, and the doors were locked.

There was a logo for United Artists that was being worked on at Omnibus at the time. The project was just getting started, and they had nowhere else to go. The three studios that could have done the project—Omnibus, Digital Productions, and Robert Abel and Associates—disappeared simultaneously. So we ended up with that job.

On April 23rd, 1987, we got our first job, which was to do a film job. So you've got to remember, with the computers back then it was really, really hard to do a commercial, let alone having to do a high-resolution film job. Very few people in the United States even had film recorders. In order to record it, we had to messenger tapes to the supercomputer center data in San Diego. They had the closest film recorder down there. Because one of the computers at Robert Abel and Associates was financed by the father of Allen DeBevoise, we were able to lease that Celerity computer too. In return for using the computer, we would make payments on it. Now we had one Celerity computer and one Silicon Graphics workstation. We were working out of my apartment on Melrose Avenue, and then Charlie Gibson said "I'm not going to work here anymore; you have to get a real office." So we found a real place.

We found a basement of a dental office in Culver City, and we moved in there. I had let Wavefront use my computer where Jim Keating wrote the modeling software. When Wavefront (Figure 2.8) went public, they needed to control everything. We had to agree to let them control the modeling software in return for shares of their stock. They had been paying Jim Keating all along, but their agreement was that we could use the modeling software but we would both own it. They didn't like that agreement. Once the more financially astute guys got involved with Wavefront, the agreement had to change. So we got shares of stock in return for them getting control of the modeling software, which at the time was called *model*.

> **At the beginning of 1987, I had the replacement value insurance, which got us a brand-new Silicon Graphics computer ...Our studio had one state-of-the-art computer ...**

Bill Kovaks wrote the animation software for Wavefront, Jim Keating wrote the modeling package, and Roy Hall wrote the rendering software. Jim and Bill were working out of my studio when they were writing the software, and Roy was working at home.

**TOM:** *What would you consider your dream project?*

**JOHN:** I am a big fan of John Lassiter and the work that is being done at Pixar. If I had to choose a dream project, it would be to have an animated feature film done here at Rhythm & Hues with the same production values as the work being done at Pixar. John Lassiter is a terrific director, and the films coming out of that studio are of the same quality and subject matter of the kind of work I would like to see being done here.

## Bill Kroyer, Animation Director

*Some milestones define digital imagery. These projects were there first, setting the bar much higher than was thought possible. One of these projects was* Tron. *This Disney film was not originally intended to include computer-generated animation. But, as it turned out, the 1982 release became the first film to produce more than 20 minutes of computer-generated imagery. One of the people who was involved with* Tron *was Bill Kroyer.*

*Bill served as the animation director for* Tron *and continues to direct animation today on feature films and commercials. His animation of the light-cycle sequence in* Tron *still inspires digital artists. Bill's more recent achievements include directing animation on* Cats and Dogs *(Warner Bros.) and* The Flintstones in Viva Rock Vegas *(Universal Pictures).*

*Bill has produced many traditional animation pieces including titles for* Honey, I Shrunk the Kids, National Lampoon's Christmas Vacation, *and* Blake Edwards' Son of the Pink Panther. *He directed the animated feature* Ferngully: The Last Rainforest *for Twentieth Century Fox, and he received several awards for his 1988 computer-animated short* Technological Threat. *This film is considered by many in the field of computer graphics to be one of the seminal pieces of work that define the craft.*

**TOM:** *Can you describe the technical and creative challenges associated with creating the groundbreaking work you did on the movie* Tron.

**BILL:** *Tron* was the first movie that I worked on that used computer graphics, and I think it was one of the first feature films that had computer graphics. It was not originally conceived as a computer film because that technology was not widely used or widely known about.

**Figure 2.8**
The original code for Wavefront Technologies, the first off-the-shelf software available for creating broadcast graphics, was written on the computer that belonged to John Hughes.

*Tron* was conceived as a conventional animated film but the subject matter was about life in the computer so it lent itself naturally to that kind of medium. When we first developed the story we were going to do it with like a back-lit technique so it had kind of an electronic glow feeling to it. But then, as word spread around the industry that we were actually going to do a computer-animated film, people who were interested in this new art form of computer graphics started coming out of the woodwork. I mean, we were getting calls from all over the country asking about this film. When Disney picked up the option, it became really the rage. Of course, the computer graphics community in 1979 was a lot smaller than it is today. A few of the key people, like Alan Kay, heard about the project and started flying down on their own money from Xerox PARC to Los Angeles. Every Friday night after work he would fly down on the shuttle and come over to our studio and just ask to sit around and consult with us on story bull sessions. And when a guy like Alan Kay finds out about a movie in those days, he makes a couple of calls and the next thing you know, everybody in the computer graphics business, all 47 of them, knew about *Tron*.

So, when we got to Disney, we started getting all these film samples sent to us. There were no video-tapes. People didn't send you a cassette or a 3/4 tape. You actually had to get film. There were only four companies in the whole country that could do a computer-animated film, and they all sent stuff to us. Steve Lisberger said, "We could actually do this film with computer animation, like real computer animation." I think there were no people in the business that had any experience at that. Since I was animation director of the movie, I automatically inherited the computer animation director job.

> **Steve Lisberger said, "You know what, we could actually do this film with computer animation, like real computer animation." I think there were no people in the business that had any experience at that. Since I was animation director of (Tron), I automatically inherited the computer animation director job.**

It turned out that the kind of animation I was used to at Disney was exactly the kind of thing you needed for this movie. In those days you needed to visualize very precisely what you wanted for computer animation because there was no ability to preview it like we do today. There were no workstations that could play back imagery. You couldn't even play five frames at a time on a com-

puter. All you could do was look at one frame and often a wire frame. There were no flipbooks, there was no SGI that had the graphics pipeline technology where you could actually watch it play. And consequently, viewing or doing that movie *Tron*, meant you had to completely envision and almost animate in our heads and then describe the detail with numbers and graphs and literally describe the channel band and exactly how the objects would move. And we literally handwrote x, y, z translation, and rotation six channels per frame for the light cycles and so forth (Figure 2.9). We wrote exposure sheets with all those numbers on it about how those vehicles get moved.

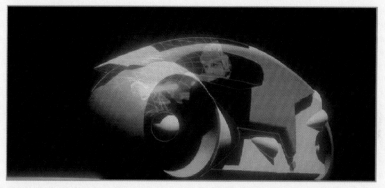

**Figure 2.9**
The light-cycle sequence in *Tron* had to be animated by writing down the values for each channel for each frame on an exposure sheet. © DISNEY ENTERPRISES, INC.

The animation on that picture was interesting. As I said, we would do the graphs, we would do the plans, we would do the exposure sheets, then give them all to the programmers at the animation companies. They would type it all but they couldn't see how it would move. The first time anybody saw it was when they filmed it out onto a film recorder. They sent it to us, and we put it up on a 70 mm projector (Figure 2.10), and that's the first time we saw anything move. That was our very, very, very, very first look at the animation. That's what you tweaked. You tweaked a 70 mm wire frame pencil test. And, consequently, if you didn't have it very close, you would have spent a lot of money.

The other issue in those days was that there was no standardized software. Literally, every company in the business was writing their own software in-house. There were no commercial companies. Alias|Wavefront didn't exist yet. No one was writing modeling packages or animation packages or lighting packages. So the four companies we used, Triple I, Magi, Robert Abel, and Digital Effects in New York, all had absolutely different software, completely incompatible—they never

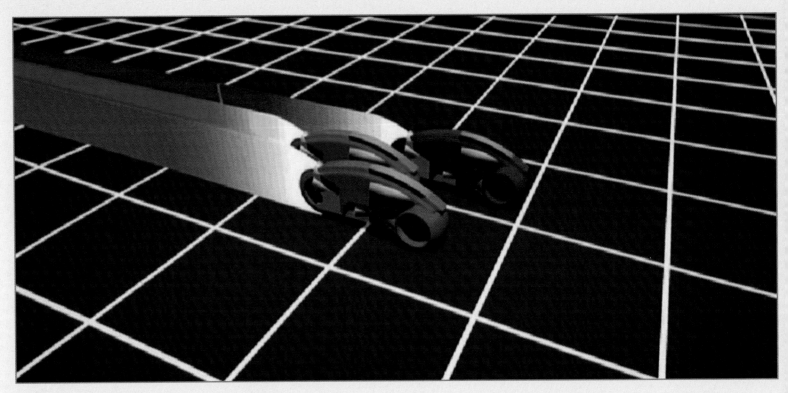

**Figure 2.10**
The animation in *Tron* had to be shot to 70 mm film just to preview it. © DISNEY ENTERPRISES, INC.

talked to each other—they were incapable of talking to each other. Triple I even went as far as to build its own computer. They did the whole movie on their own piece of hardware called the Foonley, which was their personal computer that they built. It crashed every couple of hours.

The only company that modeled in wire frame in a way that has become sort of traditional, with polygons, shaded polygons, was Triple I (Figure 2.11); they were using shaded polygons. Robert Abel and Associates didn't have any ability to shade at all. Their work was pure vectors, and they actually output cels, you know, acetate cels. Digital Effects did some kind of polygonal modeling. They only did one shot for us. And then Magi, of course, did this thing called Synthavision, which was their software that was based on principles of ray tracing. They did solid geometry. All their objects had to be built with solid geometry that were really mathematical formulas. They can only build things by adding or subtracting geometric shapes that were easily described by formulas.

**Figure 2.11**
The Foonley was a computer built by Triple I.

So you can only have circles and rectangles and crescents, and things like that. And everything you built, like the light cycles or the solar sailor, had to be made by simple solid geometry (Figure 2.12), which was then rendered in the system, the Synthavision system. Dr. Phil Mittelman, who founded Magi, was the guy who invented ray tracing. What he developed wasn't ray tracing for animation, it was to CAT scan. I think he was a medical doctor, and he used the same technology that he used for a CAT scan to do this. So anyway, it was a very

*...it was a very iterative process where we constantly had to learn about this brand new technology, what it could and could not do, and then literally design the film. The content of (Tron) had to be designed around what could be done and what couldn't be done.*

iterative process where we constantly had to learn about this brand new technology, what it could and could not do, and then literally design the film. The content of the film had to be designed around what could be done and what couldn't be done.

**TOM:** *Could you describe the production environment you created for the film* Technological Threat?

**BILL:** After *Tron* I worked in the computer industry for about four years, and I really enjoyed computer animation even though it was very primitive at the time. I liked a lot of things about it, but I still missed the organic, instant nature of hand drawing animation, so I wanted to find a way to bring the precision, accuracy and the power of computer generated geometry into the world of hand-drawn organic imagery. This friend of mine, Tim Heidmann, had been doing some work in computer graphics, and developed a little software program where you would plot things out on a plotter, and so I talked with him and said "What if we developed

**Figure 2.12**
The models of the light cycles in *Tron* had to be described as a series of solid shapes that were added to and subtracted from each other. © DISNEY ENTERPRISES, INC.

this software and we could make computer animation on a plotter?" I went out and got some funding to do this. I borrowed some from my father-in-law. I took a loan out, then I spent all this money leasing an SGI for Tim so he could sit there and write this code.

Nobody had ever seen computer animation plotted out on paper. So we thought, well, we'll go ahead and make our own film as a demo. So I started thinking what would be a fun film to show off the difference between computer animation and hand-drawn animation. I thought, "I'll do a duel between computer-animated characters and hand-animated characters. And I'll do the computer-animated characters by computer, and I'll do the hand-animated characters by hand." I mean, the philosophical depth of that was just amazing. But we didn't have any money. You know, there were only three of us: my wife and I, and one computer guy.

We recruited a lot of friends to work on the film who subsequently became famous. Rob Minkoff, who directed *Stuart Little*, animated. Chris Bailey, who directed the animation for *Mighty Joe Young* at Dreamquest, was an animator. Brad Bird, who later directed *The Iron Giant*, helped us out. Rich Moore, who directed the some *Futurama* episodes, helped us out too. We had really great people helping us out.

We did this short little film called *Technological Threat* (Figure 2.13), and we did it by doing exactly what I said. We boarded it all traditionally and then I animated all the computer stuff myself. We plotted it all out on paper, and then we did the hand animation, and then I took it all to Korea to a studio. We inked and painted the whole thing in three days and came back. And that was our movie. And, of course, that movie got an Oscar® nomination and won festivals all over the world, and then we became really well known and we got so much work that we never made another short film again because we were too busy.

> I thought, "I'll do a duel between computer-animated characters and hand-animated characters. And I'll do the computer-animated characters by computer, and I'll do the hand-animated characters by hand." ... the philosophical depth of that was just amazing.

**TOM:** *You've been involved with many traditional animation projects, as well as computer-animated projects. Can you explain your favorite and least favorite things about each medium.*

**BILL:** Computer animation has been evolving a lot, but what I've always liked about it, I guess, was that you didn't have to draw. The thing that separates animators from most other human beings is that an animator has the ability to draw a character over and over and over again in any position, from any angle, and make it look like it's the same character. And that pure drafting skill is very rare. But then you combine that drafting skill with the ability to add movement to those drawings, so that drawing to drawing to drawing it appears as if you have the illusion of life—that's a skill that a minute, portion of the human population possess. I mean, literally, the number of good animators that can draw in the Disney style in the whole United States of America. Out of 275 million people, there's literally 1,000 human beings that can really do that well. It is a really, really rare skill. And it's hard, really hard. You have to love it, and so I love doing it, and I can do it but it is really difficult to do; it is a lot of work.

And you slave away. I worked at Disney for a year, and I did 60 feet of film. I created 40 seconds of animation in a whole year of my life. So at that rate, you know I could work for 50 years and I would end up with a half hour's worth of work, you know. That's my least favorite thing, is how slow it is and how long it takes. Computer animation, on the other hand, is great because once you build a model, you've built it, it's there. And that model looks the same from all angles, and when you move it, at least it still looks the same. So a huge amount of the difficulty and labor of hand-drawn animation has been replaced. You can now just focus on performance, how it moves and how it acts. With me as an animator, that's always been the most advantageous part of the medium. And because of that, if you're a good computer animator, you should be able to rip through much more footage. And we do, actually!

> And you slave away. I worked at Disney for a year, and I did 60 feet of film. I created 40 seconds of animation in a whole year of my life. So at that rate... I could work for 50 years and I would end up with a half-hour's worth of work...

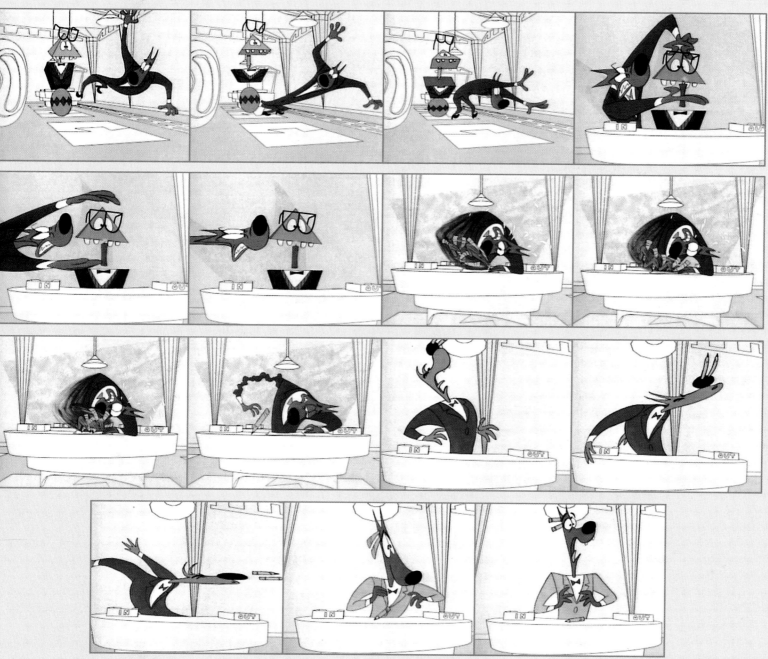

**Figures 2.13**

*Technological Threat* was a hilarious mix of traditional and computer animation.

The difference between computer animation and hand-drawn animation, and the problem with computer animation is this: Literally anyone can move a character in computer animation. Most of the people who would call themselves animators are not really very good animators. They're just people who can move things, but you don't really notice it because they always look the same. So, consequently, in the whole computer animation industry now there haven't been that many really, really great animation performances, but they're getting better, and the standards are being raised, and you look at movies like *Shrek* and look at the business. Computer animation's got to be 19 years old. Characters started being animated in the early '80s, you know—Tony De Peltrie something like '84 or '85. It took 16 years to really get the Disney quality performance animation to start showing up.

# PART II

# Modeling and Texture Mapping Techniques

# chapter 3
# Modeling Overview

In the world of 3-D modeling, several realms of technology have come together to create a specialized area of expertise. The process of creating a complex 3-D model is an exercise in sculpting, strategy, engineering, design, and programming. The 3-D modeler must be familiar with all of these disciplines. Only a handful of 3-D modelers today thought they would be building 3-D models with a computer to earn a living. Lighters, animators, compositors, and even texture painters are far more likely to say that they studied their skill for the sole purpose of doing it for a living than are 3-D modelers. Modelers depend much more on skills developed outside of the computer to accomplish their tasks. Computer modelers generally evolve from a specific background and from this training develop the skills required to create art in a technical environment.

In defining a 3-D modeler, first, you must differentiate computer modeling for design and manufacturing from computer modeling for entertainment. This book will focus on computer modeling for entertainment, which includes computer modeling for film and video and video games. Modeling for design and manufacturing involves the same basic steps required to do computer modeling for entertainment. The mechanical aspects of the two jobs are essentially the same.

Modeling is the only field in the computer graphics industry that has this manufacturing connection. It may not *seem* exciting to people just entering the computer graphics field that opportunities for their profession are available in other industries, but with the volatility of computer graphics in the entertainment industry, you should think about the possibilities of having opportunities outside the realm of entertainment. Other alternatives to entertainment for a modeler include architectural and design visualization, medical illustration, rapid prototyping, and engineering modeling (Figure 3.1).

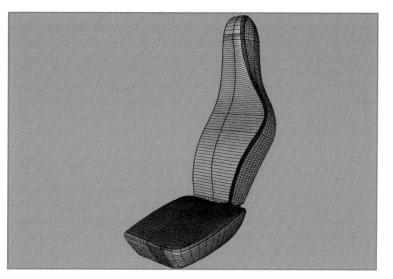

**Figure 3.1**
Modeling for manufacturing and design.

## Computer Modeling for Manufacturing

In computer modeling for manufacturing, the modeler must pay close attention to manufacturing requirements and tolerances. When modelers create surfaces for manufacturing from data derived from a 3-D digitized clay model, they must be able to maintain tolerances of up to 1/4 mm deviation from the actual digitized data. This type of surfacing is called *class-A surfacing*. Modelers and designers who work in the automotive industry and do this type of work are considered some of the most highly skilled modelers.

Modeling for manufacturing requires strict adherence to manufacturing tolerances and specifications. Manufacturable models are generally models that are created to make a tool for creating this model. These tools are fabricated from very hard and expensive metals. The labor put into making a model is quite expensive as well. The process of making a mold can require numerically controlled milling machine operations, casting, or forging. Each of these processes adds another series of requirements on the final model. When a model is created that is intended to be used as a manufacturable part, several criteria must be met before it can be approved:

◆ The part must have adequate draft angles to be released from the mold.

◆ The model cannot have any parts that could interfere with the part being released from the mold.

◆ The texture on the part must be machined, etched, or cast into the tool being used to make the final product. Many times the texture will be treated as a separate entity and put in the mold after the mold has been machined.

◆ The surfaces must maintain very tight tangency requirements to ensure that the mold can be machined with a milling machine.

◆ The surfaces of the part must stay within very tight tolerance specifications. The part must have very precise dimensional stability in order to be manufactured and used in an assembly with other parts.

The demands of creating computer data of surfaces that are turned into manufacturing molds or tools are very stringent. The tools needed can cost upward of $1 million each. If there are any errors in the data, the cost of the tool is wasted, and costs are incurred from the resulting consequences upstream in the manufacturing process. Every part has a variety of other parts that depend on it. When one part is manufactured incorrectly, it affects the entire process. Some of the consequences associated with inaccurate modeling in the manufacturing process include misaligned parts, gaps in seams between parts, excessive stress on parts, and potential deformation or warping of parts during assembly.

## Computer Modeling for Design

Computer modeling for design is a field in which industrial designers submit conceptual artwork derived from computer data to clients for potential approval to create new manufacturable products. The technical requirements for this type of modeling are not as stringent as modeling for manufacturing (Figure 3.2). While the design is in the conceptual phase, the designer may take many liberties with the actual model data. When the client is in the design approval process, the only important thing is that the model looks good. As the design gets closer and closer to final approval (Figure 3.3), the model needs to be transferred to an engineering program to create manufacturing data. This manufacturing data has very stringent

**Figures 3.2, 3.3**
Modeling for design proceeds in stages, ranging from loosely created initial models to detailed and complete data sets for manufacturing.

requirements similar to class A surfacing but is generally created by design engineers on a solid modeling program. When a model is created on software specifically suited for manufacturing, maintaining the stringent requirements for the manufacturing process is more automatic.

A typical scenario of how the process works goes like this: The designer creates the conceptual art in a free-form surfacing program similar to the modeling program Alias, and one or more iterations of client approval will take place to narrow down the design. After the client is close to approving the final design, the data will be transferred to an engineering program, such as Pro-engineer. In the engineering program, the data will be tuned so that it can be made with the appropriate tools for manufacturing. Details, such as draft angles and radii for part edges, are included to make it easy for the engineers to create a manufacturable part.

## Modeling in Different Studios

The methods for creating models vary from studio to studio. Generally, a 3-D modeler can use any software package to create geometry as long as that geometry can be exported into the software package where animation and rendering take place. A 3-D model used for production must conform to many requirements, but most companies allow some latitude when it comes to the specific package that is used for modeling.

A brief introduction to some basic modeling principles is required at this time. Modeling on the computer is done using mathematically based geometry types. Two major modeling entities used in modeling for entertainment are polygons (Figure 3.4) and surfaces.

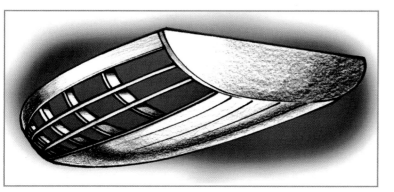

**Figure 3.4**
The exterior of the boat wraps around contoured shapes that define the hull.

Although polygons are simple geometric entities, there are several derivations of surfaces based on the mathematical algorithm used to create the surface. These surface types include B-Spline, Bézier, and NURBS surfaces.

To visualize surfaces, think of the hull on a boat (Figure 3.4). When the boat is constructed, cross-members are put in place to support the profile shape of the boat hull. These contoured pieces of wood create the framework for the outside of the boat. Once these cross-members are covered with the slats that create the final exterior surface of the boat, these supports are no longer visible, but are still necessary. Surfaces are built the same way. The construction of a surface begins with

**Figure 3.5**
Each polygon is represented by one of the mirrors.

drawing curves that define the shape of the surface. The curves have surfaces applied to them to create the final shape. The final rendered image has no trace of these curves, but they are still a necessary part of the model.

To visualize polygonal models think of a mirrored ball (Figure 3.5). Each small mirror on the ball can be thought of as a polygon. A polygon is simply a face that rests between three or more points (Figure 3.6). Polygonal geometry comprises simple geometric entities that span across three or more vertices. As more polygons are put together, models become more complex. As the number of polygons

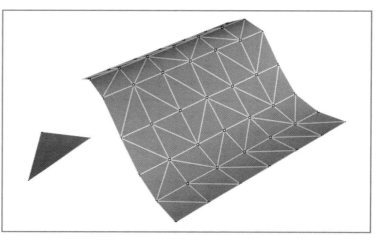

**Figure 3.6**
Complex shapes are made from joining polygons into larger meshes.

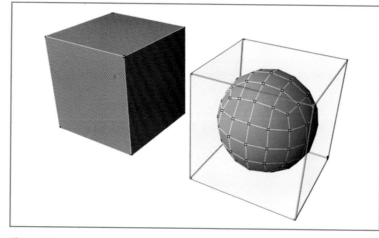

**Figure 3.7**
Subdivision modeling begins with the creation of a polygonal "cage."

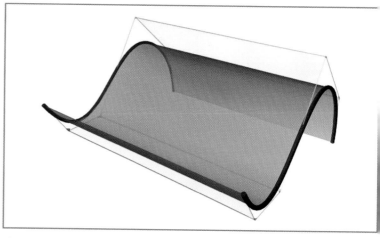

**Figure 3.8**
NURBS surfaces use control vertices to shape the overall surface.

increase and their relative size to each other decreases, the ball appears smoother and smoother. This process is called *subdivision modeling* and was made famous by Pixar.

A new development in modeling is *subdivision polygons* or an entity type called *subdivision surface* (Figure 3.7). Modeling for a subdivision model is done the same way as modeling a low-resolution polygonal model. Certain tips and tricks are required for a subdivision model to have adequate detail where it is desired using lower-resolution polygonal modeling techniques, but the overall workflow is the same. A good modeler can use either entity type. The basic workflow begins with a good model built with as few polygons as possible. The subdivision algorithm will then use a curvature routine to subdivide the polygons into smaller shapes and smooth the overall form at the same time. The result is a lifelike and organic shape created with little effort.

Another important entity type is spline-based surfaces (Figure 3.8). For every type of spline curve, there is a corresponding surface type. The two primary splines used to create surfaces in the computer graphics industry today are *B-Spline* surfaces and *NURBS* (Non Uniform Rational B-Splines) surfaces. (The *B* in *B-Spline* stands for *basis*.) NURBS surfaces are more mathematically evolved than B-spline surfaces.

When spline-based surfaces were first introduced, the philosophy was that any given shape could be made from a single surface. The first model that many modelers made was a face constructed from a single spline-based surface. This technique, although convenient to maintain tangency along a single surface, had

problems when creating complex forms that rested along smooth areas. An example of this is a character's ear placed along the side of the head. The geometry to create the ear is fairly complex, whereas the side of the head is not complex. The point at which the ear is stuck to the head is a point where complex surfaces meet simpler, less complex surfaces. The conditions at which these dissimilar surfaces came together required a blending treatment of some type. Sometimes it was desirable to create a blending surface (Figure 3.9) or *fillet*. In other cases, the modeler took the end of the surface that was joining another surface and positioned the points so that one surface appeared to be resting on top of the other surface, creating a smooth blend condition.

Many studios create models using large single surfaces that need to blend at the points they came together. Many studios still do a lot of video work and small film jobs that create models using this technique. This technique was considered state-of-the-art when the digital effects classic *Jurassic Park* was created. Studios, such as Cinesite and VIFX, created many models using this NURBS modeling technique.

Blending surfaces with dissimilar topologies created problems for animation setup, which requires creating deformation conditions where two surfaces come together. When these two surfaces have very dissimilar topologies, it is difficult to create a smooth deformation at the point where the surfaces come together. The solution is *patch modeling*. Patch modeling requires the modeler to make more surfaces than is necessary to create a character from single surfaces. These patches have topology and curvature identical to the patches that lie adjacent to them. The end result is a model constructed of NURBS surfaces that appear to be a smooth continuous surface (Figure 3.10).

**3. Modeling Overview**

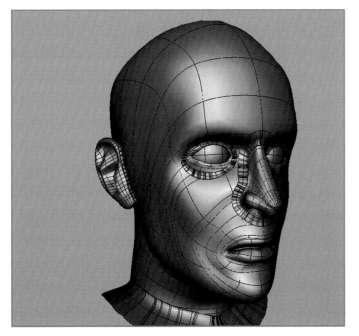

**Figure 3.9**
NURBS modeling using single surfaces to create shapes can lead to the complex problem of dealing with "blend surfaces."

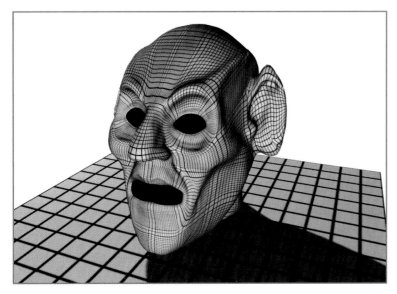

**Figure 3.10**
Patch modeling is a process that creates surfaces that align evenly and deals effectively with changes in topological detail without creating blend surfaces.

B-Spline surfaces, as opposed to NURBS surfaces, have two rows of points that extend beyond the boundaries of the surface on all four sides. Modelers keep the model smooth by making sure that the points on each border coincides with the adjacent surface, and the points on the rows that fall outside of the surface coincides with points that fall two rows inside the adjacent surface.

Sony Pictures Imageworks built its modeling production pipeline around NURBS patch modeling technology. The models created for deformation must be constructed very carefully using the patch modeling process. These models are time-consuming to set up for animation and deformation. The initial problem with NURBS models is keeping the overall surface smooth where individual patches come together. To describe how each patch appears, the software uses information about all the points in a patch but does not take into account what the points of the neighboring patches are doing. Because of this, one patch can tear away from another or appear to have a crease. The most common solution to using models constructed this way is the need to have software "stitch" the surfaces back together when the model is animated. Initially the model is constructed with all the surfaces having tangency at the points where the surfaces meet, so no seams or creases are apparent. Maintaining this tangency while the model deforms is more complicated than it may seem. Several ways exist to stitch the surfaces together. One way is to use a software program that monitors the position of the points near the edges of each surface. This software maintains a tangency condition along each edge while the model is animated. Another way to maintain the appearance of continuous curvature is to animate a low-resolution model as a deforming object. The high-resolution patch model is controlled by the lower-resolution deforming model, and tangency is maintained because the low-resolution model smoothly affects the high-resolution surface and does not break the seams of the model while deforming.

Many people feel that this technology is still considered state-of-the-art. Although there are many good things to be said for creating models of this type, multipatch NURBS models are complex to set up for animation and generally require each patch to have its own texture map.

Other studios have production pipelines set up to be similar to the Sony Pictures Imageworks paradigm. In the movie *Dinosaur*, Walt Disney animation studios used a NURBS patch model workflow similar to the one that Sony uses.

At Rhythm & Hues studios, where special effects for films, such as *Babe*, *Cats and Dogs*, and *Scooby-Doo* were produced, the final model is constructed using polygons. The earliest version of the software that is used for most production at Rhythm & Hues used polygons all through the pipeline. Part of the software methodology is the same today. To understand the current technology used to

**3. Modeling Overview**

create models at Rhythm & Hues, you need to look back at the original modeling process created by Robert Abel and Associates.

In 1985, the early days of the first computer graphics, modelers were referred to as *encoders*. The Brilliance commercial (Robert Abel and Associates), commonly referred to as the "Sexy Robot" commercial, became famous because it introduced one of the first computer-generated character animations. The ad was remembered for the natural feel of the robot's movement, as well as the incredible look that was achieved.

Encoding was not a glamorous job. The modeler simply digitized 2-D data in the computer. The modeler, or encoder, was responsible for making sure that the number of points per digitized line was identical, and even more difficult, the points on these lines had to line up exactly with the points on the adjacent line. The modeling software written by Robert Abel and Associates was not user-friendly, and everyone in the production process had to manually do many things that modern software does for modelers today. This process of digitizing layers gave only a framework of data (Figure 3.11). The final model derived from this data needed a more artistic approach to create the final model data.

The task of the encoder became more straightforward when the 3-D digitizer was developed. It was no longer necessary to cut a sculpture into thin slices to get 3-D data. With the 3-D digitizer, the modeler could create a mesh on the surface of the sculpture itself to digitize the model directly in the computer as 3-D data. Using the 3-D digitizer is not an adequate way to create 3-D models for rendering, nor is slicing the model into thin slices. The actual model for the final render requires the data to be structured so that the light falls on the surfaces naturally, and any stretching, folding, or creasing takes place along the lines appropriate for those deformations. This type of careful delineation of where surfaces fall is something that must be done after the digitizing process. Although the digitizing can be set up so that you will get the necessary data in the necessary places, the final model will require careful placement of surface borders and surface direction.

This process of using 3-D digitized data to create models is snubbed by modelers who create 3-D models from 2-D drawings or from scratch. This is not considered real modeling by modelers who do not digitize data. However, this process is complex and demanding. It requires the modeler to maintain tight dimensional tolerance to the original sculpture to work around the limitations of the sculpture.

Because the creative part of the modeling process is performed by the sculptor, the modeler is simply a technician responsible for the interpretation of the 3-D form into the computer. However, new modeling processes, such as subdivision modeling techniques, have rendered the process of digitizing nearly obsolete. No longer

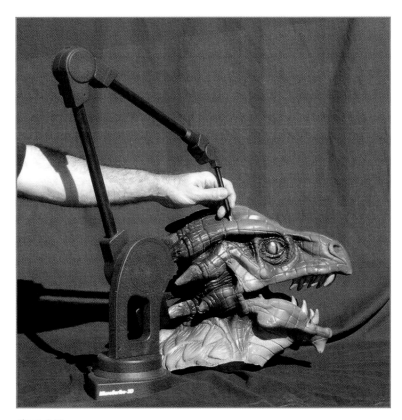

**Figure 3.11**
A digitizer can create fast 3-D reference data but not a good 3-D model.

is the creative process left solely to the sculptor. Although the main characters for major productions will frequently require a digitized sculpture, each modeler is also responsible for creating usable models from drawings or from scratch for incidental characters, props, and environments.

Many procedures occur after the model is created that require skill and creativity that would be difficult to create using a digitizer. The process of creating facial poses and similar 3-D morph targets is a necessary and time-consuming part of many studios' production processes. Many production requirements that the model must have cannot be created using scanning or digitizing technology. These processes, such as creating texture coordinates, material groups, and deformation groups for animation, require technical knowledge and attention to detail. At times, props that are used in production need to be matched in the computer, and therefore, creating an exact computer replica from an existing object is still a useful skill.

# Modeling for Games versus Modeling for Film

Modeling for games requires a different emphasis than modeling for film. When you model for film or video, the emphasis is on creating a model that is lifelike or aesthetically pleasing. The resolution of the model is relatively unimportant compared to the process of modeling for games (Figure 3.12).

The process of modeling for games is focused on creating models that fit within a strict guideline that dictates the exact number of polygons allowed per model. Each game has its own budget for geometry and textures that can be seen on any given frame. This budget needs to be allocated based on graphics' performance and the performance of the game engine. As the performance of consoles increases, more polygons can be seen on the screen for any given frame. This gives the modeler much more creative freedom and the ability to model much more lifelike forms than similar consoles previously allowed only a year ago. Figure 13.13 shows a car model that was used in a video game that was produced in 1995. (By today's standards, this model is very low-resolution, even for a video game.)

The increase of realism in game models is directly related to the increase of performance of the game consoles. The increase of performance of the game consoles, like all computing equipment, is an accelerated evolution that has dramatically changed the cost and performance of new computers. There is no single reason for this; however, Gordon Moore, co-founder of Intel, put a name on this phenomenon: Moore's Law.

In 1965, Moore observed that the number of transistors per square inch on integrated circuits had doubled every year since the integrated circuit was invented and predicted that this trend would continue. This observation became known as *Moore's Law*. The actual number varies somewhat from the original estimate, but the premise that technology will dramatically advance every year and the cost will drop every year still holds true.

In the video game industry, high performance for real-time movement of polygonal models is essential. The polygonal models that are built for video games are lower resolution than the models used for film and video. The video game models depend largely on texture maps to achieve a high level of detail. Over the years, the number of polygons allowed in a polygonal model for video games has increased dramatically. Very early real-time graphics for video games required that the models have no more than 5 to 10 polygons each. The models required for video games now can have several hundred polygons each. It will simply be a matter of time before real-time video game models will have tens of thousands of polygons

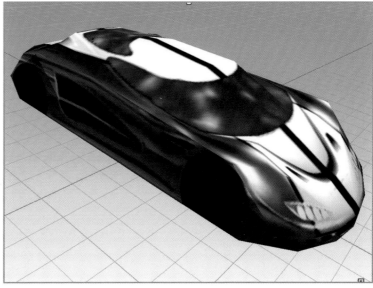

**Figures 3.12, 3.13**
Models created for film and video have higher resolutions and are more detailed than the models created for video games.

per model. With this increase of realism, the games themselves will get closer to the visual detail found in television and film.

Video games are becoming a major market for potential modelers. Video games offer more opportunities to create not only models but also animation, textures, and other graphics. In game development the need to get much more work done by fewer people is the major factor that separates it from the process of developing graphics for film or video. For this reason, a game artist has many more opportunities to work in other areas of the production process. Figure 3.14 is a model for

**Figure 3.14**
Modelers in a video game studio have a wide range of responsibilities.

The video game industry is experiencing a resurgence in revenue and high demand for graphically intensive game content. Several console manufacturers are battling it out for dominance in the marketplace. The weapons in this battle are the new game titles to play on these consoles. It is too early to say who the potential winners will be, but within a year or so it will become evident which consoles will survive this round in the battle. It is safe to say, however, that as the graphics potential of these video game consoles gets closer and closer to film, the more video game manufacturers will have to carefully watch their budgets.

Whether that means the salaries for artists or the number of titles released per year will drop considerably, no one can say. As is the case with any question regarding video games, it will not be the game company with the best graphics that will sell the most games. The indisputable rule in the video game industry is that gameplay rules. If this were not the case, the Game Boy would have been a marketing failure. However, the Game Boy is making more money than nearly all the consoles combined. It is probably no coincidence that the art staff required to create a Game Boy title consists of just a couple of hard-core game artists.

## Modeling in the Production Process

Each production environment places modeling in the production pipeline after the creation of the conceptual art and before final animation and rendering. But where exactly modeling falls in between those places in the production pipeline varies slightly from studio to studio. In some studios, modeling is part of the art department. The modeler is considered a sculptor working for the production designer and answers to the art director and the production designer for final approval.

In other studios, the modeler begins working after all the conceptual art is finalized. In a production environment like this, modelers will have their work approved by people more closely associated with the production part of the process. As with every part of the production process, modelers must create work that is approved by the various creative directors associated with the project they are working on. In most cases, this means modelers must have their work approved by an art director, a lighting director, an animation director, or a production designer. Any or all of these various creative directors could be involved on a project that the modeler is working for, and the modeler must be prepared to create work that conforms to the wishes of all the directors involved.

The approval process does not end with the approval of the creative director. Throughout the entire process until the film is delivered to the client, the model can go through many iterative changes. These changes can be required by the various departments that are using the model. For example, once the model is

a video game that was designed, modeled, texture mapped, and set up for animation by a single person. This range of responsibility in the production process is very rare at a film production facility.

As the consoles for video games become more powerful, the crew required to create graphics for each video game is getting larger. The typical video game five years ago would require no more than five artists to develop the entire game. The graphic requirements for today's video game consoles have exploded. What used to take 5 artists to create now takes more than 20 artists to create. The number of people that it takes to create effect shots for film is getting closer to the size of the crew for a typical video game. As the number of people required to create video games increases, the profit margins for video games is bound to decrease. As the film industry has seen in the last five years, profit margins have become smaller and smaller because of increasing overhead and competition.

approved by the creative directors, it might have problems during the setup process and require changes. It might also require changes during the lighting and animation phases of production.

Often, a model created to match something that appears in the live action footage requires modifications from one scene to another. In some cases, a model that appears perfect in certain shots will not work in shots with different lighting and camera setups.

The reasons vary based on the model and the production. In the case of modeling for face replacement, it is common to model an animal's face that will later have to talk. These animals must be modeled very accurately, and the reference data available for modeling is usually high-resolution photography. Although digitizing the head seems more convenient, it would require removing it from the body of the animal, which is not possible.

An animal might look exactly right in one shot, but the angle of the camera will make the model appear wrong in other shots, requiring models to be fixed on a shot by shot basis.

Another reason for modification would be if the animation changes after the model is built. If the model is built according to storyboards that never require the mouth of a character to open, it will not be necessary to build the inside of the mouth. Leaving this out may seem irresponsible, but saving many hours of modeling, lighting, and texture mapping is not irresponsible—it is efficient.

One more reason you might need to revise your work would be if there is not enough detail on the model for a particular shot. Generally, low-resolution is used for animation, medium-resolution is used to test animation set-up and deformations, and high-resolution is used for rendering. In some cases, the high-resolution will not be high enough. If the model is a spaceship, and the camera gets an extreme close-up of the ship flying past, the modeler may be required to build additional details on the surface of the ship where the camera will be close to the ship. This model will sometimes be called an extra-high-resolution model, and will be used for close-ups only.

# chapter 4
# Modeling Tools and Techniques

Modeling is creating 3-D objects in a 3-D environment, whether on the computer or a traditional physical model and has as much to do with technique as it does technology. To make it easier for you, I have broken down the tools starting from the very basic concepts to more advanced subjects. The specific name of the tool or menu may change as technology changes, but the principles remain the same. Some tools of modeling pertain to basic geometric concepts and their digital equivalents. Many terms found on the menu of a digital modeling program can be lifted verbatim from a high school geometry textbook. Other tools are more complex or more specific to digital modeling. Modeling tools may vary between software packages, but most tools that you'll need can be found in most software packages. Because data exported from most modeling packages must be used by other software, the data must follow common guidelines and standards.

The world of 3-D space in the computer has been designed to mimic the physical space outside the computer.

Many correlations exist between 3-D computer modeling and the process of creating 3-D physical models outside of the computer. Figures 4.1 and 4.2 show some similarities between a sculpture and a digital model.

 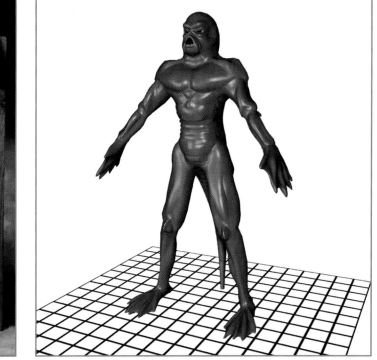

**Figures 4.1 and 4.2**
A sculpture and a digital model share geometric 3-D properties, such as width, length, height, surface area, and volume.

41

## Basic Modeling Concepts

Objects in a 3-D environment have width, height, and depth. These dimensions correspond to the dimensions in most 3-D systems used for modeling. The mathematical model that uses these dimensions to define 3-D geometry is called the *Cartesian coordinate system*. The coordinates used to create models fall on the X (width), Y (height), and Z (depth) axes (Figure 4.3). Other coordinate systems can be used to describe 3-D space, but the modeling programs that are commonly used do not use those coordinate systems.

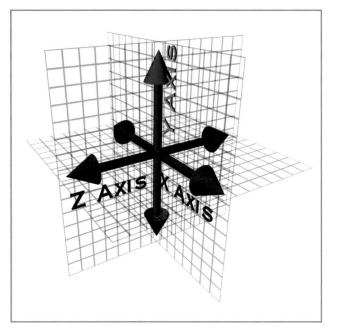

**Figure 4.3**
The Cartesian axes, X, Y, and Z, are used to define the digital workspace.

Whether you are creating models in the computer or real physical space, you have to deal with various aspects of 3-D space, including the 3-D workspace, where you can view the 3-D objects and the transformation of objects in 3-D space.

## The 3-D Workspace

The place where all dimensions begin is called the *origin*. In Cartesian coordinate space, the directions X, Y, and Z are used to show where in space an object is placed. The actual numerical values for X, Y, and Z are defined by the distance that object is from the origin. In 3-D space, the origin represents zero, and all values for X, Y, and Z are determined by moving along these directions relative to the origin.

Any direction, X, Y, or Z, is referred to as an *axis*. If an object is one unit to the left of the origin, then that value is one unit on the X axis. Generally, 3-D placement requires three coordinates, X, Y, and Z. An object that rests at "1, 1, 1" is one unit to the left of the origin (X axis), one unit above the origin (Y axis), and one unit toward the viewer (Z axis).

Different modeling software packages have different rules that define the values of these axes and dictate the value of the rotation about the axes. The most common rule is the *right-hand rule*, which defines the coordinate value direction and rotational dimension along each axis.

To understand the right-hand rule, hold up your right hand so your palm is facing you and extend your thumb—that represents the X axis moving from zero into a positive direction. Extend your index finger upward to represent the Y axis. The middle finger, which is pointing towards you, represents the Z axis. The dimensions along the Z axis get larger as they get closer to the viewer. Figure 4.4 illustrates the right-hand rule.

To determine the direction of rotation about the X axis (Figure 4.5), curl your fingers around as you extend your thumb. The direction of the fingers curling around represents the positive rotation around the X axis. The direction of the Y and Z axes can be determined by orienting the thumb along those axes and curling your fingers.

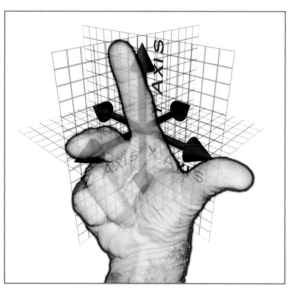

**Figure 4.4**
The right-hand rule helps you grasp the idea of axes.

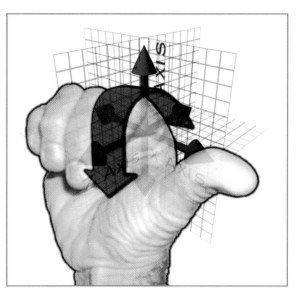

**Figure 4.5**
Determining rotation direction using the right-hand rule.

## 3-D Objects and Components

Computer modeling has several building blocks that are common to all objects that can be built. These components all build upon each other to create complex entities with additional functionality over what pertained to the individual components. The entities are points, lines and edges, polygons, curves, and surfaces.

### Points

The *point*, or *vertex*, has no area or volume but can be located by using numbers given in the X, Y, and Z dimensions, as shown in Figure 4.6. (A vertex is more often associated with polygonal geometry.)

### Lines and Edges

A *line* is defined by the X, Y, and Z locations of its two endpoints (Figure 4.7). An *edge* is a type of line that is defined by adjacent sides of polygons or surfaces (Figure 4.8). A *polyline* is a type of line that comprises a string of two or more straight line segments attached to each other.

Modeling packages manipulate lines and edges in different ways. Traditional polygonal modeling packages use polylines to construct models from. Some packages use *winged edge modeling* to construct models. A winged edge modeling system treats edges as the primary modeling entities. Winged edge modeling software does not usually use polylines. Modeling software that uses polylines generally does not acknowledge edges as objects that can be picked and manipulated.

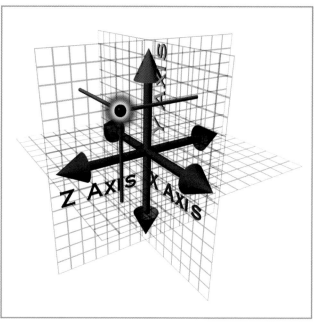

**Figure 4.6**
A point is a theoretical place in 3-D space that is designated by three coordinates along the X, Y, and Z axes.

**Figure 4.7**
A line is the entity that spans directly between two points.

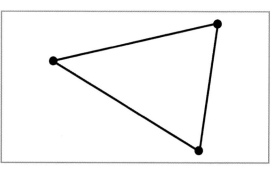

**Figure 4.8**
Edges are the lines that surround polygons.

## Polygons

A polygon is a face that exists between three or more edges (Figure 4.9). Polygonal models are used in a variety of applications, such as video games, military simulation exercises, animation software for television and film, industrial prototyping systems, and high-end medical visualization.

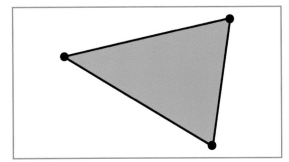

**Figure 4.9**
A polygon.

**Figure 4.10**
Models made from simple polygons can appear very realistic and complex.

Polygons that are used in most models have information stored for each corner of the polygon. The basic polygon is conceptually simple and needs only three pieces of information for construction—the location of the three vertices that make up the corners of the polygon. Each of these corners is defined by three numbers: X, Y, and Z coordinates. As requirements for the model get more complex, so does the information stored for each vertex.

A *polymesh* is a series of polygons grouped together to create one object. In most instances, the polymesh should consist of a continuous region with all the polygons facing the same direction. Polygonal models are built by combining polymeshes into one final model. Polygonal models can appear ultra-realistic (Figure 4.10), and are capable of tremendous movement and flexibility.

### Face Normals, Vertex Normals, and UVs

Every polygon has a front and back side. *Face normals* indicate the direction the polygon is facing. Polygons are connected to their surrounding vertices using a clockwise or counter-clockwise ordering of points. The direction of the polygon is determined by the order in which the vertices flow along the edges of the polygons. Generally, counter-clockwise ordering of points creates a front-facing polygon. A face normal can be visualized as a vector that proceeds at exactly 90 degrees to the surface of the polygon.

Polygonal models, like the facets on a diamond, can appear very jagged on the surface. The facets' appearance is the behavior of all polygonal objects that have not had *vertex normals* applied to them. Smoothing a polygonal model is called different things in different modeling packages. Some packages call this the application of smoothing groups, and some call it the softening or hardening of normals.

Vertex normals are created in areas of the model that are supposed to appear smooth. The normal that is assigned at the vertex interpolates the display of the adjacent polygons, smoothing out the entire region. This normal is calculated by averaging the direction of the faces that are attached to a common vertex.

A vertex normal can be visualized as a vector that emits from a common point between several polygons, with a direction that is the average value of all of the face polygons that surround that vertex.

### Advanced Polygon Concepts

Each polygon in a polygonal model has a number designated to it, which is generally based on the order of creation. The vertices surrounding each of these polygons are also assigned a specific number, also based upon the order of creation.

To understand the inner workings of a polygonal model, examine the structure of a polygonal file format. One popular file format is the Wavefront *.obj* file format. The .obj file format is a text-based file format, so the information in the file can be edited by hand. The first character of each line specifies the command that the line is performing; the command is followed by arguments.

The example file shown next is very simple; many entity types supported by this file format are not listed here. This example shows the correlation between the polygonal entities within a single file. The first thing that usually happens—after a comment about which software wrote the file and maybe how many vertices and faces are contained in the file—is to list the group name:

g sphere

The second thing is to list all of the vertices in order of creation:

v 0.000000 -0.707107 -0.707107

v -0.707107 -0.707107 -0.000000

v -0.000000 -0.707107 0.707107

v 0.707107 -0.707107 0.000000

The numbers listed for each vertex represent the X, Y, and Z values for each vertex. The order of these vertices indicates their identity. The first vertex listed is vertex one (1), the second is vertex two (2), and so on.

Until now, not one polygon has been called out in the file. The other things are listed first, and then the final part of the file puts it all together. The last entity is the face command:

f 1 2 6 5

f 2 3 7 6

f 3 4 8 7

f 4 1 5 8

Here the face command assembles the various parts of the polygon into faces. The order in which the vertices are listed determine whether the polygon is front facing, and the order that the faces are listed determines the polygon (face) number within the model. Polygonal ordering is crucial in situations that use morph targets, where several polygonal models must have identical ordering.

When building models using polygons, there are some important things to remember. Polygonal modeling tools work best when the model is clean. That usually means that duplicated edges, vertices, and faces will screw things up. Another problem is *back-facing polygons*. Back-facing polygons do more than simply control the display of the polygon. If all of the polygons do not face the correct direction, polysets will not merge correctly or render correctly. One way to check for back-facing polygons is to turn face normals on in the display options. Another way is to turn the display of the polyset to single-sided. In single-sided mode, the back-facing polygons will disappear, and holes in the model will indicate problems. Another problem is *concave polygons*. Concave polygons are polygonal faces that will have problems during render and display (Figure 4.11). Faces that have sides that are concave need to be subdivided into smaller polygons until the concavity is eliminated.

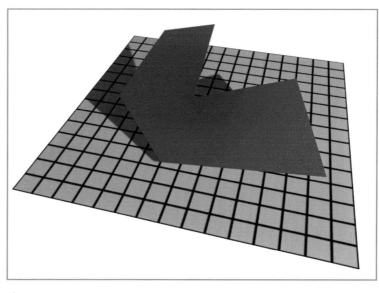

**Figure 4.11**
Concave polygons cause many problems with display and rendering.

Before any model is completed, coincident vertices and edges should be deleted, and the model should be cleaned up to eliminate coincident faces, and faces that are facing the wrong side should be cleaned up.

4. Modeling Tools and Techniques

## Curves

A *curve* is a type of line that is usually defined by several points and deviates from a straight path. These points define the overall direction of the curve. Different curve types use different mathematical algorithms to determine curvature or change in slope along its path. *Splines* are curves that resemble the thin strips of stiff material that an engineer or craftsperson uses to draw smooth curves between two or more points.

A *linear curve*, shown in Figure 4.12, resembles a polyline but has higher math functionality. The changes of curvature between the points is determined by a linear algorithm, resulting in a sharp break in the curve at each point.

A *cardinal curve*, shown in Figure 4.13, has a path that passes through each point. Its shape is controlled by moving one of these points.

A *Bézier curve*, shown in Figure 4.14, also passes through each point along its path, but the Bézier curve has handles on each side of the point that control the curvature at that point.

A *B-spline*, shown in Figure 4.15, passes through only the first and last point along its path. The placement and curvature throughout the rest of the curve is determined by the placement of the *control vertices* that will usually fall outside the curve itself.

A *NURBS curve*, shown in Figure 4.16, uses the position of all its control vertices, as well as the ability to assign weight to each control vertex individually, to control shape and slope along its path. The weights at each control vertex are represented

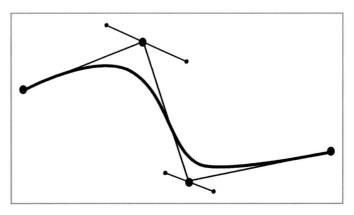

**Figure 4.14**
The Bézier curve uses handles that extend from the control points to adjust the weights of each point.

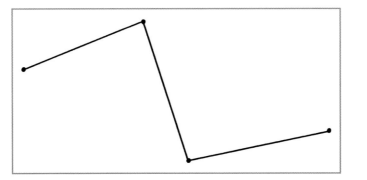

**Figure 4.12**
A linear curve resembles several two-point lines laid end to end.

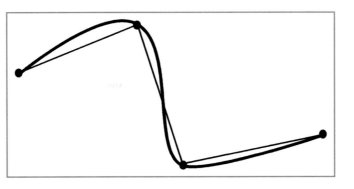

**Figure 4.13**
A cardinal curve has control points that rest along the path of the curve.

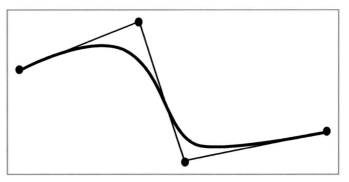

**Figure 4.15**
The B-spline has points that rest outside the curve that control the shape of the curve.

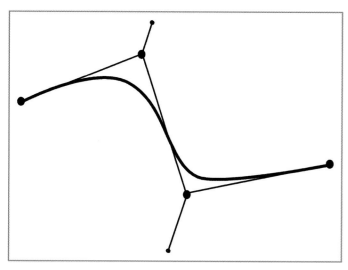

**Figure 4.16**
The NURBS curve has a weight associated with each vertex that allows the geometry to be more complex and flexible than B-spline geometry.

as vectors. These vectors are not usually visible in the modeling program but are shown in the figure to illustrate the effect of these weights.

## Control Vertices, Hulls, and Edit Points within Curves

A *control vertex* is not the same thing as a point on the line. The points along the line are usually referred to as *edit points*. NURBS geometry creates control elements known as *hulls*. These hulls rest outside the NURBS geometry and control the shape of the actual geometry. The hull of a curve is represented by a sequence of straight lines that come together at specific points. The point at which the hull changes direction is the control vertex. In a curve that contains four control vertices along the hull, the curve itself could have no more than two edit points, one at each end of the curve. The space between the edit points is referred to as a *span*. Figure 4.17 is a diagram of a typical NURBS curve. The wide tube indicates the actual curve, the thin black line indicates the hull, the green boxes are control vertices, and the red balls are the edit points. There are two additional control vertices toward each end of the curve. The spans of the curve are the spaces in between the edit points.

The length of the curve in world space is the *arc length* of the curve, and must be calculated in X, Y, and Z units. If the curve exists between the points zero and one in any single direction, the curve will have an arc-length of one.

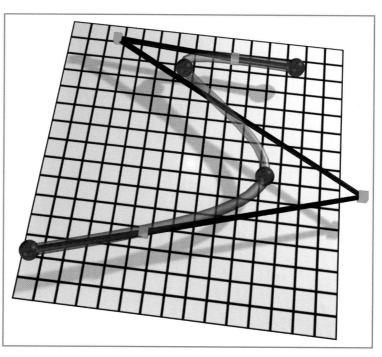

**Figure 4.17**
This diagram of a NURBS curve shows the components that make up a curve.

Curves are three-dimensional entities, but travel in only one direction, the *U direction*, along the length of the curve. This is an alternate coordinate system to X, Y, and Z, and the curve can also be measured using this new system. The U dimension measures the parameterization of the curve. Generally, if there is one span between edit points on a curve, the curve will have a parameterization of zero to one. If there are three spans in a curve, the parameterization of that curve will generally be defined as zero to three.

## Curve Parameterization

The direction of the curve is determined by the order in which the edit points are placed, and the values of each edit point's parameterization on the curve is based on the order and location of the point along the curve. Parameterization can be defined in terms of the number of spans (*uniform parameterization*) or by defining the entire curve in terms of "zero-to-one" (*chord-length parameterization*). The points along a curve can be identified based on the order in which they were created. The first point in the U direction on a curve is zero, the second is one, and so on.

**4. Modeling Tools and Techniques**

47

## Surfaces

A *surface* is the theoretical fabric that spans two or more curves. For each curve type is a corresponding surface. Surfaces can be created in several major ways. The technique used to create the surface is the definition of the surface type. Whether a B-spline surface or a NURBS surface is created using a loft function, the surface is considered a *lofted surface*. Even polygonal modeling programs use these surfacing tools, like lofting, to create areas that contain many small adjacent polygons known as a *polymesh*.

The lines within and surrounding a surface when a surface is constructed from curves are called *isoparms* (Figure 4.18). In most cases, when a surface is created from splines, the number and placement of these isoparm lines correlate with the number and placement of the edit points on the curves that create the surface. *Isoparm* is a term used to define the generic separations within a spline-based surface. These separations define the points at which additional geometry is added to the surfaces to define the shape.

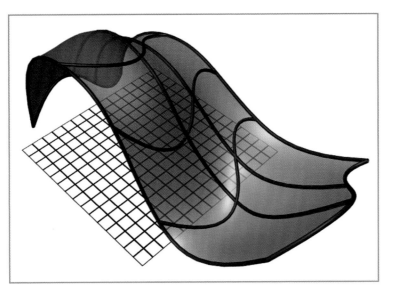

**Figure 4.18**
An isoparm is the place in a surface where a surface span ends. Isoparms can occur at surface borders or within a surface.

## Surface Parameterization

A spline-based surface has an inherent parametric range of values along each side. These values, measured in U and V, are also related to the number of isoparms and thus the number of edit points in the curves that created the surface. The *U direction* is the primary direction of the surface. In the case of the single span lofted surface, it is the direction in U that the curves that are used to create the surface are running in. The *V direction* is the secondary direction of the surface. In the case of the single span surface, V indicates the direction between the curves. The numerical value of V is based on which curve was picked first when the surface was built.

The directions of U and V determine the direction of the *surface normals*. Surfaces, such as polygons, are front-facing or back-facing. You can determine which way the surface will face during the construction of that surface, but it is always a good idea to check the surface direction after building the surface, by turning the display mode from double-sided to single-sided. You can also check this by using a directional texture map that will only read correctly when the surface is front-facing.

Unlike polygons, surface normals run normal to the surface in any direction the surface is facing at any given point. A single surface can be very complex, and because the surface is a theoretical, infinitely smooth skin, it can have an infinite number of theoretical normals. Surface normals can be visualized as vectors that emit 90 degrees from the front of a surface along the surface, like steel bristles covering the entire surface.

Each direction, length and height, of the surface can be measured in U and V. In the case of a single span skin surface (using the same curves on each side to construct the surface), the U values correspond to the number of edit points on the curves on each side. The V value would be 1 by default. These values relate also to the number of spans. By selecting the single span skin surface, and reading the information window statistics on the selected surface, you can see that the spans relate to the way the surface was constructed. When you begin to attach, detach, insert, and rebuild surfaces, you begin to make changes to the number of spans in the surface and thus the parameterization.

Different curves with equal number of points can create surfaces with radically different parameterization. Surface parameterization is similar to curve parameterization. If the spans on a surface correspond to the placement of edit points on the curve, the parameterization is uniform; if the segments are evenly distributed along the length of the surface, the parameterization is chord length (Figure 4.19).

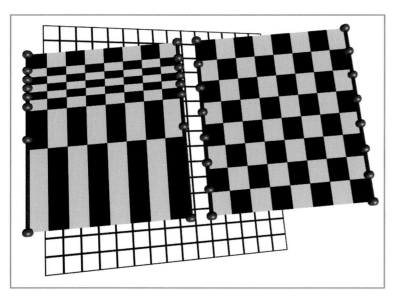

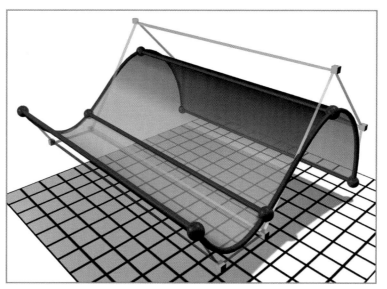

**Figure 4.19**
Curves with uniform parameterization were used to construct the surface to the left. Curves rebuilt using chord-length parameterization were used to construct the surface on the right.

**Figure 4.20**
This diagram of a NURBS surface shows the various components that make up a surface.

Parameterization is useful for building models and laying out assemblies of NURBS patches and can be easier to visualize when a texture map is applied to the surface. When a model is created using NURBS surfaces, the parameterization of those surfaces can be visualized using texture maps. The parameterization of each surface places the texture map cleanly inside the boundaries of the surface.

## Control Vertices, Hulls, and Edit Points within Surfaces

Surfaces are a mathematical extension of a given curve type. B-spline curves create B-spline surfaces, and a NURBS curve creates a NURBS surface. Surfaces, like the curves that create them, contain control vertices, hulls, and edit points. Figure 4.20 is a diagram of a NURBS surface. In this diagram, the control vertices are represented as green boxes, the edit points are represented as red balls, the hills are represented by the straight colored lines, and the isoparms are represented as curved blue lines. Just like the curve diagram shown earlier, there is an additional row of control vertices toward each end of the surface, and the edit points separate the spans. In the case of the surface, the edit points are located at points where isoparms meet.

Each vertex within the surface has a unique identifier based on the location in UV space and the order in which the point lies relative to the first point in U and V. The first point in U and V would generally have a parameterization of zero in U and zero in V (0,0). Each point spreading out in U and V away from the 0,0 point will be given an identifier based on the direction in U and V, and the number of the point relative to the point 0,0.

## Surface Types

A *lofted* surface is the simple spanning across two or more curves. A lofted surface can be very basic, creating a simple flat rectangle, or it can be very complex, creating an entire organic character with one surface. This type of surface is also known as a *skin* surface (Figure 4.21).

A *revolved* surface is created by using a simple curve and spinning it across one axis to create a shape. This action mimics what a lathe would do in the physical world (Figure 4.22).

An *extruded* surface is created by either extending the curve off in one direction or by "sweeping" that curve, the profile curve, down the length of a guide curve, the path (Figure 4.23).

A *swept* surface is created by "sweeping" one or more profile curves along one or two paths. Whereas a revolved or an extruded surface is a type of swept surface, the swept surface category is broad and includes more complex surfaces. The swept surface type includes swept, bi-rail, and animated swept surfaces. Generally, the term *swept surface* is reserved for surfaces constructed from more than one profile curve or path curve (Figure 4.24).

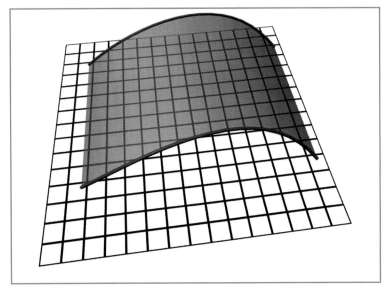

**Figure 4.21**
An example of a lofted surface is a boat hull.

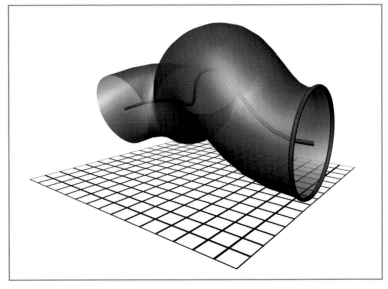

**Figure 4.23**
Extruded surfaces can be used to create long, thin items, such as tentacles and phone cords.

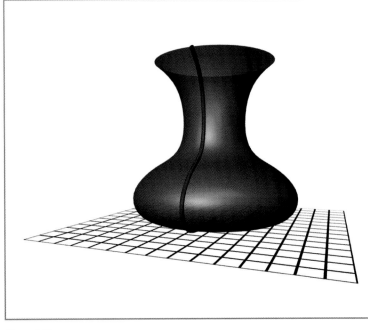

**Figure 4.22**
An example of a revolved surface is a wine glass.

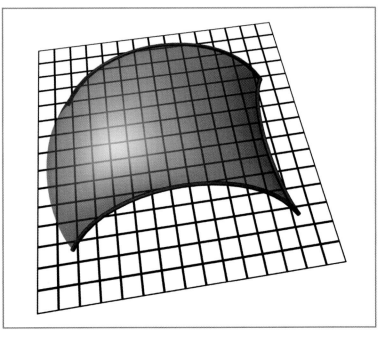

**Figure 4.24**
One kind of swept surface is the bi-rail surface. Bi-rail surfaces are good for modeling many hard-to-create surfaces, such as vehicle components.

A *boundary* surface is created by defining the exterior edges of an area by three or more curves and filling that area with a surface. The boundary surface type includes square, boundary, and N-sided surfaces. A square surface is a type of boundary surface. Square surfaces are versatile surfaces that are used for surfacing operations where accuracy is required (Figure 4.25).

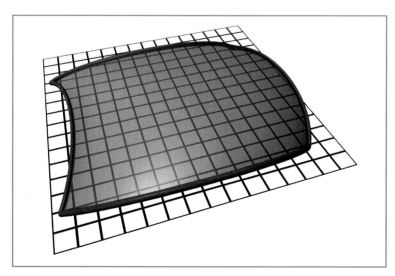

**Figure 4.25**
A square surface.

An *animated sweep* (Figure 4.26) is a complex version of a lofted surface. This surface is created from one curve that serves as a path of animation and another curve that serves as the surface profile. The profile curve is animated by moving it along the animation path, and at given time intervals the profile curve will be duplicated. These duplicated curves are skinned together to create a surface. An animated sweep (Figure 4.26) uses a profile that is animated through time to create geometry. This specialized surface is good for creating organically animated effects, such as jet exhaust.

A *primitive* (Figure 4.27) is a geometric entity that usually comprises one or more of the surface types listed in the preceding text. These primitives usually represent geometric solids that make up a library of 3-D shapes that are considered common objects. These shapes include *spheres*, *cubes*, *cones*, *cylinders*, and the like.

A *free-form shape* (Figure 4.28) can be a spline-based mesh, multiple meshes, or a polymesh. This kind of modeling requires the modeler to create meshes that approximate the correct shape and to pull points to create details and smooth rough areas. This kind of modeling was the way modelers would work when

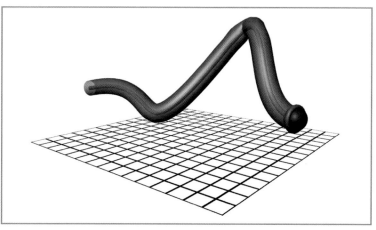

**Figure 4.26**
An animated sweep.

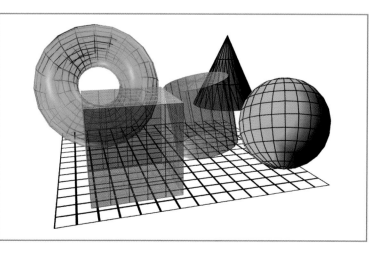

**Figure 4.27**
Primitives are surfaces that have been premodeled into easy-to-use common shapes.

creating the "single-surface head" type models that were common when NURBS-based modeling programs were initially being used in production. The process of creating a model using this technique is called *free-form modeling*. When a modeler is creating a model using polygonal free-form modeling techniques, it is sometimes referred to as *virtual sculpting* or, more accurately, *point pulling*. This procedure does not require that the initial shape be anywhere close to the desired form, but as the modeler continues to work on the shape, the model will acquire the desired form through the sculpting process.

**4. Modeling Tools and Techniques**

51

Modeling with freeform shapes is the basis for creating complex polygonal objects using *subdivision polygons*, or *polygon smoothing*. Polygonal smoothing creates a model that is visually smooth and continuous along the surface. The polygons are subdivided into smaller sizes. The surface is smoothed by calculating the position of the vertices in the original polygonal shape and smoothing the surface through those points. This smoothing is analogous to the smooth shape of a NURBS curve as it travels through the shape of the segmented shape of the NURBS hull.

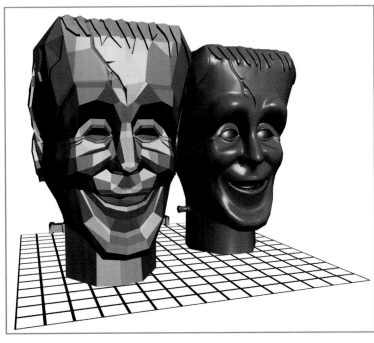

**Figure 4.28**
A freeform shape can be a polygonal shape that is manipulated by pulling points to create the shape (left). Polygon smoothing creates a smooth model from the original shape (right).

## Continuity between NURBS Splines and Surfaces

When two NURBS splines or surfaces come together, where the end of one is coincident with the end of another spline or surface, a continuity condition will define how the surfaces blend together. These continuity conditions range from the type of sharp corner found at the side of a box to a very smooth transition between them where the point at which they come together is invisible.

These continuity conditions are described mathematically. The three main continuity conditions used to model an object for the entertainment industry are

*positional continuity* (Figure 4.29), *tangential continuity* (Figure 4.30), and *curvature continuity* (Figure 4.31). Positional continuity is where two NURBS edges simply share the same position. In the case of curves, the end condition is a shared point; in the case of surfaces, the end condition would be a shared edge. The edge where a simple cube has two sides come together is a positional

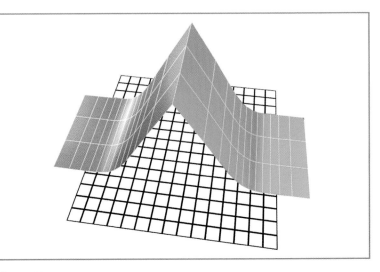

**Figure 4.29**
Positional continuity.

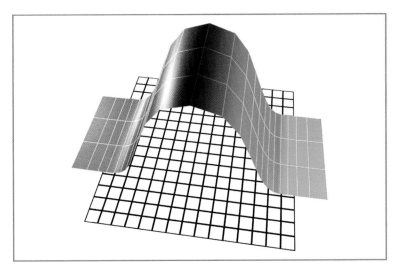

**Figure 4.30**
Tangential continuity.

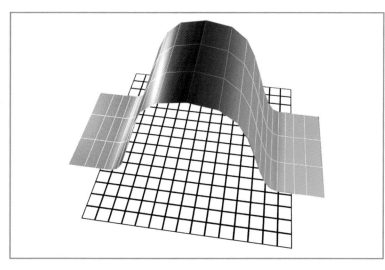

**Figure 4.31**
Curvature continuity.

continuity condition. This type of continuity is sometimes referred to as *C0* or *G0 continuity.*

Tangential continuity is the point at which two NURBS spline entities come together, and the end conditions align with each other within the range of one point on either side of the actual point where the two entities meet. In the case where two surfaces meet and there is a tangency condition, the point that rests inside the point at which the two surfaces meet would be represented as a hull, or a line of points that follows the edge of the surface. If you were to look directly to the side of the tangency condition, the points resting next to the actual point at which the curves or surfaces meet would be aligned in such a way that the path between them would be represented as a straight line. This type of continuity is sometimes referred to as *C1* or *G1 continuity.*

With this knowledge, the modeler can build curves and surfaces next to each other that would have the tangency built in. By making sure that the points resting next to the point where the two spline entities come together are aligned with each other and a straight line, the modeler can build each of these spline entities to be tainted with each other.

Curvature continuity is a condition where two surfaces or curves come together in the tangency condition but have aligned the edge points with the next two rows of points on both surfaces instead of just one row. Curvature continuity is not usually necessary when building a model for the entertainment industry. If two surfaces

look like they come together, generally that is continuity enough. Curvature continuity is very useful when building tools and for surfacing products in the manufacturing and design industries. This type of continuity is sometimes referred to as *C2* or *G2 continuity.*

## Hierarchical Nodes

In many 3-D software programs, when a modeler creates a new entity, such as a curve or surface, it is represented as a *node*. The geometry itself is a description of a certain number of vertices, curves, and so on stored inside or beneath the actual node structure. These nodes keep track of the number and names of entities and also allow the modeler to make groups of entities and position these groups as single entities. When one or more nodes are grouped beneath another node, the modeler is creating a *hierarchy*.

The easiest way to visualize how the software package Maya interprets the objects in a scene is to open the hypergraph window. In that window is a graphic representation of all the objects in a scene. These objects are represented as rectangular boxes. When several boxes are grouped together, a hierarchy is created. Hierarchies are used in almost all models that require more than one surface. When creating models that will be animated, whether they be cars or dinosaurs, proper hierarchy is essential (Figure 4.32).

**Figure 4.32**
Relationships within a modeling scene are visualized with the scene graph in Maya.

Whereas each piece of geometry is part of a node, not all nodes have geometry. A use for these empty nodes is to simply be a reference that is placed in 3-D space to represent an X, Y, Z coordinate. When a modeler creates a node simply for having a reference in Cartesian space, it is called a *null*.

## Picking

Different modeling packages have different work paradigms. For the sake of simplicity, the material covered here will focus only on the work paradigm in Maya.

In Maya, the workflow mandates that an object is selected and then acted upon. This paradigm of "select and act" is common in modeling packages. It is intuitive to be able to apply an action to an object that is already selected. In my opinion, it suits the English-speaking mind to be able to identify the object and then act upon it. This follows basic sentence structure for the English language. It is the same paradigm as the noun-verb structure found in the speech patterns of English-speaking people.

Maya allows the user several options for picking objects in a scene. The options available for picking in Maya are based on the scene graph structure inside Maya and relate to the scene hierarchy. Once an object hierarchy is picked, Maya allows the user to move up and down the hierarchy, or, if the user is at a hierarchy level where this is possible, move from left to right within the hierarchy using the *pick-walker*. The user uses the arrow keys to move up and down and from side to side through the hierarchy.

### *Hierarchy*

When selecting an object in Maya using the Select by Hierarchy menu, modelers are given three modes by which they can select geometry.

### Root

Using this menu item, the modeler selects the highest hierarchy node. Maya describes the scene as a series of hierarchy nodes, and the node at the top of an individual hierarchy is considered the root. When this menu item is used, only the root nodes will be selected.

### Leaf

In any hierarchy structure, unless the hierarchy consists of one node, there will be lower nodes beneath the root node. Each lower node is referred to as a *leaf*. In a complex assembly of objects, there will be a major hierarchy and then several smaller hierarchies within that hierarchy. A leaf node can be considered to be the top node within a subhierarchy. When using this menu selection, the user picks a leaf node within the hierarchy (Figure 4.33).

**Figure 4.33**
The root of a hierarchy and a leaf within the hierarchy are nodes that lie within a typical scene diagram.

### Template

This menu selection will allow the user to select only items whose display type has been turned to *template* mode. An object that is displayed as a template (Figure 4.34) can be picked, transformed, and displayed in 3-D space within the viewing panel. However, an object that is displayed as a template cannot be edited at the vertex level.

One reason a user may decide to "template" an object would be to keep from inadvertently picking that object while working on something else. Because normal picking modes do not allow the selection of a template, to "untemplate" an object or to transform a template object, the user must have a "pick template" option available.

### *Object Type*

Different object types in Maya are described as *objects*. A hierarchy can be considered an assembly object. Each object is represented as a single node within a hierarchy. The Select by Object Type menu serves as a selection filter. If the user is simply working on NURBS surfaces and the scene is filled with other entity types, the user can simply isolate the surface selection menu and work on only surfaces. This is a huge time-saver and will allow users to keep from having to manually

**Figure 4.34**
Templated objects are shaded.

isolate many other objects in order to pick the ones they want to work on. The different object types that are available to be filtered using this menu are fairly self-explanatory and will not be covered here.

## Component Type

Different objects have different components that can be edited. A NURBS surface can be edited by selecting control vertices, edit points, isoparms, hulls, and surface points. It is with the Select by Component Type menu that enables users to filter which component type they want to work on. This filter mechanism is useful if you are working for a long time on one component type. For example, a modeler spending an entire day pulling points on a surface would definitely want to use this menu to make the task easier. A user simply pulling points for a short period of time and then pulling edit points shortly after that would probably want to choose the option of using the right mouse button placed directly over the object to be edited to get a pop-up menu for the component selection.

## 3-D Transformations

When the modeler takes an object that already exists in 3-D space and moves it, rotates it, scales it, or affects it with any other type of movement or deformation, the modeler is *transforming* the object. Transformations can be applied in space relative to the Cartesian axes themselves, referred to as *world space transformation*, or can be applied relative to a user-defined axis, referred to as

*local transformation*. Sometimes a transform is referred to as an *xform*. Transformations can include moving an object (Figure 4.35), rotating an object (Figure 4.36), or scaling an object (Figure 4.37)

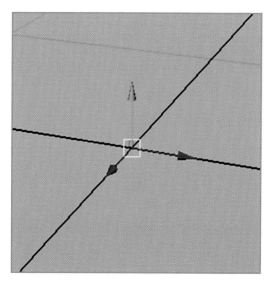

**Figure 4.35**
The move object in Maya.

**Figure 4.36**
The rotate object in Maya.

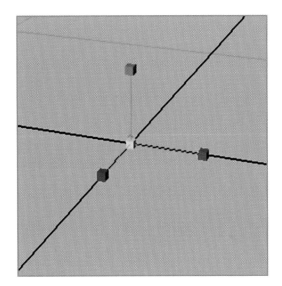

**Figure 4.37**
The scale object in Maya.

When an object is created, it has its own coordinate system associated with it. The object will have its own definition of where the origin is and its own definition of axis orientation. Some modeling packages differentiate the local axis from the object's own axis, and these packages allow the user to transform using *object transformation*.

When the model is transforming a component of an object—a point on a surface, for example—the modeler can transform the point along the surface's *normal*. The normal is the vector along the surface that stands perpendicular to the surface at any point along the surface. When a modeler uses this type of transformation, it is referred to as *normal transformation*, or simply moving along the normal.

Transformations are descriptions of the translation (movement), rotation, and scale of an object. These transformations utilize the translation, rotation, and scale *channels* to move the object from one position to another. A simple transformation is sometimes referred to as a *linear transformation*. A linear transformation does not necessarily mean that the transform goes directly from one position to another in a straight line. A linear transformation is where the movement of the object can be described using linear algebra.

### Translate

*Translating*, or *moving*, an object from one place to another is the simplest transformation. When a move takes place in modeling, it usually consists of relocating from one point in Cartesian (X, Y, Z) space to another but keeping its original size

and direction. In some cases, the modeler may want to use a local coordinate system for moving an object, but not for the most part.

### Rotate

An object can be *rotated* about the X, Y, or Z axis. When you are rotating an object, it is generally critical that you are certain about which coordinate system you are using. Usually when you are rotating an object about the world origin, it is only the correct axis to use if the object itself is placed at the world origin. More often than not, the modeler will need to establish a new origin for the object prior to rotating it either by moving the local axis to the point where you want the object to rotate around or by grouping the object to itself and then relocating the origin for the group (null) node.

### Scale

An object can be *scaled* in four ways. The object can be scaled along each axis, X, Y, or Z, or the object can be scale uniformly along all axes. The scale process is also very dependent upon the origin about which the object is being scaled.

For example, the object you want to scale is 1 unit in length and is centered at the origin. If you scale the object along the X axis by a factor of 2, the object will be 2 units in length with 1 unit on each side of the origin.

If the same object, 1 unit long, is centered at 10 units away from the origin along the X axis, and the object is scaled by a factor of 2 along the X axis, the object would once again become 2 units long, but the object would move to be centered at 20 units along the X axis. The scale function not only scales the object, but it also scales the space the object occupies from the origin.

### Duplicate-Xform

To create an array of similar elements, the modeler will duplicate an object and then modify that object by transforming it, which is the fastest way to create a complex scene without doing much modeling. It is also the fastest way to make the scene so computationally intensive that the scene cannot be rendered. The *duplicate* function, or *duplicate-xform*, (Figure 4.38) must be used judiciously.

### Mirror

*Mirror* is a variation of the duplicate-xform function and is included in many modeling programs. Mirroring (Figure 4.39) an object is simply duplicating the object and then scaling it by a factor of –1 across any given axis and flipping the normals of that object's surfaces by clicking a button. Note that the mirror function is essentially a scaling function, and for this reason it is as sensitive to the position of the origin about which the object is scaled as any other scaled object.

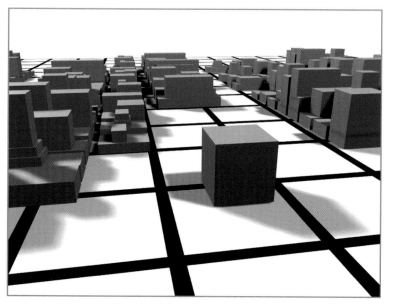

**Figure 4.38**
Duplicate is a fast way to propagate a scene.

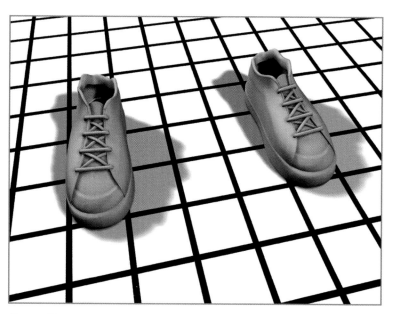

**Figure 4.39**
Mirroring is a specialized way to duplicate an object.

## Hierarchical Transformation

While using transformations, the modeler may want to have control over the point at which the object is scaled without changing the local origin of the object itself. In cases like this, the modeler should use a hierarchy to control this point of origin. A very common occurrence for this will be the mirror function. When you create and modify an object, the origin of the object has probably moved away from the world axes. To flip the object across the world axis, the modeler will probably create a *group* that contains the object and then reflect the group across the world axis. When the model is grouped, a *node* is created above the object in the scene-editing window. By creating this node, the modeler has reset the object origin to the world axis. If the modeler needs to rotate the object using the object's origin, the object's subnode can be selected beneath the group node and transformed without affecting the group's orientation to the world axis.

For some objects, the modeler will create more complex hierarchies to enable the simple animation of the object. One way to illustrate this would be to group an object to itself three times, creating three nodes above the object node, as follows:

1.  The bottom, or object, node will be left alone to be used for modeling transformations (Figure 4.40). Be sure to lock all the channels for this object. In some packages, the transformations of the nodes above the object node are inherited by the object at the bottom of the node stack. Although "baking" in the transformations applied to the object saves time and makes things conceptually simple for the modeler, for the sake of this exercise, it is better to lock all the transform channels so that the object will be transformed only by the nodes above the object node.

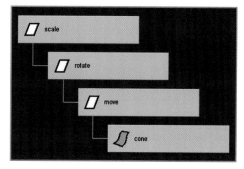

**Figure 4.40**
The nodes of this hierarchy are specifically assigned different transformations per node. This keeps the contribution of each transformation easy to control and keep track of.

2. The second-to-the-last node will be used to apply scaling transformations to the object. On this node, it will be necessary to isolate only the channels that are being transformed. In this case, the translation and the rotation channels will need to be locked to ensure that there will be no transformation other than the scaling transformation applied to the object. Name this node Scale.

3. The second node from the top will be used to apply rotation transformations to the object. Again, the channels that are not being used will need to be locked. In this case, it would be the scaling and the translation channels. Name this node Rotate.

4. The top node will be used to apply movement transformations to the object. Lock the channels for scaling and rotation. Name this node Move.

5. Select the Move node, and key in a value of 2 for the X channel.

6. Select the Rotate node, and key in a value of 90 for the Y channel.

7. Select the Scale node, and key in a value of 2 for the Z channel.

This way of isolating the transformations to separate nodes accomplishes two things: First, it allows the modeler to keep track of the transformations. Second, it gives the modeler control over multiple points of origin.

Another benefit is that by using this process, you will be able to understand the effect of transformation ordering.

## Transformation Ordering

While applying multiple transformations to an object, each transformation will not only act upon the object but will also act upon the other transformations as well. In the exercise described earlier, the order in which the transformations were applied had a very significant effect on the final location and appearance of the object.

If the model has these nodes moved around, the final position of the model will be very different. If the translation node is moved below the rotation node (Figures 4.41 and 4.42), the model will be rotated first and then translated. This will cause a model that originally was located at a Cartesian position of X=2, Y=0, and Z=0 to have a new position of X=0, Y=0, and Z=2 because the object was rotated prior to the translation. This is an important point to consider when you are using packages that have a different order of channels than another package that you may be used to.

## Complex 3-D Transformations

Complex transformations do not simply move an object. These transformations generally change the shape of an object and may also change the position of an object. Some of these transformations are created using tools that are traditionally

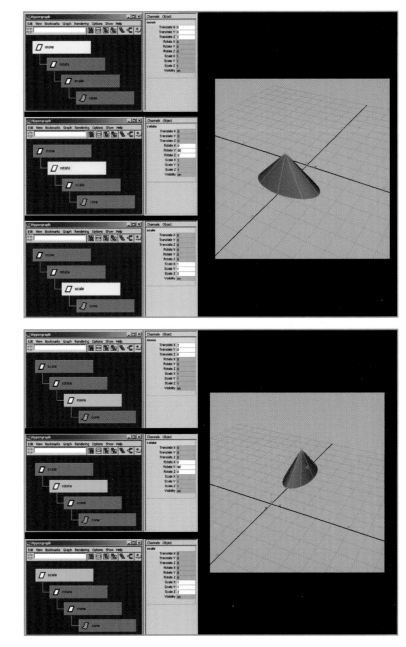

**Figures 4.41 and 4.42**
Rearranging the order by which transformations occur within a hierarchy enables you to transform a model in different ways.

defined as *animation tools*. When an object is being deformed during animation, this is a complex transformation. These complex transformations are used to modify an object to create 3-D models. A complex transformation can affect all or part of an object. Different modeling packages will deal with these transformations in different ways. The following sections discuss these techniques to give you a basic introduction to the principles of these useful tools.

## Nonlinear Transformations

In order to understand what a *nonlinear transformation* (Figure 4.43) is, you must first understand that a linear transformation is an action that will move, rotate, or scale an object using a linear interpolation—that is, a motion that is consistent and constant, such as moving in a straight line or at a constant speed.

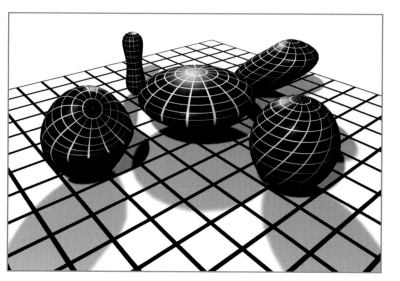

**Figure 4.43**
You can use nonlinear transformations to create effects that would take a lot of time and setup to accomplish using other techniques.

Nonlinear transformations affect the object in ways that may vary or change over time or in space. These transformations include bend, flare, sine, squash, twist, and wave. The actual names associated with these transformations vary from one modeling package to another.

## Nonproportional Modification (Move, Rotate, Scale)

*Nonproportional modification* acts upon the points within the entity being modified. Generally, there is a falloff control that will refer either to world space dimensions or specifically call out rows of *control vertices* (Figure 4.44) that designate the affected distance from the main focus of the deformation.

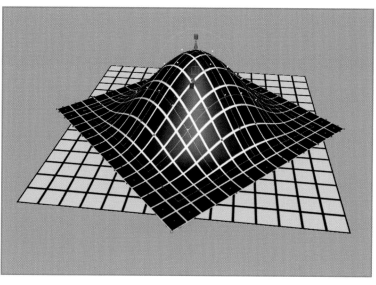

**Figure 4.44**
Nonproportional modification is used to create subtle changes to complex geometry.

The focus point for the deformation is weighted at 100 percent for the transformation so when the focus is nonproportionally translated 2 units along the X axis, the focus itself, whether it is an arbitrary marker in space or an actual vertex on the surface, will move 2 units along the X axis. The points at the farthest edge of the deformation area defined by the falloff control will have a scalar value equal to or close to zero. That means when the focus of the deformation moves 2 units, the points along the edge vertices will not move, or they will only move a small amount. The points between the focus and the edge of the affected area will have a weighting ranging from 100 percent to 0 percent depending on how far away from the focus they are. This creates a smooth deformation of the surface when the focus of the nonproportional modification is transformed.

## Deformers

Deformers are tools that were originally created to help characters move with realistic bending in the body parts. Instead of constructing characters with ball joints at the shoulders and elbows, a character can bend at those areas the way a live-action actor would bend.

Deformers are also a great way to make changes in a model. The toolset that has been created to make flexible and lifelike movement in characters can be used effectively to create changes in a model. Deformers behave differently than other modeling tools because they become a permanent part of the modeling file. Throughout the modeling process, construction history is being recorded. As the

**4. Modeling Tools and Techniques**

mouse-clicks and keystrokes exceed the history buffer, the history is eliminated. Deformers stay with the file.

Another issue that arises when using deformers is layering deformations. Deformers respond to ordering the way that hierarchical transformations respond to ordering. When one deformer is put before another, the results of the final deformation will be different than if the order of the deformers is switched.

When a deformer is used to change the shape of an object, the only way to keep the changes and remove the deformer, is to delete the construction history. When a model is passed off to the lighting or animation set-up phase, the model should be as clean as possible. This requires that all surfaces, polygons, and subdivision models have all deformers removed from them. The best way to ensure this is to delete the history on the objects that have been deformed.

## Clusters

A *cluster* is a specialized type of group that puts points in a group so that the group can be moved as a whole. Sometimes it is advantageous to put a single point in a cluster so it can be moved using a different mechanism than normal point pulling. Clusters (Figure 4.45) become useful when the modeler can create a cluster that has a falloff of point weighting that allows the modeler to use the cluster as a sculpting tool. The modeler will create a cluster and assign weights to the vertices within the cluster. These weights will range from 100 percent for the part of

the cluster that needs to move the most and drop off to 0 percent on the edges of the cluster where it does not need to move at all. Clusters work much like nonproportional modification tools. In this case, however, the focus of the deformation is user-defined and can be any configuration of points; plus the shape of the area that is deformed is defined by the modeler as well.

## Lattices

A *lattice* (Figure 4.46) is a special kind of deformer that allows a complex piece of geometry to be manipulated within a single, simple rectangular volume. This 3-D rectangular shape has a certain number of editing points along the edges, which can be pulled in various ways to modify the complex piece of geometry within the lattice.

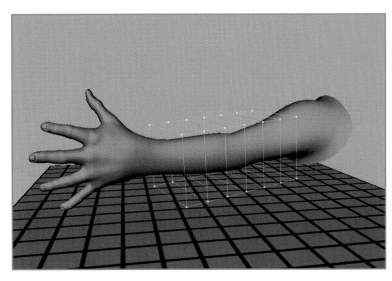

**Figure 4.46**
Lattices allow easy manipulation of complex geometric forms.

The process of binding an object to a lattice usually requires that the complex geometry maintain a historical correspondence to the rectangular shape during this transformation. This relationship assigns point weights to the complex geometry based on the proximity of those points to the editing points on the lattice. When the modeler pulls a point on the lattice, the underlying complex form within the lattice is being pulled fluidly.

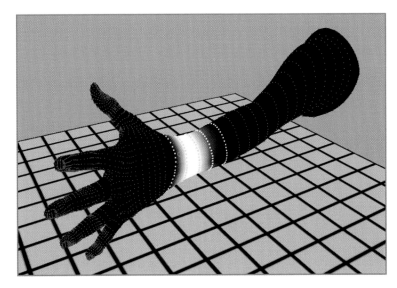

**Figure 4.45**
Clusters are specialized groups of points.

## Wrap Deformers

A *wrap deformer* (Figure 4.47) works similarly to the lattice. Instead of using a rectangular solid that deforms the object, the wrap deformer uses an object that is created by the modeler to deform another object. One common way to create this kind of deformer is to use the high-resolution model to create the low-resolution wrap deformer. Simplifying a high-resolution model can be achieved in several ways, but it is useful to begin with the high-resolution geometry being deformed because the low-resolution model will have a geometric topology similar to that of the original high-resolution model. This means that there will be distinct similarities in density and placement of vertices between the two pieces of geometry, which helps the modeler control the amount of deformation along the surface in a predictable way.

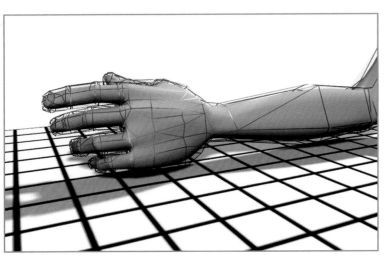

**Figure 4.47**
Wrap deformers are used like lattices to manipulate complex objects with simpler objects.

The wrap deformer is uniquely suited for creating *blend shapes*, or *morph targets* (Figure 4.48), for animation. The easiest way to create models for 3-D morphs is to modify an existing model. Sometimes these modifications are extreme and simply pulling points to get the blend shape model to look right is nearly impossible, in which cases, a wrap deformer is a great tool and is indispensable for creating some shapes.

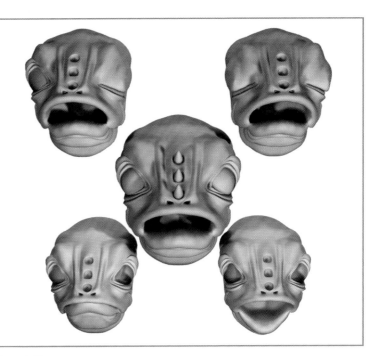

**Figure 4.48**
Blend shapes, or morph targets, are used to create facial shapes for expression and speech.

## Sculpt Deformers

A *sculpt deformer* creates modifications to an object through simple-to-use spherical shapes. The sculpt deformer acts as a tool that can be repositioned and scaled to create bulges or indentations along the object's surface. As with most deformation tools that can be used for modeling, the sculpt deformer will maintain a historical relationship with the object being modified. This can be a problem as well, so when the modeler is finished using the deformer, all history related to this deformer should be deleted. The modified object should maintain the intended shape if this is done properly (Figure 4.49).

## Wire Tools

The *wire tool* (Figure 4.50) is a unique tool that is not often used in modeling, often because many modelers are not aware of it. The wire tool, like the wrap deformer, can be used in the creation of morph targets.

The wire tool can be used in combination with other deformer types. For example, the model that is being modified is already bound by a dense lattice mesh, but it is

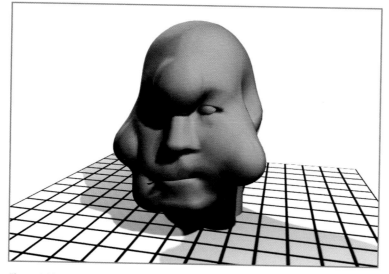

**Figure 4.49**
Sculpt deformers are specialized deformers that are good for creating spherical dents or bumps.

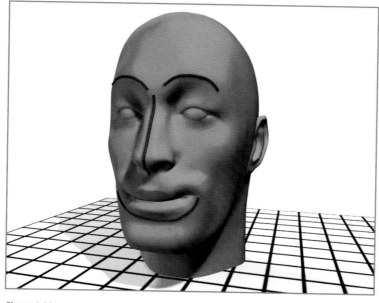

**Figure 4.50**
Wire tool can be used for creating morph targets.

difficult to control the exact vertices to modify your geometry the way it needs to be modified. One way to get control over a specific area on a lattice is to create a curve on the geometry in the area that needs to be modified. This could be a curve that is drawn on the lips of a character if the modeler is creating face shapes. Then the modeler binds the curve to the lattice, not the geometry, using the wire deformer tool. Because the geometry is already bound to the lattice, modifying the lattice will create changes in the geometry. The wire deformer is used to control the lattice in a predictable way.

## Sculpting Tools

Recent advances in software development have made tools available that artists thought were simply impossible to have in the past. In the past, point-pulling techniques to create free-form shapes were not just the state of the art but were the only way to create organic models. Tools are available now in several software packages that allow the artist to interactively move the surface of the geometry the way a sculptor would interact with a piece of clay. These tools have made the process of adding details to freeform shapes much simpler, and tools, such as smoothing functions, have made a huge difference in the way models are created.

These tools, however, are not the solution to all modeling tasks. Most of these sculpting tools (Figure 4.51) are dependent on the underlying surface resolution

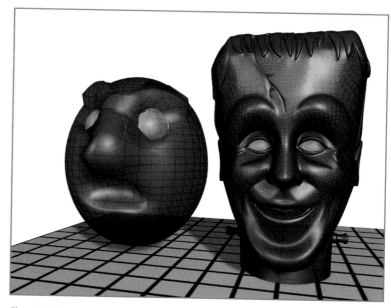

**Figure 4.51**
Sculpting tools, such as Maya Artisan, can capture some added detail, but for major modeling tasks, they may not offer the control achieved through more traditional methods.

and parameterization. If the surface that is being modified does not have the necessary number of vertices in the area being modified to support the detail being added by the tool, the surface will simply create a blobby version of the detail being added by the sculpting tool. If there is enough resolution in the model to create the detail that is being added by the sculpting tool, chances are that the model has too much resolution, and the detail could be added much more effectively by building the detail into the model geometry.

## Modeling Tips

Every modeler needs to be aware of certain things before starting on a project. Now that you understand the tools that are used in the modeling process, a few tips can be introduced. In later chapters, these tips will be elaborated on as they relate to the individual modeling specialties they apply to.

### Get Reference Material

Modelers must have a clear idea in mind of what they are trying to accomplish before they sit down at a computer to start on any modeling task. Modelers must have adequate reference material for any model that is intended to be built on the computer. The computer is a very powerful tool, but the software packages are not nearly interactive enough to be cost-efficient as sketching tools.

When building an original concept, modelers should first carefully draw the front and side views of the object to be built and scan these views into the computer. When building a photorealistic character, the modeler should require photographs that are as clearly shot from one side or another as possible. The goal should be to have views that are as directly in front of the subject, or as directly to the side of the subject, as possible and with minimal distortion. The longer the lens on the camera, the less the curvature or distortion in the image. For feature film quality productions, 80 mm is better than 50 mm, but 200 mm or longer is best. Modelers building a specific piece of architecture or an environment should obtain detailed plans and technical drawings that describe the building or buildings they intend to build.

For some models, it may be necessary to rent a specialized architectural camera or get a professional photographer to take the picture. Even with 200 mm lenses, a tall building will appear foreshortened at the top when the viewer is standing on the ground. Special cameras can adjust the perspective within the lens to correct for this foreshortening.

This type of preparation will save many hours of interactive design work on the computer. Finding reference data is a critical part of the modeler's job and should be something that every modeler does before starting a project.

### Use Reference Material

The modeler should pay careful attention to the reference material throughout the entire process of building a model. This is easier said than done. As anyone who has ever taken life-drawing classes will tell you, the mind thinks it knows how something looks, but in many cases it is wrong. It is crucial to pay attention to what the reference data is saying about the model. Several techniques can be used to enable the modeler to objectively view the reference material. One trick that artists use when they are sketching from life is to step away from the subject and blur their eyes somewhat to compare the reference data to the model. Another trick is to view the material from another angle or even upside down. This change in perspective disorients the "logical" mind and allows artists to objectively view the material without making value judgments.

A modeler building a product, such as a toaster or shampoo bottle for a commercial, should obtain as much accurate reference data as possible. When I have been in similar situations, I took actual scans of the product off a flatbed scanner, 3-D digitized data from a 3-D digitizer, and physical measurements of the actual product using calipers or a micrometer as reference data. You can never be too careful when clients need to have their products modeled accurately. There is no room for judgment calls when money is at stake.

### Document Changes

Sometimes, it will be necessary to make changes based on the supervision of an artistic director or supervisor. In these situations, it may not be possible to make the changes that are being asked for in real time. It is normally impossible to make all the changes that are being asked for while the director is sitting at your workstation. If this is the case, the modeler should try to document all the necessary changes in writing. Whenever possible, obtain additional reference data, photography, physical properties (such as props from the live-action set or additional product samples from the commercial shoot), and sketches drawn by the art director.

Many times, when the art director is sitting at my workstation, I have found it useful to draw on the computer screen using a dry-erase marker. These markers will not leave permanent marks on your computer monitor and are an excellent way to quickly indicate what it is you intend to do while you are having a conversation with a supervisor. If the modeler chooses to use this technique, it will be important to also document the sketches that are drawn on the workstation in writing on paper somewhere else.

Anytime there is feedback from a supervisor or a client, it should be documented. This not only protects the modeler from unnecessary repercussions but is also a way to keep track of the changes that are being made for production-tracking and cost-tracking purposes.

## Minimize Geometry

Economy begins with minimizing the number of vertices (for polygonal modeling) and the number of control vertices (for NURBS modeling). The determining factor for deciding how many points are required in any given piece of geometry is based on how the object looks when shaded, rendered, and animated. Whenever possible, the modeler should try to load the animation of the camera into the modeling window to determine the amount of detail that will be required in the model.

The modeler should also try to load in a default shader that has a certain amount of highlight that lets the modeler know if there are surface discontinuities that need to be fixed prior to rendering. A neutral-colored Blinn shader with a bright highlight color should be used for flat shaded evaluation, and the model should be rendered using the software renderer to predict errors that could be found when rendering. Many modelers are required to apply UVs to polygonal and subdivision models, in which cases, the modeler should create a grid texture (Figures 4.52 and 4.53) that has enough resolution to cover the surface to determine if the texture will stretch when applied to the surface.

When using polygons, the profile of the surface will appear jagged (Figures 4.54 and 4.55) if there are not enough polygons. If you increase the number of polygons, this jaggedness will disappear. If there are too many polygons, the model will take too long to render, and the animation setup will be difficult and time-consuming. Be aware of the distance the object is from the camera. If the object is seen far away, there is no need to render the object full-screen to determine if there are surface discontinuities.

When you are using NURBS surfaces, each spline in the construction process needs to be carefully thought out. If there are not enough vertices, the form of the model will appear blobby and undefined. If there are too many control vertices, the appearance of the model could look rough and wrinkled. Too many vertices will also cause problems further down the road in rendering and animation.

When a surface has a number of spans that are not appropriate for rendering but look fine for animation and animation setup, the modeler would be well advised to increase the number of rendering subdivisions before increasing the number of

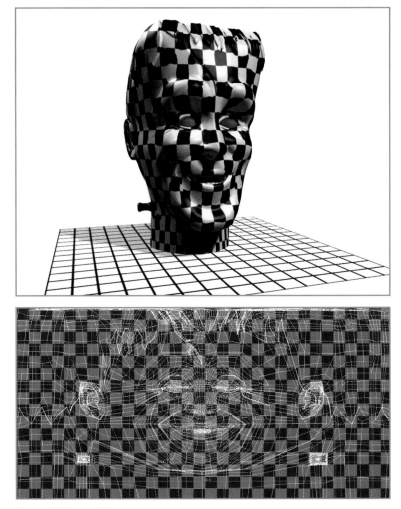

**Figures 4.52 and 4.53**
When unfolding UVs on a model, check the model for stretching using a texture map, such as a grid texture.

actual spans in the surface. Although this will not really speed up the rendering process, the animation and animation time savings will be noticeable.

When a surface has a parameterization that is sloppy, uneven, or just inappropriate for rendering and animation, the modeler can rebuild the surface using the rebuild surface tools. These tools allow the explicit number of spans for the U and V directions to be dialed in, creating surfaces that are evenly built and very clean.

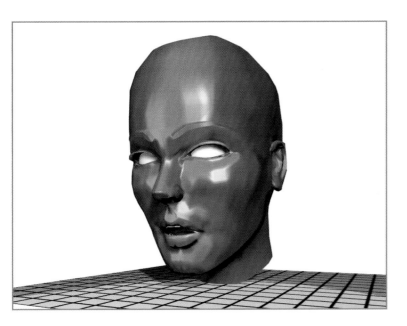

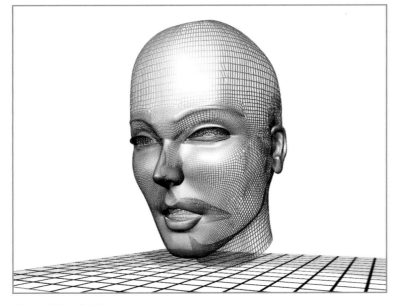

**Figures 4.54 and 4.55**
Low-resolution geometry will have obvious jaggedness along the edges, and geometry that has too much resolution will cause problems when animating and rendering.

## Never Build Something When You Can Copy It

Never, ever, model anything that can be duplicated from another object in a scene. This rule may seem like a cheat and a dodge, and in some ways it is, but when many modelers are just starting out, they are not attentive to opportunities to speed up their work by duplicating objects in their scenes, which causes two major problems. First, these modelers are wasting twice as much time modeling the object again. Second, whenever anything except the most simplistic models are created, it is difficult, if not impossible, to create the object exactly the way the previous object was created, which causes inconsistencies in the scene. Both objects may be modeled correctly, but because they appear different, one is bound to appear wrong.

## Always Use the Right Kind of Geometry for the Task

Certain production pipelines are set up around different types of models, and in those cases, the modeler is bound by the geometry type preferred by the production pipeline. But when there are choices to be made, modelers should know the options available so they can make the correct choice when deciding what to do in a certain situation.

### Adjust the Defaults

When there is a simple NURBS column on a building to be modeled and the building will be viewed from a great distance, there is no reason to build the column with the default eight spans across the diameter and degree three spans along the height. A cylinder with eight spans may be necessary when the column will be viewed full-screen, but in this case, the column could be built with four or maybe even three spans across the diameter and a degree one span along the height will suffice. This reduces the memory consumption of the column geometry to one-eighth the original memory footprint. Figure 4.56 shows two spheres. One sphere has eight spans in one direction and four spans in the other, which creates a default number of 576 triangles at render time. By simply adjusting the defaults, a sphere that would look identical in the render has four spans in one direction and three spans in the other, creating 216 triangles at render time. This is less than half the geometry that the renderer has to compute. If this sphere is multiplied many times, the time savings would be significant.

### Degree 1 Surfaces versus Degree 3 Surfaces

Many surfaces that are used in modeling are simple flat surfaces. Unfortunately, most modeling packages will default to degree 3 geometry for these flat surfaces. Degree 3 geometry will create about as many times the memory consumption that degree 1 NURBS geometry will create at render time. Figure 4.57 shows the difference between a degree 3 NURBS plane (shown left) and a degree 1 NURBS plane

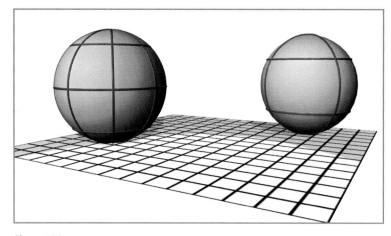

**Figure 4.56**
Never model using the default resolution for geometric primitives.

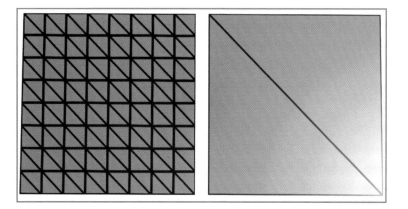

**Figure 4.57**
Degree 3 NURBS plane (left) and degree 1 NURBS plane (right).

(shown right). The triangles indicate the triangles used by the renderer. This triangulation, known as *tessellation*, is used to determine what will be precalculated before rendering.

## Polygonal Geometry

The modeler should not ignore *polygonal geometry*. In cases where there are small rectangular-shaped objects in the scene, the modeler can save a lot of time and rendering memory by creating low-resolution polygonal objects that will take the place of high-resolution NURBS surfaces.

## Surface Types

The modeler should choose the proper *surface type* for modeling. When modeling a character or an organic shape, the modeler will seldom need to use a surface type other than a lofted surface. These lofted surfaces are carefully constructed to ensure that each surface has the appropriate amount of detail.

When you construct a model of a car, product, or piece of architecture, there may be times when the more advanced surfacing tools should be used to ensure proper tangency conditions between surfaces. These advanced surface types (such as the bi-rail, square, and swept surfaces) were designed for complex surfacing tasks requiring extreme control.

## Trimmed Surfaces

*Trimmed surfaces* are sometimes referred to as *logical operators* because the trim process turns the area inside the trim region on or off. In a production environment, the modeler will seldom, if ever, find an appropriate opportunity to use trimmed surfaces. Trimmed surfaces are surfaces that use a curve-on-surface to define an area on the surface that will either be removed from the display of the visible surface or have the surrounding area removed from the visible surface. Trimming a surface is an extremely fast way to create a great looking model. However, some serious problems are associated with trimmed surfaces in film, video, and game production. When the surface is trimmed, the remaining part of the surface remains intact but is simply not visible or rendered. This makes the memory footprint of the surface at least as large as the original larger surface. Furthermore, when the surface is trimmed, the renderer makes the trimmed edge smooth in appearance by multiplying the geometry around the trim curve until it appears smooth. This can be very computationally expensive, consuming both time and memory for the renderer.

## Booleans

A *Boolean* is a type of logical operator. This is an operation that uses solid forms to create other forms that are a combination of the original forms. These combinations are usually defined as a *union* or a *subtraction* of the original form. Other variations exist, but generally the original forms are either being added to each other or one is being subtracted from another. An example is a model that describes the impact of a meteor being forced into a spherical object, such as a planet. The planet would have the shape of the meteor removed from it, one spherical object being removed from another, creating a spherical dent in the original sphere.

Booleans (Figure 4.58) generally work best with polygonal shapes that are absolutely watertight (continuous surfaces with no breaks, holes, or reversed faces). Some programs can perform Boolean operations upon NURBS surfaces too, but generally this does not work as well as the polygonal alternative.

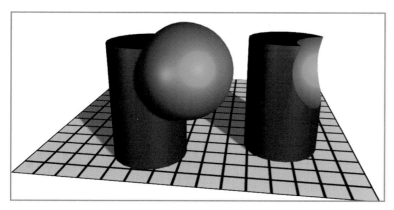

**Figure 4.58**
Booleans are useful when creating shapes that are simple combinations or subtractions of other shapes. Animated Booleans can also create interesting effects.

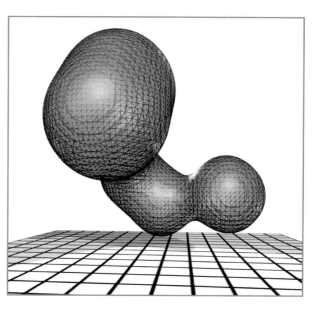

**Figure 4.59**
Metaballs are modeling tools that can save time when creating blobby organic shapes.

## Metaballs

In the attempt to create a modeling form that was intuitive and organic, the blobby surface, or *metaball*, was developed. Metaballs (Figure 4.59) appear in the modeling interface as spheres that are moved around in combination with other metaballs to create organic shapes. When these shapes are complete, the final rendered geometry will consist of a single surface that wraps the metaballs and smoothly blends the shapes together into one blobby shape that has a smooth continuous topology.

## *Use the Tools to Your Advantage*

Some tools and techniques do not fall conveniently into specific categories. Some of these functions are not really tools, but are practices that should be considered as a valuable part of the modeling process. Workflow, optimization, rendering, and data transfer issues are factors throughout the modeling process.

## Attach

One way to allow several surfaces to become one surface is to *attach* the surfaces, which replaces two surfaces with one individual surface. The problem when you use attach to merge two surfaces is the attach tool will create extra isoparms. Sometimes it is impossible to see the extra isoparms with the naked eye, but you can check the surface using the attribute editor to see if extra geometry was added to the surface (Figure 4.60).

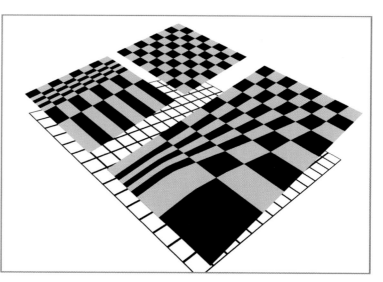

**Figure 4.60**
Attach makes one surface out of two or more surfaces.

## Rebuild Surface

In cases where there is an extra isoparm added to the surface, the modeler can *rebuild* the surface explicitly to ensure that the surface has the exact number of spans that the modeler desires (Figure 4.61).

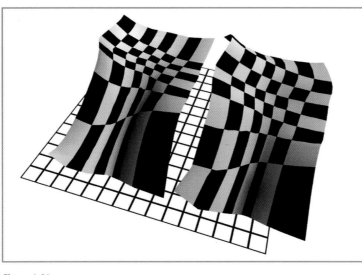

**Figure 4.61**
Rebuild surface creates clean surfaces from uneven surfaces.

When the modeler rebuilds the surface using the rebuild surface tool, sometimes the isoparms will not line up the way the modeler wants the surface to look, in which case, the modeler may need to reconstruct the surface by pulling curves directly off the surface that was created by the rebuild surface tool. This will generally give the modeler explicit control over the surface to be constructed and will give a better result. Although initially this process may take more time, the surface that is constructed using this technique will give the modeler exactly what is desired and will save time in the long run.

## Vertex Weighting and Multiplicity

Some modeling packages allow the modeler to adjust the *weight* of individual control vertices to enable explicit control of hardness at the point of each vertex. This can be a time-saving technique that will allow the modeler to keep the models light and easy to edit. The problem with applying weights to vertices and adjusting a *multiplicity* for each vertex is that these settings will not transfer well into the animation setup and will not transfer into other software packages. Unless there is a specific reason why the modeler would want to adjust a multiplicity or the weight for each vertex, a good rule to follow would be to simply add more vertices to the

existing curves to get the desired shape. This eliminates potential problems down the road and gives the modeler one less thing to worry about when passing off the model to the other departments.

Figure 4.62 shows a surface that has had vertex weighting applied to the curves that the surface was built from. Curves that have vertex weighting are unstable when exporting geometry from one software package to another and should be avoided under these circumstances.

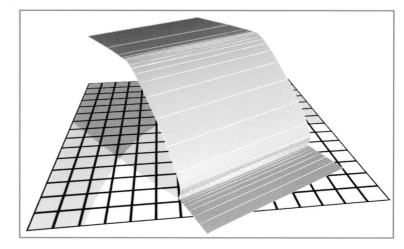

**Figure 4.62**
Vertex weighting is great for creating detail without adding geometry.

## Beveled or Radiused Edges

In all models, it is usually a good idea to include some type of *radius* or *bevel*. An object in the real world will never have an infinitely sharp edge. Even a razor blade, with an edge perceived to be extremely sharp, has a microscopic bevel that appears at that edge. One way to ensure that your objects will look realistic is to include some type of bevel or radius at the edge. Figure 4.63 shows the difference a radiused edge makes on a simple cylinder.

The exception to this would be if the object is something like a building seen from far away. Including a radius or bevel will make the geometry appear small and closer. Sometimes it is advantageous to leave out details like this if it helps tell the story.

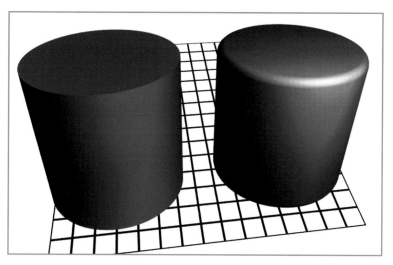

**Figure 4.63**
Adding beveled or radiused edges is one of the easiest ways to ensure a model will appear more realistic.

## Viewing Tools

Certain tools allow the modeler to work on specific objects or complicated objects. You should become acquainted with all of these options because at one time or another, the modeler will need to use these tools when he is given a complex modeling task. By isolating the part of the model that is being worked on, the modeler has more control over that part and can work on it much faster while getting higher-quality results. The time spent isolating a part of the model being worked on will save hours in the long run. Following is a list of *viewing tools*:

◆ **Layers.** Using *layers* to break up the scene is one way to have absolute control over which part of the model you are working on and which part of the model will remain unseen. Layers can be used for many things, but they are especially useful for controlling the visibility of certain parts of the model.

◆ **Isolate Selection.** Maya has a tool in the viewing panel called *Isolate Selection*. In this menu item, there are several options. Each of these options allows the user to control what is being seen and what is not being seen. Using this menu option even allows the user to control individual polygonal faces that are being worked on within a large polyset.

◆ **Clipping Planes.** Sometimes the modeler is working on a single large complex surface. Isolating other surfaces and other objects in the scene will not solve the problem of making the single large complex surface easier to manage. In cases like this, the modeler can limit how much the camera sees by adjusting the *clipping planes* in the viewing panel. The clipping planes represent the near and far limits of what the camera should display, so as to isolate specific parts of a large surface. This can save the modeler hours of frustrating work and can provide higher-quality results because of the control the modeler will have over that surface.

◆ **Hide Selected/Hide Unselected.** When the modeler is working on a single component, there are several components that are part of a larger scene, and there'll be times when the modeler will want to simply see a couple of things for a short time while working on them. In cases like this, the modeler may choose not to create a separate layer for the object but rather to use a simple *Hide Selected* option or a simple *Hide Unselected* option. This is a very quick way to get the geometry isolated on-screen.

The modeler cannot exist in a vacuum. Although the modeler has many options and tools available, many restrictions will be placed on the modeler based on production requirements and deadlines. Sometimes a particular method may seem ideal, but the rendering package will simply not support that solution, the model will become too computationally heavy, or unable to support the textures. It is critical for the modelers to become familiar with the restrictions of the particular production pipeline that they will have to work within before attempting to use every tool in the toolbox. With those restrictions in mind, the modeler can make much better decisions about which tools will be the best for everyone on the job.

**4. Modeling Tools and Techniques**

# chapter 5
# Modeling Resources

New technologies are constantly being introduced that enable faster and easier ways to use real-world objects and images when creating 3-D computer models. These technologies include scanning 3-D objects in new ways, using 2-D photographs to create 3-D environments and objects, and using haptic interfaces to sculpt 3-D objects. Some of these technologies have been around for many years, and some are still being perfected.

In the grand scheme of computer modeling, however, not much has changed in the last 10 years. The process of constructing geometry from reference data is still pretty much the same as it was in 1990. Each new technology, while making a profound difference in its particular niche, has not replaced the process of intelligently placing the correct geometry in the correct place on the computer model. Each computer modeling application has its own standard for what is optimum for geometry construction. Hard surface models are built with different construction criteria than environment models. Animated character models are built differently than models of character statues. This knowledge of the appropriate method of constructing a model for a particular purpose is difficult to automate. Although the general rules for constructing each type of model is fairly standardized, each studio will have production criteria that will change these rules somewhat on a case-by-case basis.

If anyone were to perfect the automation of correct model construction from acquired 3-D data, the criteria for construction would probably change due to the changing needs of the production environment. The companies that are trying to capture this market are chasing a moving target. However, some great new products are making a real difference in acquiring and creating useful 3-D geometry. Some of these new technologies are useful for creating models, and some are useful for creating reference models.

Accurate and high-quality reference data is critical to the production of high-quality models for film, video, and video games. Without adequate reference, models created by highly skilled artists may be inaccurate enough to look wrong. If the model that is being created is an original concept and based on a real object, a sufficient number of drawings and plans must be used to create the object that is being modeled in 3-D without too much guesswork.

Sometimes models need to be derived from or directly created from 3-D scan data. 3-D scanners enable likenesses of actual people and things to be created very quickly. The quality of 3-D data ranges from easy-to-use 3-D NURBS surfaces with accurate texture maps to blobby globs of polygons that do not look like anything. Figures 5.1 and 5.2 illustrate the difference between good scan data and bad scan data. This sculpture of a swamp creature was scanned using two techniques, one which provided clean, accurate data (Figure 5.1), whereas the other is not even recognizable (Figure 5.2).

New technologies provide the ability to sculpt inside the computer. SensAble Technologies created a sculpting interface called *FreeForm*, which enables the modeler to mimic the process of creating physical sculptures inside the computer.

Examples of providing reference material include creating a 3-D perspective sketch to begin modeling from, using 3-D scan that needs to be edited or tweaked to be animated and rendered, and sculpting a 3-D sculpture that will be surfaced for animation are all examples of providing reference material.

## 2-D Reference Material

A 2-D image can be a sketch or a photograph that is scanned into the computer and used inside the modeling program as a background for the modeling window, called an *image plane*. Gathering reference material, especially 2-D images, is a

the product from design to production. In order to understand orthographic images, you must first understand the concept of orthographic projection.

## Orthographic Drawings

*Orthographic projection* is a way of viewing objects that puts the object in a theoretical box. The surfaces of this box represent the top, bottom, back, front, left, and right sides of the object. If the person viewing the object were to stand so the view was perfectly perpendicular to one of the surfaces of this theoretical box, this would be an *orthographic view*. The modeling views in most modeling windows enable the modeler to work in this orthographic mode, generally from the top, front, and right sides. In cases where the modeler is not creating an original design, photographs taken of the object in orthographic views are suitable images for constructing a 3-D model. Orthographic views (Figures 5.4–5.6) also enable the modeler to work in views that are not distorted by the perspective camera, allowing for the accurate interpretation of the drawings onto the actual model.

**Figures 5.1 and 5.2**
Scan data can range from very high quality (left) to unusable or even unrecognizable (right).

requirement for most modeling projects. In cases where a 3-D reference is available, 2-D images can be used as image planes in addition to the 3-D reference data.

## Perspective 2-D Reference

When creating an original concept on the computer, a modeler usually begins with a 3-D sketch, or a *perspective sketch* (Figure 5.3). This perspective image can also be a photograph in cases where the model will not be an original design. Some modelers will choose to model from a perspective image in the perspective window, but the more accepted practice is to use the orthographic windows. This way the modeler can ensure that details seen from one view line up with details seen in another view.

Whereas a perspective sketch or photograph may be adequate at the earlier stages of design development, the 2-D orthographic projection—a plan and two elevations—is the conventional way of communicating the form and geometry of

**Figure 5.3**
Perspective sketches are required to nail down the concept, but modeling from them is difficult.

The method of orthographic projection is to "float" the designed object inside this imaginary box (Figure 5.7). Imagine the box as a window that you look through—the silhouette or projection of the designed object onto the top horizontal window is called the *plan*; the projection of the same object onto the front vertical window is the *front elevation*; and onto an adjacent side vertical window is an *end* or *side elevation*. Now imagine the box to be hinged. The horizontal plan is swung up through 90 degrees and the end elevation is also swung around through 90 degrees so that all three projections now lie on the same plane.

**Figure 5.7**
The sides of the box represent the views used in orthographic projection.

## Image Planes

When starting with an image plane in a modeling program, consider the following process for setting up the plane. The images should be in a usable digital format and at a usable resolution. For most modeling packages, TIFF format is universal, and for modeling purposes, an image that is about $300 \times 400$ pixels will suffice. Sometimes an image this large will bog down older systems, and sometimes this resolution will not be nearly enough to get the detail required for the model you are trying to build. These decisions have to be made on a case-by-case basis. The best results for using image planes come from getting two or three images of the object that is to be modeled shown from different orthographic views and having

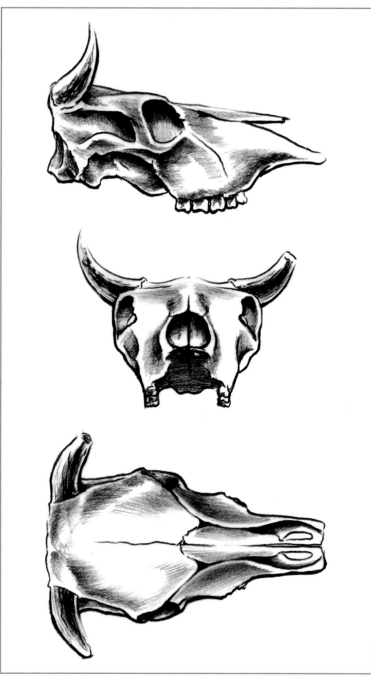

**Figures 5.4–5.6**
Orthographic views are side views of the object shown without perspective distortion.

these images scanned at identical resolutions and dimensions to each other. One trick I use when scanning image planes is to have the images I am scanning lined up on a single piece of paper in the exact orthographic layout that I want them to appear on the screen (Figure 5.8). I scan the entire sheet at once. When I crop the images to load them into individual windows on the screen, I use guides or rulers in my paint program to crop the images to ensure that they will have the same edges that create the sides for each image. For example, if you are creating three views, with the top view directly over the front view and the side view directly to the right of the front view, the left and right margins of the top and front views should be identical, and the top and bottom margins of the front and side views should be identical. For this to be truly exact, the height of the top view should exactly match the width of the side view. Paying attention to small details like this early in the process will save you a lot of work down the road.

When loading the image planes, the modeler should begin with a new file and a new set of viewing windows set to default viewing size for all windows. The reason for this is that when you load an image into your file, most modeling packages will scale the image to the existing window size. If the file has already had the windows resized to another viewing angle or dimension, the planes will load in at a different size, and all your work to get the images scanned at accurate sizes will have been wasted.

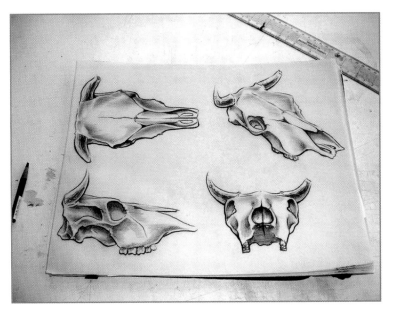

**Figure 5.8**
Drawings laid out in orthographic mode.

When you load the appropriate images into the appropriate windows, and the edges line up along the appropriate sides, you are almost ready to begin modeling. First, however, you should make some decisions about what types of surfaces will be constructed and where these surfaces will be placed.

## 3-D Reference Material

*3-D reference material* refers to processes that sample data from actual objects and make the data accessible in 3-D applications on the computer. These processes generally fall into the categories of 3-D digitizing and 3-D scanning. 3-D digitizing and 3-D scanning result in the creation of a digital version of an object that exists in the real world.

A scanner cannot replace a modeler for several reasons. One reason is that scanners will scan only objects that already exist as real physical objects. In modeling for entertainment, a lot of models are objects that do not exist in the physical world. Another reason is that the modeler spends a lot of time optimizing the geometry in the 3-D model to suit the particular purpose of the 3-D model. Because computer systems and video game platforms are becoming more and more powerful, the modeler will usually add more things in the scene. It doesn't matter how powerful the rendering software is or how powerful the video game CPU is—efficient modeling practices will always be used. As platforms become more powerful, directors and producers will simply ask for more and more stuff to be put in the scene. The opportunity to blindly add more geometry onto each model simply to save time by using the 3-D digitizing and scanning applications listed earlier never seems to materialize.

However, the companies creating these products are taking enormous strides. As these companies become more and more accustomed to the needs of the film and video game industry, the applications and equipment these companies make are becoming more and more usable. It won't be long before there will be a solution for acquiring 3-D data that can be used directly by the film and video game industries.

## 3-D Digitized Data

3-D digitizing is a manual process. When the 3-D property is digitized, the data acquired from this process is limited to vertices, polylines, and polygonal faces. Depending on the interface used during the 3-D scanning process, other entity types can be acquired as well. If the 3-D digitizing tool is interfaced with a fully functional 3-D modeling program, the digitizer can access any tool in the 3-D modeling program toolbox. The process of hand digitizing a 3-D object can be time-consuming and tedious (Figure 5.9). Most production houses that use 3-D digitizers simply use the digitizer to sample points and lines off the surface of the sculpture and complete the modeling process in the 3-D modeling program on the base. As with most 3-D sampling programs, digitizers and scanners, magnetic digitizers require that the X, Y, and Z-axes are defined relative to the origin. Once this orientation is established, the digitizing process can begin. In Figure 5.10, Ian Hulbert, a modeler and an animator at Rhythm & Hues, shows how difficult-to-reach areas can be accessed using this type of device. Other digitizers could not gather data from a complex model like the one pictured here.

The benefits of using magnetic digitizing equipment are that very large and complex physical models can be digitized quickly and easily. The size of the model that can be digitized is limited by the magnetic field of the digitizer base. The complexity of the model that can be digitized is limited by the size of the detail that can be accessed by the stylus. The stylus, which is the size of a large pen, is attached to the magnetic base with a thin flexible wire, or it can be cordless and have the signal transferred to the magnetic base through wireless transmission.

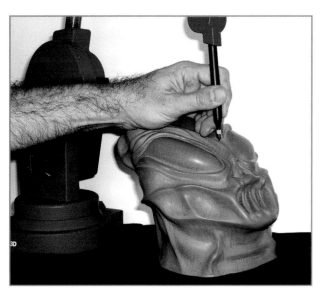

**Figure 5.9**
A 3-D digitizer traces the exterior of an object's surface.

computer. In some cases, however, the entire mesh will be modeled entirely with the digitizer. This is common when the modeler is using an oversized digitizer and the model is something very large, like an automobile.

When a 3-D digitizer is used on a 3-D property, map out each vertex that will be sampled by the digitizer by simply drawing lines on the object in an organized grid pattern along the surface. In cases where you cannot permanently mark the surface of the object, like when the object is an actual prop used on a film that must be returned, you can use thin, black pinstriping tape. The pinstriping tape creates a bold grid pattern on the surface of the object that can be cleanly removed or edited.

When sampling digitized data, gather data that will flow in line with the directions of the surfaces that you will build later. During the process of marking on the model for the purpose of planning the digitizing process, you should be planning each surface that will be built after the digitizing is completed. If you sample the data in an organized way that corresponds to how the surfaces will be laid out, you can save a lot of time. The two main types of 3-D digitizers are magnetic and mechanical.

## Magnetic Digitizers

*Magnetic digitizers* can be very flexible and can enable the modeler to access areas of the 3-D property that would normally be hard to get to. The reason for this is that magnetic digitizers use a central data-gathering location to electronically triangulate the position of the stylus and 3-D space relative to the magnetic

**Figure 5.10**
Magnetic digitizers enable great freedom of movement.

The drawbacks of using magnetic digitizing equipment are related to the nature of magnetic fields themselves. The magnetic fields used in digitizing are sensitive to metal. Any metallic substance in the property being digitized or surrounding the property being digitized will distort the accuracy of the data. A small amount of metal will create a small field of distortion, and a large amount of metal creates so much noise in the data that it will be unusable. Most objects that are digitized are sculptures created for a production. If the sculptor who worked on the sculpture used any metal in the armature, that will cause distortion in the digitized data, rendering the sculpture unusable. Sculptors who are creating sculptures for digitizing are forced to invent ways for building armatures out of wooden dowels, string, and glue.

## Mechanical Digitizers

*Mechanical digitizers* are inexpensive compared to magnetic digitizers. The stylus on mechanical digitizers is located at the end of a jointed assembly that resembles the arm of a robot. When the stylus moves along the surface of the 3-D property, it gathers 3-D information by triangulating the angular movements of the joints within the arm of the mechanical digitizer. Each time the stylus moves, the joints within the arm of the digitizer rotate and record different information based on the rotations of those joints (Figure 5.11).

**Figure 5.11**
Yeen-Shi Chen, a modeler at Rhythm & Hues, shows how this bulky arm can be used to capture details on a model.

The benefits of using mechanical digitizers instead of magnetic digitizers are mechanical reliability and lower cost. Even though the mechanical digitizers have moving parts, the mechanics involved with these parts are simple and reliable. These digitizers last for many years. It is much more common for these digitizers to become obsolete because of the software than it is for the digitizers to break and become unusable. These digitizers can sample 3-D information off the surface of just about any material. The limitations of what these types of digitizers can sample are based on the integrity and stability of the surfaces being digitized. For example, a mechanical digitizer can sample data from a metal object, whereas a magnetic digitizer cannot. But neither type of digitizer can accurately sample data from a surface that is unstable, such as a kitchen sponge or a stuffed animal toy. This is a factor relating not to the mechanics of the digitizer but more to the ability of the modeler to manually sample a flexible surface.

The disadvantage of using mechanical digitizers over magnetic digitizers is that the arm itself can be heavy and cumbersome. Mechanical digitizers are sturdy pieces of industrial equipment that can be fairly large. Some mechanical digitizers are large enough to digitize a car. When the mechanical arm is large enough to digitize a large object, the arm itself can get pretty heavy.

The weight of the arm is just one problem when dealing with a mechanical digitizer. Because the jointed arm is constructed so that it will measure rotations around a limited number of joints, the range of motion of the digitizer's stylus is limited and constrained by these joints. This can make it very difficult to digitize the surface of an object that has even a moderate amount of 3-D detail.

## 3-D Scan Data

The main difference between digitizing a model and using 3-D scan data is that the modeler is usually the one operating the digitizing stylus. But most 3-D scanning devices and software are too specialized and complex for the modelers to operate themselves. This is not to say that modelers cannot learn to operate this equipment if they wanted to; it is only that this equipment is not as automatic as the equipment manufacturer would like the customers to believe. People who have been using the equipment for many years do the best scans. When it comes to 3-D scan data, the modeler must understand what it is used for and how it is obtained. It is not important, however, that the modeler uses the 3-D scan system to get the data.

A 3-D scanner samples points from the surface of the 3-D object. The output that can be expected from a 3-D scanner normally consists of a polygonal mesh that is the actual size and shape of the object being scanned (Figure 5.12). In recent years, scanners have become more sophisticated. Scanners have expanded their capability to include the acquisition of color and texture data as well as 3-D

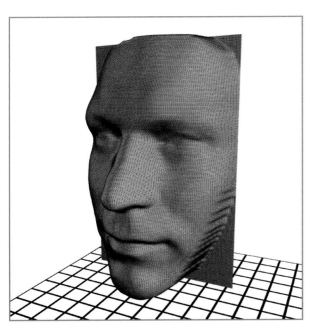

**Figure 5.12**
A 3-D scanner provides excellent 3-D reference material for modeling, but the data is too dense to be used in production.

geometry data. The properties of an object that can be captured during scanning include shape, size, color, and texture.

*3-D scanning* is the term that describes several different technologies. Recent developments in 3-D data acquisition from physical objects are more like photography than actual scanning. However, because the data that is rendered from the processes is similar to the data that is gathered from traditional 3-D scanners, these processes will be included in this section as well. The two primary ways that 3-D scanners are used for computer modeling are laser scanning and structured light scanning. Other methods of acquiring 3-D data are out there, but if the modeler understands the basics involved with these two main types, the other techniques will be easier to grasp if they are needed for a project.

## Laser Scanners

Laser scanners use a laser. The laser is a device that emits a single beam of intensely directed light. The laser is mounted in a moving device and gathers 3-D information by bouncing the laser light back into one or more cameras mounted in the moving device. A laser diode and stripe generator can be used to project a laser line onto the object (single point, line, or multiple lines). The line is viewed at an angle by cameras so that height variations in the object can be seen as

changes in the shape of the line. The resulting captured image of the stripe is a profile that contains the shape of the object.

Laser scanners use the principle of triangulation to gather 3-D data. A laser line or pattern is projected onto a part. An optical camera offset from the laser source views the laser light on the object being scanned. The 3-D data is obtained by calculating the differences between the points measured closer to the laser and the points farther away from the laser.

Advantages of laser scanning include fast 3-D data acquisition and no contact with the object. The physical prop does not need to have a surface hard enough to be digitized manually, so soft objects can easily be scanned. Because there is no contact, fragile models can be scanned as well. Laser scanners quickly sample a large number of points. Only the parts of the object that are in the line of sight of the scanner can be measured. Multiple scanner positions are required to cover the complete object. Sometimes laser scanners work in cooperation with part turntables that enable the part to be precisely moved instead of the scanner.

Because an optical device is making the final measurements, laser systems have a hard time on shiny objects that reflect a lot of light and dark objects that absorb a lot of light. Problem parts can be painted white or sprayed with a white powder to make them more visible to the laser.

Some laser scanners have large scanning heads that are rotated around an object, capturing all the surface data, geometry, and textures in one pass. Some laser scanners utilize a turntable or similar device that moves the model in front of the digitizing head of the laser scanner. In the case of the turntable, the laser still needs to move vertically to capture the 3-D sections of the object being rotated in front of the digitizing head. There are other configurations as well, but what they all have in common is that the laser is moved in some way relative to the object to capture 3-D data.

As a modeler who is required to use data received from a laser scanner or from any other scanning facility, certain things need to have careful attention in order to get satisfactory data. The modeler must clearly define the expectations to the person operating the scanning equipment. The modeler needs to ensure that the data has no gaps or visible seams; that criteria needs to be clearly spelled out to the vendor. If the vendor needs to deliver texture maps as well as 3-D data, that should be spelled out as well. The best way to define expectations is to put them in writing.

A studio on a limited budget may have some latitude when it comes to locating a scanning vendor. Normally, however, a studio should use a vendor that has a good reputation and has been used by many other clients. Although the equipment manufacturers that sell the scanners are quick to tell customers that it is the equipment that creates the quality data, the truth is that the people operating the equipment are the ones creating the quality data. This is identical to the situation visual artists find themselves in every day. Every time a new tool is introduced to the digital production market, there is a claim that this new tool will automate the job of the digital artist. The fact is, the artist—not the equipment or the software—is the one creating the work. For this reason, the studio contracting out the scanning work needs to use the best people for the job, not necessarily the best equipment.

A modeler who is responsible for the collection and final use of 3-D scan data represents the studio as a buyer. As a buyer, the modeler will be responsible for ensuring that the data is usable, as well as the following tasks:

◆ Inspecting the data received to ensure that no holes are in it. Check carefully for any gaps or seams in the surface of the data. Figure 5.13 shows problems at the fingers and the sides of the head.

◆ Turning all the display of the software that is being used for viewing the data so the polygons are single sided. The modeler should make sure that the entire surface of the model has the polygons all facing the same direction.

◆ Examining the wire frame (nonshaded view) of the data to see if there is floating data resting inside the exterior surface of the data.

◆ Examining the surface data to ensure that when merged scans in a single data set are used, two or more layers of data are not resting on top of each other. This causes many problems when the modeler is trying to use the data.

After the data is received and approved, it is usually too late to fix the kinds of things mentioned in the preceding list. This is why it is crucial to make sure these things are checked immediately after the data is collected. Figure 5.14 shows scan data after it has been cleaned up.

A few companies are known for producing the best laser scanners. Following is a discussion of these well-known and respected manufacturers.

## Cyberware

Cyberware is one of the oldest and most widely used laser scanner manufacturers on the market today. Cyberware has equipment located at scanning centers in many large cities and makes products that address specific 3-D scanning applications. Cyberware makes several high-resolution scanners for capturing 3-D data and texture data from models and sculptures. These scanners are not considered specialized scanners, but they are considered some of the highest quality scanners for general use. These high-resolution scanners operate by using a turntable to move models in front of the digitizing head. The data that is acquired from these

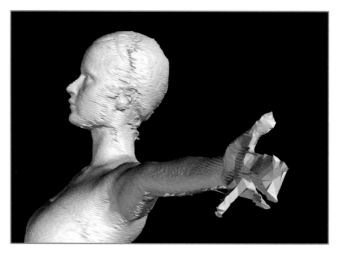

**Figure 5.13**
Common flaws in scan data include holes, missing data (shown here), flipped normals, and floating data.

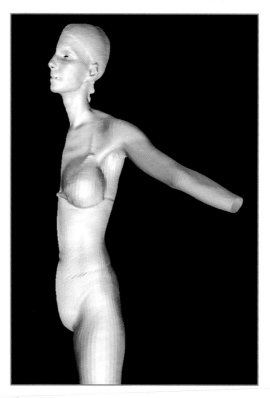

**Figure 5.14**
Cleaned up scan data.

scanners has to be acquired in multiple passes. The major reason for this is that the models will generally have an arbitrary shape that has occlusions (where one part of the model interferes with the scanner's ability to see the part of the model beneath it) and surfaces that cannot be seen unless the model is rotated to another angle.

Data that is acquired from 3-D scanners is commonly sampled in multiple passes. The problem usually lies in assembling the data into one continuous polygonal mesh after the multiple passes have been completed. Cyberware was one of the first companies to develop software that makes this task simple and easy to perform.

Two other products that Cyberware is famous for are the head scanner and full body scanner (Figure 5.15). These scanners are specialized for sampling 3-D data from the human body, and they generate color texture information as well as 3-D models of the people being scanned (Figure 5.16). The color information can be stored as texture maps in the traditional sense, or the color information can be stored per vertex in the database. In the latter case, thousands of vertices packed very close together give the impression of continuous color across the 3-D mesh, but there is no map associated with the data.

The problem with these scanners is that the scanner's digitizing head rotates around the body around the vertical axis. This captures more than 90 percent of the information required to digitally re-create the person being scanned. The last 10 percent, however, is located at the top surfaces of the human body. These surfaces include the tops of the shoulders and head. Whenever the 3-D data that has been directly acquired from the scanners is viewed, it is obvious that the tops of the heads have to be completely redone in order to be used as a digital model.

Also, because the scanners are so specialized for the purpose of gathering head and body data, they are almost useless for anything else. This is why most places that provide scanning services using Cyberware scanners need to have more than one scanner available to the customer.

Cyberware has pioneered many technologies related to 3-D scanning. The original program that was developed by this company to create NURBS surfaces from scanned data is called CySurf (originally known as Ntest). This program seems simple when compared to some of the other programs available for surfacing today, but this functionality of wrapping NURBS surfaces onto polygonal surfaces

**Figure 5.15**
The full body scanner creates fast and clean scans of an entire person. *Image courtesy of Cyberware Corporation.*

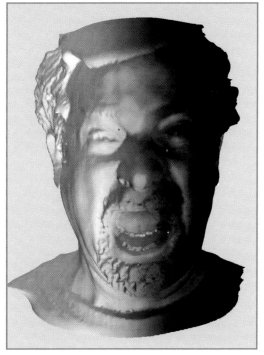

**Figure 5.16**
The head scanner creates a dataset of a person's head including the color information.

was the first step toward making scan data truly usable for a film and video production pipeline.

Less expensive laser scanning options are available. These devices offer the advantages of flexibility and lower cost, but, as was stated previously, these are instruments that require a certain amount of skill and labor to get usable results. These machines are not office copiers that automatically spit out 3-D data quickly and easily, although this is not rocket science. Any modeler who is motivated and interested can learn to do laser scanning.

### Polhemus

Polhemus makes a unique scanner called FastSCAN. This product can deliver quick and fairly high quality scans when the user is experienced and has some basic knowledge of the scanner's settings. The software used in this system has the remarkable capability to merge multiple passes accurately and easily. This scanner also has the distinction of being very inexpensive and easy to use compared to the Cyberware scanners. The scanner itself is a handheld wand that is passed over the object being scanned. Multiple passes randomly gathered by hand are assembled and put into accurate world-space using the magnetic calibration system (Figure 5.17).

This scanner calibrates itself using the Polhemus magnetic tracking system. The problem with the magnetic tracking base is that metal objects, whether motion capture, digitizing, or scanning, will adversely affect any magnetic system. This wouldn't be such a big deal except that many objects have metal in them. When a design needs to be modeled and executed in full physical sculpted form prior to capturing the form for 3-D modeling, the sculpture has to be specially designed without any metal armatures. In some cases, the building that houses the system adversely affects the results of the scanner.

### Minolta

The Minolta VIVID line of scanners are true laser scanning apparatuses. The scanning object operates the device from a PC connected to the scanner. The object being scanned is placed in front of the scanner at a fixed distance. The scanner is then activated. In less than one second, the scanner passes a laser over the surface of the object that is visible to the scanner. Because this scanner is basically a box that sits in front of the object and cannot "see" the entire model at once, the operator needs to rotate the model to get additional views scanned. As with most scanners that require multiple passes, multiple passes need to be assembled into one continuous, clean, watertight mesh. This takes time and skill and sometimes requires an additional software package to clean up the geometry. Unlike the Polhemus FastSCAN, this scanner also captures texture mapping information, as well as 3-D geometry.

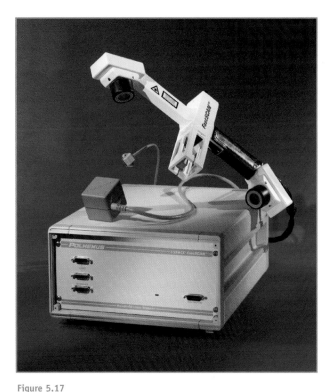

**Figure 5.17**
The Polhemus scanner is easy to use but cannot scan metal surfaces. *Image courtesy of Polhemus Corporation.*

### Lidar

A variation of laser scanning that is used almost exclusively for very large scanning applications is *lidar* (*light detection and ranging*). This type of scanner is also called a *time-of-flight* laser scanner. This technology was originally developed for scientific and military applications (Figure 5.18). It has become very useful for digitizing large structures because of its inherent ability to sample a large number of points within a short amount of time.

Lidar has been instrumental in addressing several problems related to integrating live-action photography with 3-D digital imagery. Normally when the visual effects studio receives background plates for digital effects, some guesswork is involved when creating digital environments based on the background photography. Although it is usually not necessary to re-create the environment so it can be rendered photo-realistically, it is normally required to build objects that will be used to cast shadows on and create objects for tracking purposes. If the lidar data is acquired correctly, it addresses many of these problems.

**Figure 5.18**
A scan of an actual helicopter shows how lidar can capture large data sets quickly. *Image courtesy of Alan Lasky*.

**Figure 5.19**
This hillside scan shows how reference balls can help the modeler and the person who is scanning the hillside. *Image courtesy of Alan Lasky*.

The person using the data, however, needs to pay careful attention to criteria associated with the acquisition of lidar data. Before approving any data that is received from a lidar capture session, the modeler responsible for using the data should make sure that the data meets the following criteria:

1. With each 3-D data set should be an object in the scene of a known size. For example, if the modeler is receiving data that describes a large mountain, it would be impossible to determine the size of this mountain unless there was an object in the scene, such as a box that was five feet in all dimensions, to give scale to the entire scene. Without an object in the scene that determines the scale, a lot of guessing is involved when trying to use this data. Figure 5.19 shows a lidar scan of a hillside with small green balls placed in strategic areas toward the top of the hill. These balls are a specific size, so the modeler knows how large the scene is, and the balls are also used to line up additional scans of the same scene.

2. The data that is received should be placed relative to a true horizontal plane. Although the Cartesian coordinate system cannot be exactly duplicated in the real world, there should be some attempt to ensure that the data at least rests in a horizontal position.

Whenever possible, the objects that are seen in the background plate should also be visible in the scanned environment. This includes any props, buildings, and other stationary objects that can be seen in the background images. Figures 5.20 and 5.21 show how recognizable objects in a scene can help verify a database for scale, position, and accuracy. Objects that are obscure shapes, such as rocks and plants, present a greater challenge when checking for scale, position, and accuracy.

4. If possible, the lidar data should also include 3-D data of the camera that was used to shoot the background plates. This can be useful in determining the actual distance between the camera and some of the identifiable objects in the scene.

5. The data received should be clean. Many times, the lidar data set that is received by the modeler comprises many individual snapshots of data that are taken at the sight of principal photography. When these individual small data sets are assembled into one large data set, many opportunities arise for holes and reversed faces to be introduced into the final data. Upon first viewing the data, the modeler should make sure all the faces are single sided and view the data carefully, inspecting it for holes and reversed faces.

**Figures 5.20 and 5.21**
When objects that tie the scanned scene are easy to identify and recognize, the scene is easier to check for accuracy. *Images courtesy of Alan Lasky.*

### Structured Light Scanners

A new technology, structured light scanners, provide a potentially low-cost solution to the problem of higher-priced laser scanning hardware. The tools required for acquiring data using structured light scanners can be as simple and inexpensive as a digital camera and a slide projector, or as elaborate and expensive as a structured light digitizing head and a complicated scanning rig.

What differentiates the technology of structured light scanning from the laser scanning technology is that the light that is read by the software interpreting the changes in the 3-D surface is not laser light but standard light that is readily available from a slide projector lamp or some similar white light source, such as a halogen lamp.

3-D data from a structured light scanner can be acquired in more than one way. One way is to use multiple cameras that interpret the data using stereovision. Another way is to utilize a single camera and software to extract the 3-D information from the pattern of structured light on the physical object.

Structured light scanners typically project a predefined and calibrated light pattern onto the 3-D surface of the object to be modeled. The pattern of light is distorted by the variation of the object's surface. The software in the structured light scanning system triangulates the differences in the light pattern on the distorted surface to calculate 3-D geometry.

Like some laser scanners, structured light scanners capture complete surfaces from a particular point of view. Multiple passes are made to acquire the data from multiple points of view (Figure 5.22). These multiple passes are combined into a single, seamless data set using merging software that is usually included with the purchase of the scanning package (Figure 5.23).

## NURBS Surfacing of Polygonal Surfaces

Applying NURBS surfaces to scanned polygonal data sets has become very sophisticated in the last few years. Several software packages can accomplish this task. Some are more successful than others, and some are more expensive than others. These modeling programs use as an input raw scan data. The final output of the software programs is a series of NURBS patches that have parametric alignment and geometric tangency.

Because a lot of cleanup is involved when working with scan data, programs available for creating NURBS surfaces from this data generally include tools that enable the user to clean up the data prior to creating the surfaces. This type of software works by starting with a dense polygonal mesh and uses specialized algorithms to draw a NURBS surface into the details of the scanned data. A modeler witnessing this process for the first time will see an impressive sight. The form and detail of the scan data are transferred to the surface as if by magic. When used correctly, this type of software can create amazingly accurate representations of real-life objects using NURBS surfaces that can be used in animation, manufacturing, and design. When the model is complete, it is a fully realized NURBS patch model that has been created in a fraction of the time that it would take to build a patch model by hand.

A few of the software packages that apply NURBS surfaces to scanned polygonal data sets are Raindrop Geomagic, Paraform, RapidForm, and Cyberware CySlice. Some of these packages have advantages over the others. Paraform seems to have been able to create scan data cleanup tools, curve building tools, and surfacing tools that are very powerful and easy to use. Some of the work produced using Paraform is shown in Figures 5.24 and 5.25. Paraform has been used in many films, including *Hollow Man*, *End of Days*, and *Harry Potter and the Sorcerer's Stone*.

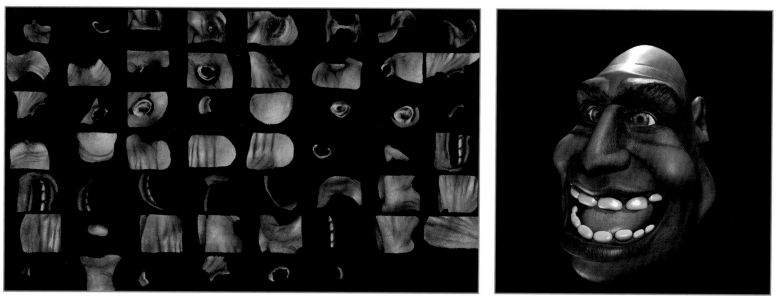

**Figures 5.22 and 5.23**
Individual scans used to complete a scan of a head sculpture, along with the resultant head model, which has been rebuilt and rendered.

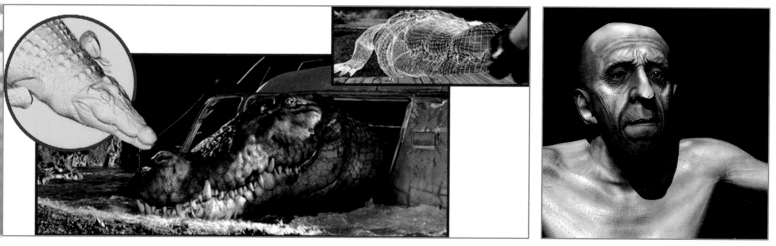

**Figures 5.24 and 5.25**
Paraform has powerful surfacing tools that can create great models. *Images courtesy of Paraform Corporation.*

5. Modeling Resources

The process of applying NURBS surfaces onto dense scan data is usually done in the following steps:

1. The scan data is imported into the system. The file format used for importing the data depends on which software is being used for surfacing and which file format was exported from the scanner.

2. The scan data is cleaned up. During the cleaning process, seal all the holes that exist in the scan data and ensure that the surfaces of the scanned data are free from surface discontinuities (noise) and irregularities caused by the scanning process.

3. The boundaries for each surface are laid out. Some software has defined a workflow for the surfacing operation so that only one surface can be made at a time. Some products, however, enable the user to lay out the entire model before creating any surfaces. Creating all the boundaries for all the surfaces can be advantageous. When this type of model is built, the success of the model depends largely on how the surfaces are laid out. A lot of time is wasted if the modeler has to reorganize the surfaces after the model is built. Paraform, one of the packages mentioned earlier, is built so that the patches can be laid out prior to surfacing. Paraform also has one of the most impressive toolkits on the market for laying out the exact parameterization of each surface and determining tangency conditions with accuracy and control.

4. The surfaces themselves are built. Sometimes, as is the case with Paraform, an additional step is required before surfacing, which requires the construction of a *spring*. A spring is a mesh that stretches between the curves that identify the surface boundaries. This mesh determines the density and accuracy of the surface that will be built on top of the spring. Although this step takes additional time, the benefits are paid back to the modeler by providing additional control. During the process of surfacing these boundary curves, there will be some areas where the curves, for some reason or another, are not exactly right for creating a surface. These conditions are places where the curves cannot meet exactly or have small breaks. At this point, the modeler must replace the curve or edit the curve to get the surface to build. Again, Paraform has excellent curve-editing capabilities.

Wrapping NURBS surfaces onto dense polymeshes holds the promise of creating complex patch models from objects that already exist. The only limitation to this technology, it seems, is that it will not create objects that do not already exist. The models that can be imported into these packages do not necessarily have to be scan data. Many polygonal objects can be quickly and easily built and imported into these packages. By building a rough polygonal model and using a smoothing function to increase the resolution of the model, the modeler can quickly create a complex patch model for a low-resolution polygonal model. Using this methodology, modelers can create anything they desire using this software.

## FreeForm Modeling and Surfacing

Modelers often throw up their hands and say, "If I could only touch the data inside the computer; if I could only use my hands." The SensAble Technologies FreeForm modeling system addresses this concern. This system uses a specialized piece of hardware that has a haptic interface. Haptics is the aspect of FreeForm's user interface design that uses force-feedback to create the impression that the modeler is sculpting with his or her hands on a model inside the computer.

Technology like this would not have been possible a few years ago. Faster graphics cards and faster processors have allowed this software and hardware combination to create amazing 3-D forms in the computer.

The data that is created by this device is similar to scan data. When exported into other packages, the data consists of thousands of small triangles that make up the data set. There are a couple notable distinctions, however. One distinction is that the data that is exported is very clean. Another distinction is the position of the data is right on the construction coordinates used for the digital modeling process.

The reason the data is extremely clean is that the data that is exported is a polygonal representation of a theoretical volume within the FreeForm software. The database that is calculated within FreeForm uses *voxels* to determine the volume of the object. Voxels are theoretical bits of 3-D information that make up a 3-D scene in a similar way that pixels fill up the 2-D screen on the computer. These voxels contain information about the 3-D sculpture in the FreeForm program. Some of this information includes the coarseness of the object, the shape of the object, and the color of the object. (Coarseness is the hardness of the model.) Because voxels are true 3-D entities, the sculptures created in FreeForm can be painted through the object. These colors on the object cannot be exported as texture maps, but they can be exported as colored point data on the surface of the object.

The coarseness of the sculpture in FreeForm is a very important aspect to using this program. Coarseness values correspond to the size of the voxels. Large voxels have a large coarseness value. If the virtual clay that is being sculpted has a very large coarseness value, the clay is very soft and can be easily sculpted. Soft clay, however, will not hold detail very well. As the sculpting continues, the hardness of the clay must be increased to get additional detail. Hardening the clay means reducing the size of the voxels. When the sculpture is finished, the clay will normally not be very coarse. The model shown in Figure 5.27 was built using the following steps:

1. Use an orthographic drawing or photograph to create a background image or image plane in FreeForm.

2. Make a large solid shape with a large coarseness size.

3. Make a curve on the front face of the shape that is used to cut the profile. Cut the profile with this curve.

4. Make a curve on the top to cut the top profile and cut the top profile with that curve.

5. Round off the edges, creating the basic 3-D form of the sculpture.

6. Decrease the coarseness one step and add detail.

7. Decrease the coarseness another step and add more detail. Continue adding detail until the sculpture is complete (Figure 5.26).

8. Create surfaces on the model using curves and surfaces available in the surfacing toolbox.

9. Export the NURBS surfaces into the animation program.

The FreeForm modeling process differs from other methods of creating 3-D models because it can create models with random complexity (Figure 5.27), and texture and graphics can be created in 3-D, unlike most other modeling packages.

Another benefit to the system is that it has a built-in NURBS surfacing program, making it a fully functional stand-alone model creation package. The NURBS surfacing package is very intuitive and reliable and the NURBS surfaces that are exported from FreeForm are very clean. The NURBS surfacing software is not as flexible as the Paraform software, but it provides about 85% of the functionality and a fantastic sculpting package as well.

Drawings, digitizing, scanning, and sculpting have not replaced modeling yet. They remain tools in the modeler's toolbox. So much about the model is tied directly to animation and rendering. Therefore, the modeler must depend on information that is specific to the production pipeline to make decisions about how to make the model, not restrictions imposed on them by the data acquisition process. One day, these process may be the way all modeling is done. In the meantime, knowing about these technologies and how they work can save the modeler hours of time. The finished product, at least for now, remains the work created by the modeler.

**Figures 5.26 and 5.27**
SensAble Technologies' FreeForm system enables the modeler to create models using an intuitive sculpting tool and enables the export of NURBS patch models. *Dinosaur model by Tom Capizzi; Demon model courtesy of Chein-Hsiung Wang.*

**5. Modeling Resources**

# chapter 6
# Modeling Specialties

Computer graphics artists should be proficient in all modeling tasks, but if they have specialties, that is, talents that will make them stand out, they will be indispensable. The specialties that modelers pursue are *hard surface models*, *environment models*, and *character models*.

## Hard Surface Modeling

The type of model most closely related to the kind of model used for manufacturing or design is a *hard surface model*. These types of models are usually props, vehicles, or products that will be rendered and can be constructed using entity types that would not be allowed in a character model. Because the geometry simply needs to be rendered, the model can consist of many more surfaces or more complex surfaces than would be allowed in a character model.

Deciding what kind object falls into the category of hard-surface model is simple. The final decision will usually come down to one question: will the model require *character rigging*? Character rigging is creating a series of deformers on the model that allows the model to bend predictably and easily. When the model is set up this way, the animator can create a deformable character performance using that model. Hard-surface models usually do not require character rigging for deformation.

Although this kind of model does not deform, it does not mean that the model is not a character model. If the model is a robot or a model of a medieval knight, the model does not need to deform. In these cases, the hard surface model is the character model.

Hard surface modeling usually attracts people who have a background in design or architecture. The skills used to create presentations for these professions are useful when defining shapes that have never before been seen in three dimen-

sions. Also, a real technological aspect to this type of modeling exists, especially when the reference material for building these models is a stack of blueprints. The modeler who is responsible for translating the detailed information into a usable 3-D model needs to accurately depict the detailed reference information in using 3-D geometry.

> For hard surface modeling, I use Alias software whenever possible. For organic or character modeling, I use Maya. All the examples used in this book feature Maya, because it has been developed specifically for the entertainment industry and has enough functionality for any modeling task mentioned in this book. The modeling tools in Maya are similar to the tools in Alias, but Alias has singled itself out in the marketplace as the modeling package preferred by designers and manufacturers. Over the years, Alias has simplified the process of creating standard NURBS surfaces so that creating NURBS models in a relatively short amount of time using their modeling tools is easy.

Some of the things that can be called hard surface models are spaceships (Figures 6.1–6.3), buildings, common household items, mechanical objects, and other props. The most challenging is building a vehicle, which requires knowledge of the modeling process and surface types and visualization skills. Modeling a car is a great way to get acquainted with NURBS modeling programs. The spaceship shown here shows some of the problems associated with hard surface modeling and how a modeler has to spend some time adding detail to achieve realism.

Adding detail is not as difficult as maintaining a smooth continuous surface along a complex form, such as the surface of a car.

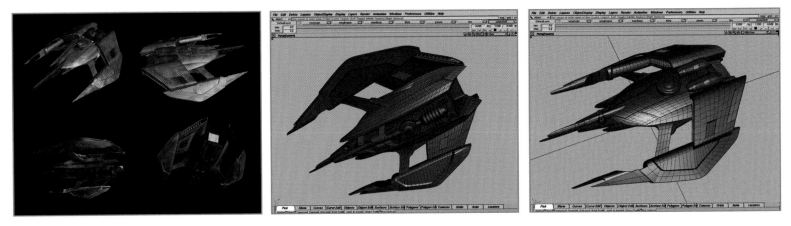

**Figures 6.1–6.3**
A spaceship is a typical example of a hard surface model.

---

### CASE STUDY: HARD SURFACE MODELING AND *SAN FRANCISCO RUSH*

The Atari arcade game *San Francisco Rush,* although a huge success, was in development for two years. Atari, then called Time-Warner Interactive, hoped to have the project done in less than two years within budget. Two years after the project was started, the budget was spent, but the game was far from finished. Most of the money was spent on the development of a next-generation 3-D graphics system created for the hardware that is installed in the game cabinets. Arcade games, unlike console games, need to include their own hardware. Developing this hardware can be more expensive and time-consuming than developing the actual game. Fortunately, 3DFX came along with a very powerful and cost-effective solution.

The art staff made several road trips to San Francisco to get pictures of the architecture and landmarks to use in the game. The levels, tracks, and worlds were built in Multi-Gen, a program that was originally designed to enable the military to model flight and battle simulation models quickly and easily.

When I was brought onto the team as art director, the environments and tracks were taking shape and were tweaked for performance and timing, and the track models and textures were in progress. However, the cars for the game were nonexistent, and the select screens and cabinet designs were not being worked on at all.

The cars that were used were ordinary polygonal models. The textures, however, were derived in a unique way, which allowed the simple translation of data from high-resolution models that were constructed for cabinet artwork, full-motion videos, and promotional materials to textures used for low-resolution car models. We started by building a high-resolution, fully rendered model of the car required for the game. Texture mapping the low-resolution car for the game is much simpler than texturing using photographs. (See Figures 6.4 and 6.5.)

Next, the cameras were positioned orthographically around the model to render orthographic views of the car. Orthographic projection is explained in Chapter 5.

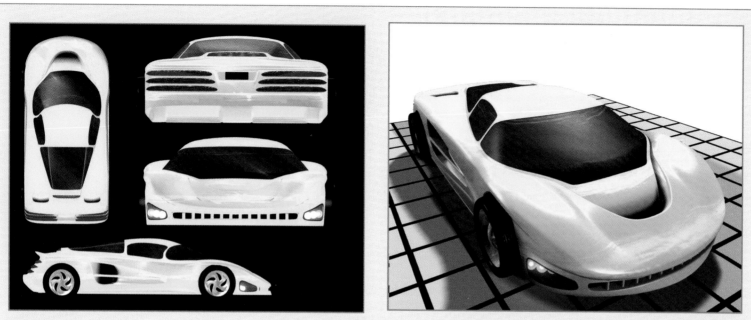

**Figures 6.4, 6.5**
Orthographic views of a high-resolution model used for texture mapping a low-resolution car (left) and a perspective render of the same car (right).

A *high-resolution* model has enough surface detail to allow the model to be viewed in shaded mode, and it appears smooth and finished looking. A *low-resolution* model has visible discontinuities in the surface and will not appear finished looking.

This is the most time-consuming part of the process. Most real-time models are texture mapped using photographs of cars or photographs that are modified in a paint package. High-resolution models were used on *San Francisco Rush* to consistent-looking textures of cars that had never been seen before and to create consistent-looking textures of commonly seen cars that had radical paint jobs. Because we did not have access to these actual cars to take photographs from, and the pipeline to get these cars done had to be efficient and clean, it was much easier to place cameras in the digital scene in the exact location as opposed to setting up professional photography for each car. This also allowed for the modification of the paint jobs and styling, which would not have been possible using actual photography.

Then, a low-resolution polygonal version of the car was built for the game. This model conformed to the size and shape of the proxy model that created the physical simulation of real-time driving. The polygonal model that the art staff created was simply a shell; the real game was played with a much simpler model that was not displayed during the game.

Finally, the texture maps derived from the orthographically rendered images were applied to the low-resolution polygonal model. The construction of the high-resolution car is the only part of this process that will be covered in this chapter. The polygonal construction of a low-resolution car is simple in comparison to the construction of a high-resolution NURBS model. Projecting UVs and texture maps onto a polygonal object will be covered later in the book.

When constructing a free-form shape from NURBS surfaces, the modeler must consider certain things, some of which are specific to free-form NURBS modeling. Other things covered here fall into that category of general modeling practices. The models that were built for the San Francisco Rush game were more high-resolution than any car ever built for a real-time game before and probably since then. These are not the kind of high-resolution models that could be used for manufacturing a real car. The details of curvature tolerances and tangency when building a car in the automotive industry is extremely different than the details of surfacing a car that simply needs to appear correct in a rendered image.

## Curve Construction

When you are constructing models using NURBS surfaces, you should begin with accurate and clean curves. The curves will determine how the surfaces will appear, and the number of spans in the surfaces will be controlled by these curves.

Every 3-D model, especially models built from real everyday objects, must have accurate reference data. Sources for reference are used to begin modeling a complex object. A common reference is a 2-D image. This image can be a sketch or a photograph that is scanned into the computer and used inside the modeling program as a background for the modeling window. An image used in this way is called an *image plane* and is a standard procedure.

When constructing a hard surface model, the modeler might begin with a perspective sketch or a photograph. A simple perspective sketch is seldom enough information to create a detailed model. To create an accurate model from 2-D reference data, the modeler is usually required to have at least two orthographic views of the intended design. Once the modeler has these drawings, and the drawings have been approved, the drawings can be used as image planes in the modeling program.

Orthographic projections of the object are ideal for image planes because they can be placed in the standard orthographic modeling views, and the modeler can literally trace the images with the modeling tools without the distortion cased by a perspective camera. When the orthographic images are placed in image planes in the scene, the drawings appear in the modeling windows.

Gathering accurate reference data at the beginning of the modeling process is a crucial step. If the model needs to be built from images, no modeling should begin until approved reference drawings or photographs are available. When 3-D reference data is available, the modeler should also have additional reference data, such as drawings, photographs, or plans. If the 3-D reference data consists of

**Figure 6.6**
The reference images need to be arranged orthographically around the object being modeled.

digitized lines from 3-D sculpture, the 3-D sculpture should be available to the modeler for the entire time that the modeler is working on the model.

### Building Curves in 2-D: Surfacing Strategy

At this stage of the model-building process, you should create a plan of action that will allow you to create surfaces in the areas that you designate instead of designing the surface layout while you are trying to model. Use the orthographic layout in the modeling program to view the object and draw curves over these image planes to outline where the surface edges will be. The curves that you build to draw these outlines will not be the curves used to construct surfaces; therefore, these curves do not necessarily have to be clean or have the appropriate number of vertices.

Once the surface edges have been outlined, these lines can remain displayed while you are modeling in the modeling windows if you set them to a noneditable viewing mode, such as template mode or reference mode. These curves describe the perimeter of each surface that you intend to build and serve as a guide but will not be regarded as the final layout of the surfaces. Throughout the modeling process, you will make many discoveries about the model that you had not previously considered before attempting to surface the model. To accurately model any complex shape or object, the modeler must be given a certain amount of freedom throughout the process to make decisions about where to place the surfaces to model the object correctly (Figure 6.7).

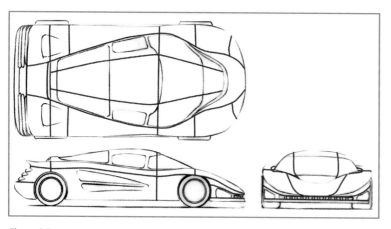

**Figure 6.7**
Using a diagram like this can save many hours of work.

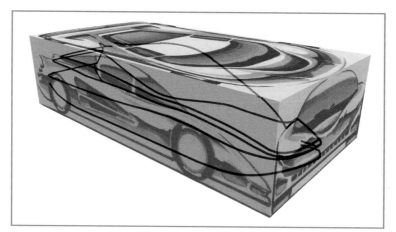

**Figure 6.8**
Laying the curves out using side views and editing the curves in the adjacent views creates 3-D curves for modeling.

## Building Curves in 2-D: Drawing Curves

When constructing curves from 2-D images or image planes, the modeler needs to spend more time interpolating the 2-D information into usable 3-D geometry. The process of modeling from images is seen as a more creative process than constructing models from 3-D reference data when the subject matter is a character or an object that allows some design input. Modeling from 2-D images allows the modeler to have input as to how some issues are resolved related to the translation from 2-D into 3-D.

When drawing curves from 2-D images, the modeler picks one image of the view that will be the best reference. The modeler will still need information from all views, but only one view will be the best. This may come in handy when making a judgment call between which view has the best details in comparison to the others. When a curve is drawn, the modeler should try to manually place the control vertices or edit points as evenly spaced as possible, while still placing any extra points or fewer points in specific areas as necessary to maintain accuracy.

When the curve is drawn in the main view, the points from the adjacent view can be modified to match that view. By drawing the curve in one view and modifying it in the adjacent view, the modeler can create true 3-D curves. Drawing the initial curves down the length of the model defines the form quickly and creates surfaces that blend together more easily later in the modeling process. In Figure 6.8, the red lines indicate the flow of surfaces moving from front to back. These curves are initially drawn in one view and then edited in the adjacent views to create 3-D curves.

To create good surfaces, the modeler should make every attempt to reuse these curves throughout the construction process. Although surfaces are constructed from the curves being built in this stage, they will inherit the spacing and placement of spans that are constructed in the curves. If the number of spans created in each curve for this surface is identical, the surface itself will appear very clean and have a consistent number of spans within the surface.

Create as many long continuous curves that stretch throughout the entire length of the model as possible. Most good modeling packages will allow surfaces to be built within long continuous curves as long as the boundary curves that run perpendicular to these long curves are constructed correctly and intersect with the long continuous curves. This is especially useful when creating models of vehicles. Most cars, planes, and boats are generally constructed of a single large, smooth shape that is broken up along areas of surface detail. If the curves that construct these surfaces can remain continuous, then a tangency condition between these adjacent surfaces is much easier to create, because the curve will remain tangent to itself throughout its entire length.

When the modeler is working on a model that represents an everyday object that is easily recognizable, artistic creativity may sometimes lead to creating models that do not exactly match what is seen in the real world. In these cases, I find it useful to begin with as much data as possible and will gladly use 3-D digitized data or 3-D scanned data if it is available.

## Building Curves in 3-D

Orthographic drawings are an acceptable way to begin the modeling process, but orthographic views do not tell the whole story. Sometimes there are details about the model that are not accurately described in the orthographic views. To visualize this condition, think of a modeler who has the task of building a sphere from scratch with no prior knowledge of the actual form of the final 3-D shape and only a front view and the side view of the sphere (Figure 6.9). Using this literal example, the modeler could come up with a shape that has sharp edges, which define the circular profiles seen in the 2-D drawings. The final shape of the 3-D model built from the drawings, while having the correct profiles, will not resemble a sphere (Figure 6.10).

When working in 3-D, the modeler must continuously check the model in 3-D space. If the modeler is creating models from orthographic drawings, he or she should have additional 3-D reference data, such as digitized data, a sculpture, or a thorough understanding of what the final model will look like.

## Building Curves in 3-D: Surfacing Strategy

While using 3-D reference data, modelers must create a plan or schematic that will allow them to surface the areas they have laid out individually. As with 2-D references, trying to create the schematic during the curve-building and surfacing process can be confusing and result in wasted time and energy. 3-D reference data takes the form of either a low-resolution 3-D model built from polygons or, more commonly, a series of polylines that have been created using the 3-D digitizer. The orthographic windows where the 3-D data will be loaded can serve as easily as 2-D image planes. Instead of drawing 2-D curves inside the image planes, the modeler draws the curves in the modeling windows. Again, the modeler must make these reference curves noneditable because the curve-building process could be complicated by the presence of other curves that are present while the modeler is attempting to snap curve points to existing data.

## Building Curves in 3-D: Drawing Curves

The 3-D reference data is not clean enough for the construction of a final 3-D digital model. This is why the 3-D data must be traced using clean and evenly spaced curves. The modeler will use a curve-snapping mode when drawing these curves along the existing data. The reference data must be separated from the work that is being done to surface the model. In Figure 6.11, the red lines indicate the main, larger curves that defined the flow of the main surfaces. The blue lines indicate the surfaces that were put in to create the rest of the curve network.

Several techniques will also help the modeler keep the reference data separated from the active modeling data. One way is to put the reference data on a separate

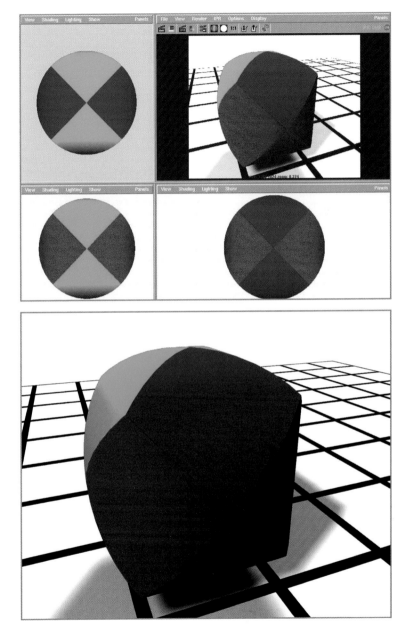

**Figures 6.9, 6.10**
Sometimes orthographic images alone do not give the complete story about the 3-D shape of an object.

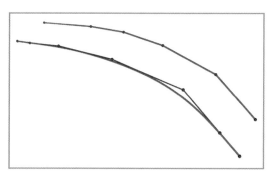

**Figure 6.11**
Curves taken directly from digitized data (top) normally need to be rebuilt as clean, evenly spaced curves (bottom).

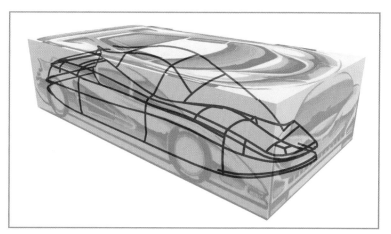

**Figure 6.12**
The curve network should resemble a 3-D version of the original surface strategy sketch.

layer while the model is being built. The options available in Maya's layer display will allow the modeler to make the reference data invisible or change the mode of the reference data to template or reference mode during the modeling process. Using this technique, or variations of this technique, allows the modeler to snap new curves onto the existing data but not to edit the existing data or pick the existing data.

Again, it is important to make sure every curve that is used to create a single surface has the same number of spans as the other curves in the surface. This is simply a good modeling practice, and the modeler should make every attempt to meet this condition if possible.

## Curve Network

When all the curves necessary to create the surfaces are laid out and the surfacing strategy schematics are complete, the final geometry should resemble a cage where the surfaces that are to be created will be placed. Figure 6.12 shows the curve network in place before the surfaces are applied. The curves shown in the final curve network match the original surfacing strategy sketch (refer to Figure 6.7).

This cage, when complete, should have every point at which one curve passes over another curve be a true intersection of curves. Many times when the modeler is learning this workflow, there will be curves that pass over other curves that appear to intersect but in reality do not. Only when the curves touch each other will there be a condition where a surface can be constructed from each curve.

When constructing the curve network, the modeler should make every attempt to avoid shapes that are not rectangular. Triangular and N-sided surfaces will have difficulty maintaining tangent edges with their adjacent surfaces. These types of surfaces are also not constructed from simple NURBS geometry. They can be a

modified standard surface or a trimmed standard surface, both of which are difficult to edit and cannot be rebuilt in such a way that the surface will line up cleanly with adjacent surfaces.

When the surfaces are applied, more problems will arise, for example, keeping surfaces tangent and surfaces clean while the details are applied. Figure 6.13 shows the surfaces in place with a diagram of the original curves superimposed on top of those surfaces.

**Figure 6.13**
The final surfaced model with the wireframe of the curve network superimposed on the model.

Allowances must be made where two large surfaces come together to include the radius, or fillet condition. In any 3-D object that exists in real physical space, there will be some sort of *fillet* or *bevel* where the two surfaces come together. In most cases, this fillet or bevel will be clearly visible to the naked eye. The highlight created when light strikes the surface in between two large surfaces gives the model the impression of being finished. Without these extra modeling touches, the computer model will appear as if it had been computer generated. With these details that exist in all physical objects, the computer model will take on a heightened level of realism.

You need not diagram every fillet condition and every bevel condition in the curve network as long as you understand that these details will be added later. In some cases, however, a large radius will be surfaced in between two large surface slabs. In these cases, the radius must be treated like a separate surface, and the boundaries laid out clearly just as if they were one of the slabs. The final model shown in Figures 6.14 and 6.15 shows the extra details, such as fillets, lights, and air vents, cut into the model.

### Surfacing

During the surfacing process, it will be necessary to rethink the surface layout created in the curve network. Although it is possible to construct the 3-D curves necessary to make these changes from scratch, the modeler may find it easier to build preliminary surfaces in the areas that require new construction. By building curves that rest on these preliminary surfaces, the modeler can quickly and easily create new curves that define new surfaces.

### Tangency

Tangency (discussed in Chapter 3) between surfaces is critical in a car model. Maintaining tangency conditions between surfaces is handled in several ways. The first requirement is that the curves, whenever possible, are built so that they create tangency conditions between surfaces. This will not guarantee that all surfaces will maintain this tangency, but it will go a long way to get the model on the right track right from the start.

Tangency can be built into the surface at the start using the continuity options in the surface creation dialog boxes or added to existing surfaces using align tools or stitch surface options (Figures 6.16–16.21).

### Trim Surfaces

*Trim surfaces* create a region that is trimmed away, or the rest of surface will be trimmed away from that region. Trim surfaces are areas within a standard rectangular NURBS surface that are defined by a *trim curve*, or a *curve on surface*, which is not a regular NURBS curve. The relationship with the surface that the curve rests on is a part of the trim curve. The trim curve can be created by drawing a curve on the surface, projecting a curve through a camera or a user-defined vector, or intersecting one shape with another shape.

A trim curve has to define a closed shape to define a trim region. A straight line that falls within the boundaries of a surface, without extending to any of the surface edges, will not successfully create a trim region. In order to create a trim region, the trim curve must create a region that can be separated completely from the rest of the surface.

**Figures 6.14, 6.15**
The final car model.

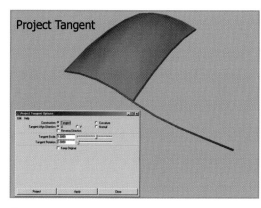

**Figure 6.16**
Project tangent options.

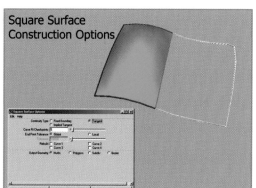

**Figure 6.17**
Square surface construction options.

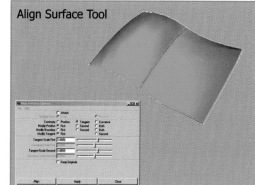

**Figure 6.18**
Align surface tool.

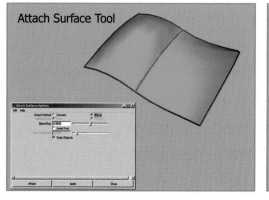

**Figure 6.19**
Attach surface tool.

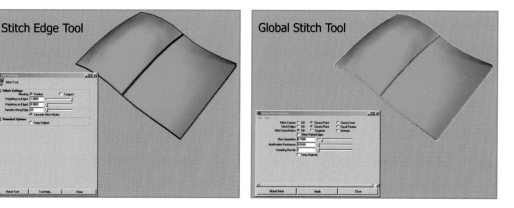

**Figure 6.20**
Stitch edge tool.

**Figure 6.21**
Global stitch tool.

A good example of a trim region is a circle. When a circle is drawn within a surface using a trim curve, the interior of the circle clearly defines a trim region. The circle can be used as the shape that will be trimmed away from the object or kept as the part that is retained when the rest of the object is trimmed away from it.

Trim surfaces are generally not allowed in models used in the production environment. Trim surfaces are not compatible for production processes at large studios for several reasons. One reason is that the boundary of the trim surface is defined by an edge of the surface where the surface no longer renders. This edge is not considered to be a real geometry border; any surface tessellation parameters and explicit parameterization settings will not apply the same way that they apply to standard NURBS surfaces. Another reason is that trim surfaces do not translate well across different rendering packages. When the production environment is set up to handle different packages for different parts of the production process, trim surfaces are usually off limits. Trim surfaces are also computationally expensive to render, in which the computer must calculate the visible region of the surface prior to rendering.

Figure 6.22 shows the difference between an untrimmed surface and a trimmed surface. The triangles shown in this diagram are the actual triangles generated by the rendering program during the surface *tessellation* process, which is used to create triangles that represent the NURBS geometry used in the scene prior to rendering. The computer calculates all the surfaces into triangles, loading all the triangles into memory before rendering. When the render is complete, this data is purged from memory. This diagram shows why trimmed surfaces are not an efficient way to create models.

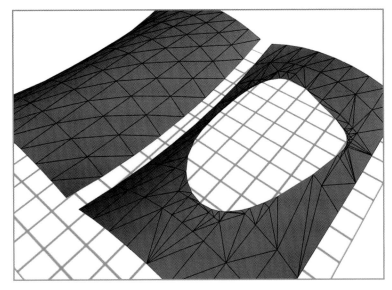

**Figure 6.22**
Trim surfaces are fast ways to build complex surfaces but are inefficient to use in production.

The reason that trim surfaces must be discussed in this section is that trim surfaces are excellent tools for creating difficult-to-create surfaces. Trimmed surfaces can save many hours of modeling time. For a hard surface product or vehicle model, trimmed surfaces are extraordinarily useful. If there is a possibility that trimmed surfaces can be used in the facility or production that the model is being created for, then trimmed surfaces can be used judiciously. One way to use trimmed surfaces and get the most use of geometry at the same time is to use the shrink surface option. This will shrink the original NURBS surface to optimize rendering time but will still leave the visible part of the trim surface intact.

One process available for using trimmed surfaces in a production environment that does not allow trim surfaces is to model the initial surface using trimmed surfaces and then build new curves for untrimmed surfaces on top of the preliminary trimmed surface. With these new curves, you can create usable surfaces while using the trim surface as a guide.

A basic rule with trimmed surfaces is to minimize their use or to eliminate their use in any project that requires animation. Multiple passes of rendering an object with trimmed surfaces is computationally expensive. Trim surfaces are fine for creating texture maps for games, however, because only one render is required per texture map. The time saved modeling with trim surfaces far outweighs the time saved during the rendering process.

# Environment Modeling

Some modelers do nothing except create environment models. These modelers generally create light resolution models of large and complex environmental scenes. These modelers tend to be highly skilled in texture mapping and lighting and use many tricks to optimize these complex scenes, knowing which details they can leave out and which can be faked using texture mapping lighting tricks.

When the modeler is dealing with complex environment models, the key to creating a really great model is creating an efficient model. When creating large-scale environments for digital rendering, rendering and animation must be included in the modeling process. If there are things that can be shown using texture mapping or rendering, then those details should not be modeled. If the animation is roughed in, and parts of the model will never be visible in the animation, then those parts should not be modeled. Much of this may seem like common sense, but many modelers overlook these basic principles.

## *Efficient Modeling Practices*

The specialty of environment modeling, as well as every other aspect of modeling, depends on the efficiency of the model to get the rest of the production finished. This section deals with the issues of optimization and provides some techniques that help create models that animate and render cleanly and efficiently.

### Copying Geometry versus Instancing Geometry

When a model has vast complexity, copying excessively can kill the entire production. *Instancing geometry* is a way to take a copy of a visual representation of an object in the scene and place it elsewhere. When the original object has a fundamental change applied to it, like the modification of vertex positions or shader assignments, the other instances will be updated to reflect these changes.

A complex environment model should not use many instances. Instances have a tendency to create rendering errors and other unpredictable results. While many modelers believe that instances will allow the render to work quicker, this is not the case. The renderer treats each instance as a separate model at render time, which saves no time whatsoever during the rendering process. But instancing does allow the modeler to work faster because the on-screen graphics update faster when using instances instead of copied geometry.

## CASE STUDY: *PARASITE EVE* (NEW YORK CITY FLY-THROUGH)

Squaresoft is a huge game company that has several mega-hit games that became video game dynasties. The most famous, *Final Fantasy*, spawned 10 sequels and a film. The games and film have very little to do with each other content wise, but all excel in graphic appeal.

A division of Square Company, the parent company to Squaresoft, had an office in the Los Angeles area (Square L.A.). At this facility, Squaresoft was producing a game called *Parasite Eve*. Many artists were employed to create this game, which was in production for a while. Square L.A. had more than 100 employees, whereas the art staff for *San Francisco Rush* consisted of four to seven people, depending on when you took a head count. Clearly, this game—as is true for many other games financed by large, mostly Japanese, companies—has a different economic structure than many of the games released by smaller U.S. companies.

*Parasite Eve* had some ambitious production goals. One of those goals was to produce many beautiful FMV (*full-motion video*) sequences that would be used to transition the player from one scenario to another during gameplay. These FMV sequences, while having very little to do with the gameplay itself other than providing some basic ideas about where the player is supposed to be in the city and what part of the game is coming up, are the most beautiful parts of the game. The FMV sequences serve as a reward for the player; upon finishing a level, the player sees the next FMV. Figures 6.23–6.25 are rendered images similar to the FMV images used in Parasite Eve. The amount of detail and geometry in these images far exceeds what is normally seen in video games. The images created for these sequences were laid out, modeled, and rendered in Alias Power Animator. The examples here were rendered in Maya.

**Figures 6.23–6.25**
These images, rendered in Maya, are representative of the kind of detail shown in the FMV sequences produced for *Parasite Eve*. *Parasite Eve* is a trademark of Square Co., Ltd. Based on the novel: Hideaki Sena "parasite EVE" (Kadokawa Horror Bunko).

I was not working at Square L.A. at this time, but there were people there who had long-standing working relationships with Rhythm & Hues, which was later called in to help on this project. Two sequences were awarded to Rhythm & Hues. One was a transformation sequence that required a character to be designed and approved by the Japanese game designer in charge of the project. The other was a helicopter fly-through in New York. Because of the realistic nature of the game FMV sequences, creating a fly-through sequence where five helicopters traverse Manhattan could not have been done by just two people, but this is pretty much what happened. There were two technical directors assigned to the project: a lighting technical director (TD) named Theodore Bialek and myself. I was called the head TD for this project, but the truth is, the work was shared evenly between the two of us—and there was plenty to go around. The tasks we performed had a huge amount of overlap, and the work that will be described here represents a joint effort from both TDs to get the job done.

All the modeling was started using 3-D databases purchased from Viewpoint. When a model that is purchased from a company like Viewpoint is used in production, it is generally changed or reworked entirely to suit the requirements of the production. *Parasite Eve* was no exception. The data we received from Viewpoint, although accurately depicting what the helicopters and New York City buildings would look like, could not be used in its current state. To determine what was needed for this production, we had to first take a look at the animation. When it was obvious what would be seen and what would not, we began the shot.

We had a production requirement to avoid using high-resolution polygonal models. For this fly-through sequence, we used Alias software. Although Alias does a lot of things well, it is not optimized for rendering or manipulating "heavy", or high-resolution, polygonal objects. The New York City dataset from Viewpoint was considered at that time to be a fairly heavy. Moreover, it did not have the necessary texture coordinates applied to the geometry that would make it possible to light for the shot.

Figure 6.26 shows a view of the original Viewpoint dataset of Manhattan. The main building that will be seen in this sequence is the Chrysler building. In this view, the Chrysler building cannot be used because it is too low-resolution for rendering at this distance.

Because Alias Power Animator is inefficient at rendering polygons, the building had to be rebuilt using NURBS surfaces (Figure 6.27). Once the NURBS model was put in place, the difference in the final rendered image was obvious (Figure 6.28).

When modeling the city, first we determined which animation we would use. Then we rebuilt the parts of the city that would be seen, in most cases replacing everything that was built in polygons with optimized NURBS models.

Figure 6.29 shows the city database in polygons. Large portions of the model were rebuilt using degree 1 NURBS surfaces to speed up render times and to create models that were easier to texture (Figure 6.30). The decisions of which parts of the model that needed to be rebuilt were based on what would be seen from the camera after the camera animation was finished. The task of rebuilding the dataset of New York City based on only what would be seen in the animation began. The criteria for building these models focused on efficiency and the ability to create a high-quality rendered sequence.

**Figure 6.26**
The original Viewpoint model of Manhattan is shown here, with the Chrysler building shown to the right.

**Figure 6.27**
The Chrysler building is shown after being rebuilt using NURBS surfaces.

**Figure 6.28**
The final render of the Chrysler building.

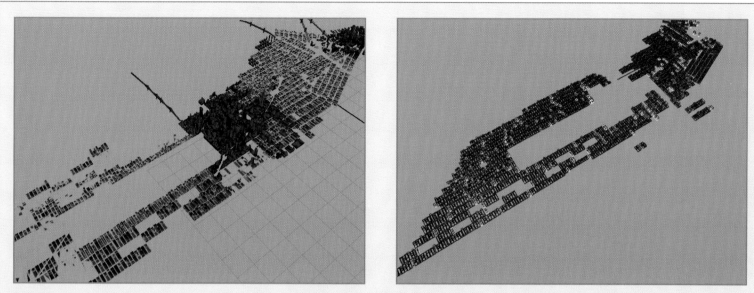

**Figures 6.29, 6.30**
We rebuilt the city using degree1 NURBS surfaces because render times and memory optimization was a high priority.

Then we determined from the preliminary animation what we could render without creating additional geometry. Based on the speed at which the helicopters flew through the city, many details on the buildings could be left out and rendered using maps, and in some cases, fog and dirt would hide a lot of detail as well.

## Modeling from Primitives versus Modeling Surfaces

Using primitives, the default shapes offered by the modeling program, is not usually a good idea when creating a complex environment model. Normally the rendering settings for these primitives, the surface types, and the tessellation settings are not efficient enough for large models of this type. Additionally, cubes have the drawback of being constructed from six individual surfaces. A simple way to create a cube from a single surface is to make a surface of revolution from a degree 1 curve that has four sections. If this is constructed correctly, the resulting shape will look like a cube. This technique also allows the modeler to add bevels and radiused edges that give the cube a realistic appearance and reduces the amount of geometry generated by the renderer at render time. By revolving a curve around an axis, a simple cube can be created that is more efficient and also has bevels at the top and bottom, which the default primitive does not have (Figure 6.31).

## Single-Sided Surfaces versus Double-Sided Surfaces

When you are using Alias and Maya, the modeling package will default to using double-sided surfaces. Many other packages available will not use double-sided surfaces as the default. *Backspace culling* is a process by which the renderer calculates everything in the scene to determine visibility prior to the prerender calculations, such as tessellation. If the surface is not seen during rendering, it is simply left off the internal list of objects that are to be rendered.

The majority of the modeling I do requires that the models created in Maya be exported into other packages. These packages are not as forgiving when it comes to double-sided surfaces. Every single surface must be modeled single-sided before the model is rendered.

Alias also has an option in its render stats that allows the modeler to choose opposite-sided versus single-sided. Using this opposite-sided option is another way that unpredictable rendering results can take place. Whenever possible, the

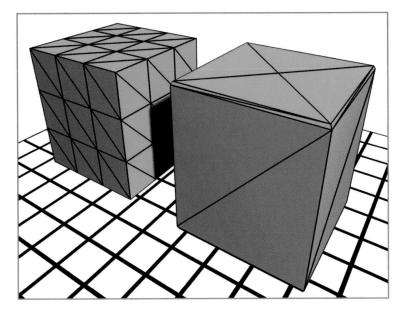

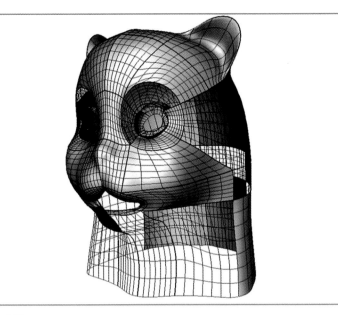

**Figure 6.31**
Tessellation of a cube made from degree 3 surfaces and a cube made from revolving a degree 1 curve about the vertical axis.

**Figure 6.32**
A model with many surfaces reversed.

modeler should make single-sided surfaces that face in the correct direction. If surfaces do not face correctly when they are modeled, the direction of those surfaces should be reversed so they do face the correct direction. Figure 6.32 shows that problems that arise when a model that is constructed using double-sided surfaces are suddenly converted to single-sided surfaces.

### No Set Planar Surfaces

Alias has two methods for creating planar surfaces. One option, available in Maya, is to use a trim surface with a trim that is automatically created from the curve that defines the planar surface. Another method is to use a special entity type inside Alias specifically created for planar surfaces. This entity type renders quickly and is computationally efficient. For this reason, you might expect the planar surface to be used whenever possible. This is not the case. Planar surfaces are notorious for creating rendering problems and should be avoided at all times. The best way to create a planar surface is to create a surface using the trim surface option and then build curves on top of the trimmed surface that will create flat standard NURBS surfaces that will take the place of the planar surface.

### Rebuild Curves and Surfaces

When creating degree 3 or cubic surfaces, you should attempt to use evenly spaced curves to create evenly spaced surfaces. This is good modeling practice and should

be the goal when you are creating any model from degree 3 surfaces. Sometimes, it is necessary to rebuild the curves so they are clean. When surfaces are constructed from these curves, sometimes there will be extra spans or a nonuniform distribution of spans. Surfaces should also be rebuilt in these cases. Uniformly rebuilding curves and surfaces produces clean and predictable results for modeling.

### Tessellation

*Tessellation* is the process where Alias software (and Maya, for that matter) will generate polygonal triangles internally in memory that represent the NURBS surfaces in the scene. It cannot be overstated that tessellation criteria, when set correctly, will optimize a render more efficiently than just about any other single thing you can do. The number of triangles generated for each NURBS surface depends on whether you use uniform subdivision or adaptive subdivision and degree 1 surfaces or degree 2 surfaces.

### Uniform Subdivision versus Adaptive Subdivision

*Adaptive subdivision* allows the renderer to decide on the number of triangles generated at render time based on surface curvature and the distance the object is from the camera. The modeler can set the number of adaptive subdivision triangles used by the renderer, but the numbers used by the renderer are limited to powers of 2 (2, 4, 8, 16, 32, 64, 128, and so on).

*Uniform subdivision* (Figure 6.33) explicitly sets the number of triangles per span in the surface. This number can be any number. By default, Alias sets the subdivision mode to adaptive, and Maya will set the subdivision mode to uniform.

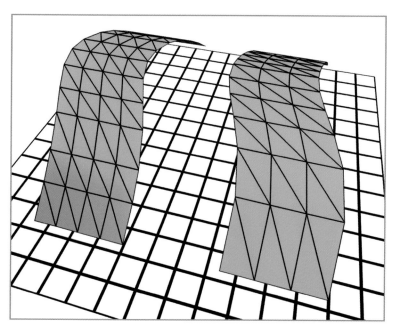

**Figure 6.33**
Uniform subdivision will tessellate an object with less geometry than adaptive subdivisions.

Trim surfaces will have adaptive subdivision set as default because the number of triangles required to display the trim surfaces correctly cannot be set correctly based on surface spans. Using trim surfaces in an environment model will dramatically increase render times. Trim surfaces should be avoided for this type of model. During the creation of the *Parasite Eve* model that we made, each surface had uniform subdivisions explicitly set. Because many of the buildings we created were copied over and over, we made sure the settings were in place prior to copying.

## Degree 1 Surfaces versus Degree 3 Surfaces

A single segment, single span degree 1 surface can be visualized as a simple polygon. The number of triangles that will be generated at render time will be two. If the modeler were to rebuild the same surface using a degree 3 surface (Figure 6.34) and the rendering settings were sent to the default settings, the number of triangles created at render time would be 18. All surfaces would be visually identical, but the degree 3 surfaces would take much longer to render. This is why it is

important that whenever there is an opportunity to reduce render time by changing surface degree type or by optimizing rendering stats the modeler takes advantage of these opportunities. During an animated sequence, these models have to be rendered many times. If the modeler can save several seconds for each render, then hours and hours of production time can be saved over the course of the entire animation.

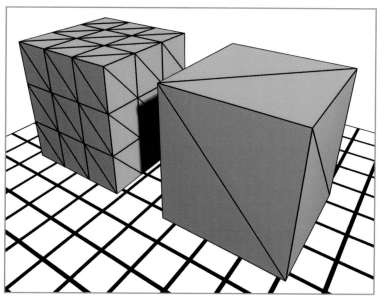

**Figure 6.34**
Tessellation differences between degree 3 surfaces and degree 1 surfaces.

When constructing architectural environments, you will commonly have many flat surfaces. Flat surfaces can easily be replaced by degree 1 surfaces. When there is a curve condition, which can commonly be seen in arched doorways and other architectural details, you must use degree 3 surfaces. Using degree 3 surfaces in these cases will not present an extraordinary load on the renderer.

### Bevels

It may seem inappropriate to represent a rectangular building as a simple cube, because a cube does not have *bevels*, or radiused edges, that could catch highlights during an animation, and a cube, by default, is made up of six separate surfaces. For smaller objects, such as a brick, a bevel would be a good thing to see on the object because it makes the brick look realistically scaled. A building should not have a bevel because it makes the building look small. The edges that naturally occur at the edges of a brick are so small when seen at the scale of an entire building that they would disappear.

### Texture Coordinates

When modeling, you need to have understanding of the way the lighters will use your geometry during the production process. Different types of productions and different software packages require different types of geometry. A primary concern when creating geometry is texture coordinates. NURBS geometry has an inherent set of texture coordinates, but polygonal geometry will need to have texture coordinates applied to it before passing the model to the lighters. Figure 6.35 shows the difference between NURBS texture coordinates and a polygonal cube with the texture coordinates applied to it.

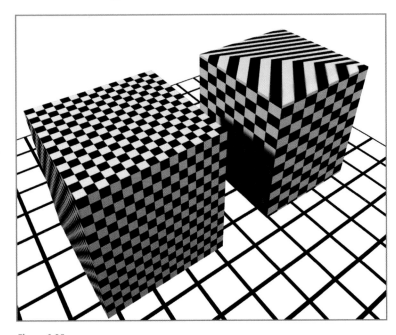

**Figure 6.35**
Inherent texture coordinates of NURBS surfaces (left) and simple spherical texture coordinates applied to a polygonal cube (right).

A single NURBS surface with the degree value of 1 and a single span can be textured so that the image rests cleanly and exactly within the boundaries of that surface. If the models were built using polygons, each individual face of the building—assuming that each face represented a single wall—would have required the application of texture vertices. This would have taken quite a long time, considering that we had many buildings, and would have left us in a position where we had to use polygons in a software package optimized for spline surfaces. This is why we decided that the small individual generic buildings would be made up of individual surfaces that represented each wall. We made individual models for the buildings seen up close, and for the signature buildings, such as the Empire

State Building and Chrysler Building. The techniques used to optimize the models for these buildings are described in the preceding sections.

## Character Modeling

Another type of modeler will create nothing except creature or character models. The creation of these models must be coordinated carefully with the various departments that will be creating animation setup and animation and the lighters creating the final render. The character modeler needs to be versed in almost all aspects of digital production. The animation setup person will depend on the modeler to correctly put in place the geometry required for necessary deformation. The lighter will depend on the modeler to make the geometry simple to split into various materials and texture groups. The animator will depend on the modeler to create attractive morph targets for animation, as well as creating geometry that can be moved easily without twisting.

People who specialize in models that deform need to be familiar with the techniques that allow modelers to create complex and refined forms using few surfaces, as well as surfaces with little topological complexity. As I describe specific modeling techniques and tools, the process of creating lightweight character models will be explained.

When people talk about character modeling, they will invariably discuss the techniques and modeling practices used when creating character models. Several philosophies exist about modeling characters that are all being used in production today. These modeling strategies are all based on technologies used for animation and rendering that are compatible with the particular modeling process used for the production. It cannot be stressed enough that the animation and rendering pipeline determine modeling strategy, not the other way around.

When determining the process that will be used for modeling, the modeler must be familiar with the various aspects of digital production that the model will be ultimately used for downstream. The modeler must also become acquainted with the various techniques used for modeling. This will give the modeler more than one option for any production scenario that may develop.

Character modeling currently has a few basic camps for model types that are used for production at various studios. This simplistic approach to defining each modeling technique only serves as a convenient way to catalog the modeling workflows. The subtleties involved with each modeling type has to be examined by breaking down these workflows. The basic modeling workflows for character modeling are polygonal character modeling (Figure 6.36), NURBS character sculpting (Figure 6.37), and patch modeling for characters (Figure 6.38), and subdivision character modeling (Figure 6.39). These all have common elements with some distinctions as well.

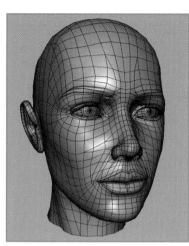

**Figure 6.36**
Polygonal character modeling starts and ends with polygons. Model courtesy of Poser Software.

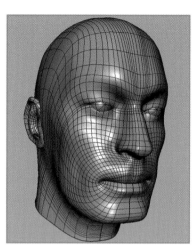

**Figure 6.37**
NURBS character sculpting focuses on using large sculpted surfaces. Model courtesy of Viewpoint Datalabs.

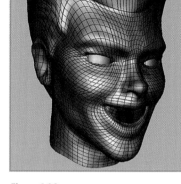

**Figure 6.38**
Patch modeling for characters uses several surfaces to create a complex shape.

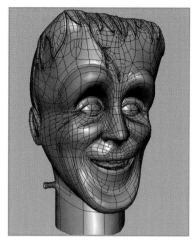

**Figure 6.39**
Subdivision character modeling starts with low-resolution geometry and creates a high-resolution model.

## Details of Characters

Character modeling is an aesthetic as well as technical exercise. Many character modelers have at least some sculpting experience. Some of the visual and mental abilities needed to translate an organic form using complex 3-D geometry are the same skills required to sculpt an organic shape from clay. Capturing the form is the key when it comes to character modeling. A modeler involved with creating a major character for a film is dealing with a character that will have the same dramatic impact on the film as an actor who would be paid millions of dollars in a live-action film. The modeler is under a certain amount of pressure to get the form of that character just right.

Many times, the definition of what's right is a moving target. When a modeler is working on a film, several people will likely want to participate in the process of designing the character. Although the modeler is ultimately responsible for getting the form executed in 3-D, many people will want to provide their opinion about whether the form is correct. On any given feature film, these people might be any of the following: the director, the production designer, the art director, the lighting director, the animation director, the producer, the lead animator, the lead lighter, the lead setup person, the modeling supervisor, the animator, the lighter, the fellow modelers, the lead texture map artist, the entire texture map department, the entire animation department, the entire lighting department, the coordinators, the caterers, the drivers, and the receptionist. This would be funny if it were not so close to being the truth.

Also, depending on the film, more than one person may be assigned to each model. This can be a great assistance, but it can also cause some confusion and communication problems. When more than one person works on a single character, a great deal of coordination is required to ensure that the areas being worked on by the different people line up and the visual characteristics of the different parts are consistent. Different modeling techniques will cause even more logistical problems than others, but the shortcomings of having two or more people working on a single character are usually outweighed by the resulting time savings. Large films that have teams of modelers will assign one person to be the lead for a character, and others will support the character lead. This helps solve many problems. Sometimes in film production so many levels of management are in place that it becomes counterproductive. In some cases, having a single contact person who can make the judgment calls is necessary to get the job done. If supervision can be counterproductive, then having several people working in an uncooperative effort is even more counterproductive. Sometimes it is just important that someone, anyone, makes the calls.

Another important aspect to creating character models that will deform predictably is the flow of the geometry over the deformable areas of the model. When an object deforms or changes shape, generally the object will bend, rotate, flex, or contract using a predictable line of action. For example, if a character moves an arm at the elbow, the forearm will rotate away from the upper arm at the elbow along an axis that projects from the elbow. The elbow will not expand or transform into something besides an elbow. Given this criteria for modeling an elbow, the modeler can make the deformation easier by constructing the geometry that creates the elbow in such a way that the geometry will flow around the arm laterally. This will allow the elbow to bend without going against the flow of the geometry.

Another is the character's mouth. The mouth is one of the most expressive and flexible parts of the character. If the mouth is constructed from a single square surface on the front of the face with ridges modeled in to represent the lips, any mouth movement aside from a knowing grin, would cause extreme twisting and tearing along the surface. This is why a good typical model of a character will have the mouth modeled so that the geometry flows away from the inside of the mouth radially, as if the mouth were a tube. When the geometry is built this way, the animation of the mouth can be much more extreme.

Areas, such as the mouth, eyes, and nostrils are all surrounded by radial perimeters. The circular regions that surround them can define all of these areas. Areas that animate have to be built so the geometry will deform in the same direction as the intended movement. Areas that are defined by circular regions need to be able to move easily in the directions defined by the shape of the circle. The mouth, for example, will expand and contract in the direction of concentric circles around the mouth region. Geometry that defines circular areas must be laid out in a circular manner. If the geometry does not flow in the direction of the natural circular movement of these areas, the model will twist and tear when it is animated. Figure 6.40 shows radial flow of geometry around the eyes, nostrils, and mouth. This flow of geometry assists in the animation and rendering of organic models.

## Character Modeling Techniques

Character modeling is more than simply capturing the form correctly. As stated previously, the modeling effort is, above all, the process of creating 3-D for animation and rendering. If the model is not compatible for the animation or rendering process, then the time spent modeling is wasted. This is why each studio has adopted its own production standards based on the specific production pipeline. The nuances for each studio cannot be listed here, but a few general techniques should shed light on some of the studios' workflows. These methods will be explained in a somewhat chronological order. Some of these modeling methods were either spawned directly from new modeling technologies as they became available or evolved from existing technologies.

### Polygonal Character Modeling

The first 3-D geometry for computer graphics was polygonal. The earliest visual representations of 3-D imagery were vector representations of 3-D polygonal geometry. Creating these models was not easy before the introduction of easy-to-understand 3-D modeling programs. Many times the models needed to be constructed using cryptic command-line instructions that described the exact X, Y, Z

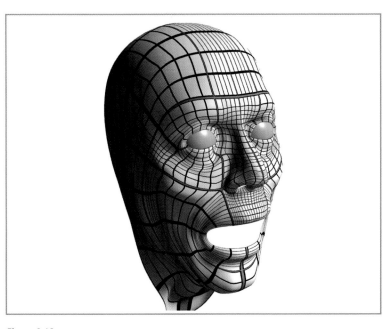

**Figure 6.40**
The radial surfaces assist in creating easy-to-animate models.

coordinates of each vertex. Loading this series of points in the computer created a numbered list of vertices. The modeler, with these numbers in place, could define polylines from them using the reference or index number that got assigned to each, not the X, Y, Z coordinates, of the adjacent points. Once a series of points was defined as a line, then a series of lines could be defined as a polymesh. This method of building models was much like programming a computer to create 3-D geometry.

I worked using this modeling method during my early years in the computer graphics industry. This primitive method for creating geometry really shows a modeler just how important it can be to have an intuitive user interface for a modeling program. While good modelers should be able to adapt to the production limitations imposed on them, it can also be said that good modeling software will pay for itself in a fairly short amount of time. Anything, indeed, is possible, but when a modeler has to overcome counterintuitive and clumsy software, the models that are created will unlikely be as high-quality or created as quickly as models created with software that is powerful and easy to use. In the current production environment, the cost of hiring people to create computer graphics far outweighs the cost of purchasing software and hardware. Therefore, most studios will not hesitate to get the most powerful software available, especially if it can be proven that this software will save time in the long run.

The method for creating polygonal models that required manual input of every vertex to create polygons eventually led to the introduction of intuitive interfaces and powerful modeling tools. During the time when modeling software with easy-to-use interfaces became available, most of the packages offered nothing except polygon modeling tools. Even modeling packages that have become famous for offering outstanding NURBS modeling tools and little else had their origins in polygonal modeling. Softimage and Alias, two software packages that became the standard character modeling tools for NURBS surfaces, originally offered only polygonal modeling tools in their initial releases.

During the years of 1981, when Wavefront Technologies started, through 1988, the programs that enabled faster polygonal modeling had an explosive effect on industry and entertainment. The requirement for building polygonal models using archaic command line interfaces led to an era where polygonal models were being built quicker and easier than ever before.

The computer-generated visual effects seen in films during this time reflected this technology as well. Examples include *Tron* (1982), *Young Sherlock Holmes* (1985), and *The Last Starfighter* (1985). While all of these films were groundbreaking, the technology used to create the films' effects had the distinct signature of polygonal modeling. Short films produced during this time also showed signs of technological limitations. Examples of short films made during this time would be Pixar's *Luxo Jr.*, (1986), Bill Kroyer's *Technological Threat*, (1988), and Pacific Data Image's *Locomotion* (1988).

Polygon models can be seen in more computer graphic applications than any other type of model. The models created for video games are primarily polygonal models (Figure 6.41), as well as many models created for high-end productions (Figure 6.42). Polygonal models offer a great deal of flexibility and can be transferred easily between different software packages.

## NURBS Character Sculpting

In the late 1980s new modeling technologies began to emerge. When Alias Research opened in Toronto in 1982, it focused on creating tools that made modeling easy and fast. Alias originally used polygons to create models in their first releases of the software, but they soon were creating models using NURBS surfaces in later releases. Upon introducing NURBS surfaces, Alias Research started a new way of thinking about models. Other companies also began putting NURBS surfaces into their modeling workflow. Another company that became famous for NURBS surfaces in its modeling package was Softimage, founded in 1986.

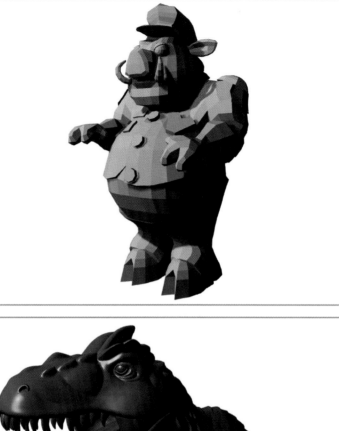

**Figures 6.41, 6.42**
Polygonal models range from low-resolution models used for games to high-resolution models used for television and film. *Game character model courtesy of Jef Shears; T-Rex model courtesy of Nancy Klimley.*

The world was introduced to NURBS modeling in the entertainment industry with James Cameron's film *The Abyss* (1989). During the water tentacle effect, the world experienced the first convincing 3-D character animation. This effect, created with Alias software, used NURBS surfaces, 3-D scan data, and 3-D morphing models to create a chilling representation of a human face made from water. Another film that typified the look of this type of modeling technique was James Cameron's *Terminator 2: Judgment Day*, produced in 1991. The word *fluid* was appropriate for the look and feel of these objects. This was largely because the NURBS model allowed the rendered image to appear as if there were no straight lines or edges at all in the object.

The processes adopted for dealing with NURBS surfaces (Figure 6.43), mathematically defined rectangular patches that can appear infinitely smooth, usually required that single surfaces envelop as much of the model as possible. In the case of the water tentacle, the entire model was created from one single surface. Creating a model from one single surface could have been considered the goal of most NURBS models built using this technique.

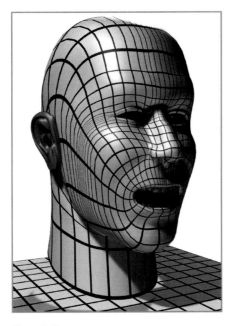

**Figure 6.43**
Construction of the surface used to create a head.

Many productions to this day are using modeling techniques where models are constructed using single surfaces to cover large areas of the model. One way to recognize this technique when reviewing a character model would be to look at the head of the character. When a modeler is sculpting large NURBS surfaces to create a model, the surface of the head, or at least the head and mouth, will be one large surface. The eyes, eyelids, nose, and ears are often modeled separately and stuck onto the single-surface head using surfaces that are tangent to the surface of the head.

This type of modeling was considered state-of-the-art during the late '80s and early '90s. Still, even today this technique is considered by many to be the best way to get models created for some productions. Many small, and some not-so-small, productions use modeling of this type. Cartoon characters are generally modeled this way because it is the fastest and simplest way of building a character. This does not mean that this process is easy. To create a convincing character using a single NURBS surface, the modeler must be a skilled sculptor. A model of this type may turn out badly in any of a variety of ways. The modeler must be patient and prepared to rebuild the model many times over to get satisfactory results, making it difficult to estimate the amount of time required to build a model of this type.

Despite the conceptual simplicity, this type of NURBS modeling presents several technical limitations. When NURBS surfaces are stretched beyond the mathematically rectangular nature of the surface, they can have uncontrollable distortion when texture mapping is applied to them. This is a common occurrence when you are attempting to model a complex shape with a single surface. Also, because a single surface is being used to approximate the shapes of complex objects, the requirement of keeping the flow of the geometry aligned with the direction of the animation is difficult, if not impossible, to maintain. This causes stretching of the surface and unpredictable twisting along the axes of animation.

## Subdivision Character Modeling

*Subdivision modeling* is a development that can be conceptualized as a hybrid of NURBS modeling and polygonal modeling. Several software packages, in one way or another, model an object using subdivision techniques. They all begin within a lower-resolution polygonal object and increase the resolution of that object using the same type of mathematic algorithms that are used to create NURBS surfaces. Following is a list of several reasons why subdividing a polygonal cage to create a high-resolution model is advantageous to the other methods of creating character models:

◆ Creating a low-resolution character model is simple and easy compared to other methods and can actually be fun. The ability to create complex details in a relatively short amount of time is very efficient and satisfying for the modeler.

◆ The application of UV coordinates gets applied to the low-resolution geometry, and then the model is subdivided, interpolating the low-resolution UV's onto the higher resolution model. This saves a great deal of time compared to applying UV coordinates to a high-resolution polygonal model.

◆ The animation setup can be applied to the low-resolution model, and when the model is converted to a high-resolution mesh, the animation set-up will still be in place. Every set-up deformation can be applied smoothly to the high-resolution model without any extra effort.

◆ The animation can be tested on the low-resolution model. The low-resolution model will show deformation and will indicate how far something will bend, but will be fast to move and animate because the geometry is low-resolution.

◆ The actual subdivision process can be put off right up until the render takes place, making the entire process streamlined and faster compared to other methods.

The specifics surrounding the actual transformation of this *polygonal cage*, as it is referred to, into a higher-resolution subdivision object (Figures 6.44 and 6.45) differ from software package to software package. Pixar is given much credit for the proliferation of this modeling technique. Although the actual history behind the philosophy of smoothing a polygonal cage precedes the research done at Pixar, this company has implemented this technology in such a way that it can be considered state of the art. Since Pixar developed its process of creating *subdivision surfaces*, several companies have made their own version of what can be considered *true subdivision surfaces*.

One thing that distinguishes the Pixar method is that each quadrangle in the polygonal cage is converted to an actual NURBS surface at render time within Pixar's proprietary rendering software RenderMan. Because of the unique way that RenderMan handles NURBS surfaces, the subdivision models appear infinitely smooth and finished looking. Due to the way that Pixar renders, this type of geometry has by nature adaptive subdivisions.

Another option available in subdivision modeling is *polygonal smoothing*. This technique is available in many software packages. Using this technique, a modeler simply creates a lower-resolution polygonal cage and then smooth the polygonal cage. This increases the number of polygons and changes the shape of the object. When using this technique, the modeler has no way to adaptively subdivide the object. Each polygon in the lower-resolution cage will subdivide the same amount as every other polygon in the lower-resolution cage. This can be both good and bad. The modeler determines where the details need to be and where it is possible to have fewer polygons without having the object appear jagged and unfinished.

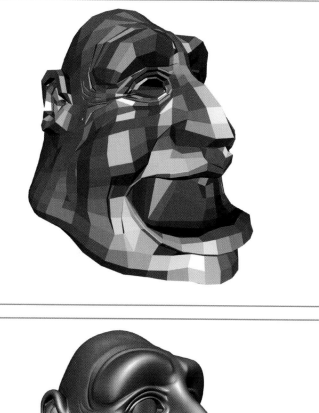

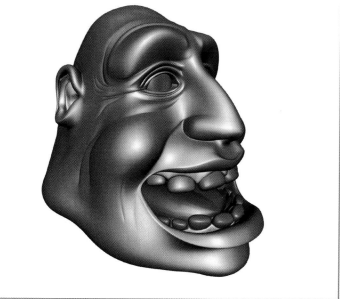

**Figure 6.44, 6.45**
A low-resolution polygonal cage was used to create a high-resolution subdivision model.

6. Modeling Specialties

## CASE STUDY: *THE FLINTSTONES IN VIVA ROCK VEGAS*

During the time that Rhythm & Hues was working on this film, the production pipeline for modeling was going through a radical paradigm shift. For many years before this production, high-resolution polygonal models were used for every model. Construction of these models was tedious and difficult. NURBS patch modeling was quickly becoming the fastest, cleanest, and most efficient way to produce clean high-resolution models. A detailed example of the model for Dino is shown in Chapter 7.

**Figure 6.46**
The model of Dino had to match the puppet used in live-action shots. Copyright © 2002 by Universal Studios. Courtesy of Universal Studios Publishing Rights, a Division of Universal Studios Licensing, Inc. All rights reserved.

Subdivision modeling, however, was being researched during the time. It was fast, easy, and produced clean models that were easy to set up and render. By smoothing a polygonal cage to create a high-resolution polygonal model, the models were perfectly compatible with the rendering pipeline. One of the biggest advantages to this procedure was that the modelers at Rhythm & Hues did not have to learn any new software. The tools used to build high-resolution models for many years did a fine job of making low-resolution models.

**Figure 6.47**
The computer generated Dino model was used for shots where the entire character was shown at once. Copyright © 2002 by Universal Studios. Courtesy of Universal Studios Publishing Rights, a Division of Universal Studios Licensing, Inc. All rights reserved.

Dino may be the last high-resolution polygonal character model that Rhythm & Hues will ever create. Subdivision modeling has allowed the modeling department to become more efficient than ever before, and the quality of the models is very high.

**Figure 6.48**
The computer generated Dino was used for many shots in the film. Copyright © 2002 by Universal Studios. Courtesy of Universal Studios Publishing Rights, a Division of Universal Studios Licensing, Inc. All rights reserved.

The Hopperoo character in *The Flintstones in Viva Rock Vegas* was constructed using a lower-resolution polygonal cage. When the polygonal model had the resolution increased, the model was ready to render for the film, as shown in Figures 6.49 and 6.50. Figure 6.51 shows the Hopperoo character in the film.

**Figures 6.49, 6.50**
Hopperoo was modeled using a low-resolution polygonal cage (top). The cage was subdivided to create a higher resolution model (bottom). Model built by Ian Hulbert.

**Figure 6.51**
The Hopperoo model as it appeared in the final rendered shot. Copyright © 2002 by Universal Studios. Courtesy of Universal Studios Publishing Rights, a Division of Universal Studios Licensing, Inc. All rights reserved.

A modeler would decide to use polygonal smoothing over true subdivision surfaces for a number of reasons. Subdivision surfaces are, by nature, tied directly to the renderer that is in the software package being used to create the model. Many production environments have a particular package for modeling and another package for rendering. When transferring data back and forth, you cannot use these special entity types. Another production environment that makes these true subdivision models impossible to use is the video game production environment. In cases where a low-resolution model is being produced for a game but needs to be used in higher resolution for a *level-of-detail* model (LOD) or a *full-motion video* (FMV), the modeler cannot use subdivision surfaces in the game engine.

Some utilities are available that allow the modeler to visualize the higher-resolution smoothed polygonal model while the modeler is working on the lower-resolution mesh. This capability to view the model in its final state while working on the low-resolution mesh is a huge time-saver. By the same token, subdivision surfaces can also be modeled in this way.

Subdivision surfaces have the added benefit of being able to have certain edges "tagged" as nondivided or as divided at a different resolution from the rest of the model. This allows for hard edges on objects and allows the modeler to use this technique to model hard surface models using subdivision modeling techniques. When you are modeling an organic shape or a character, the ability to create hardened edges within the polygonal cage is not used as much as when modeling hard surface models. Certain techniques allow the modeler to create an edge that appears harder than the rest of the model without tagging it at a different subdivision resolution as the rest of the model. One such technique is to add one or two rows of polygons along the edges that require hardening. When the entire model is subdivided, the additional rows appear as a tight edge that has a tight bevel. Generally, these extra steps make a nicer looking model than tagging edges as non-divided.

Another benefit to using true subdivision surfaces, which become true NURBS entities during the rendering process, is that true NURBS surfaces allow adaptive subdivisions at render time. This may not be necessary for some applications, but in certain circumstances, especially when the use of displacement mapping is required, this can be a major factor when deciding whether to use polygons or true subdivision surfaces.

### Patch Modeling for Characters

An alternative to modeling a complex shape from a single surface is *patch modeling*, in which you create many individual surfaces, or patches, that come together to make the final form. An example of how to create a patch model is described in Chapter 13. A modeler using patch modeling to create 3-D geometry must pay careful attention to the layout of the patches along the surface of the model. The purpose of using patch modeling in a production environment that uses NURBS surfaces is to overcome the limitations of using a single spline surface to approximate a complex shape. For instance, a modeler who would attempt to build the head of a character from a single surface would spend a great deal of time working on one single surface and would still have to deal with the limitations of uncontrollable deformation stretching and uncontrollable texture stretching. A modeler who is using patch modeling techniques would spend time working on a network of surfaces, where each surface in the network would have spans within each surface that would be relatively equal to each other. Following is a list of several advantages and disadvantages related to using NURBS sculpting instead of NURBS patch modeling:

◆ NURBS sculpting requires fewer surfaces to keep track of during the setup process (Figure 6.52).

◆ NURBS sculpting requires fewer texture maps. NURBS patch modeling requires a separate texture map for each surface; for an entire character, this could easily result in more than 100 texture maps.

◆ NURBS patch modeling maintains a more uniform distribution of geometric complexity (Figure 6.53).

◆ NURBS patch modeling does not require blend surfaces to transition detailed areas into smooth areas.

A detailed tutorial that discusses patch modeling is presented in Chapter 7.

### *Organic Modeling*

Character modeling is actually a subset of organic modeling. Character modeling has been discussed more in detail because a production facility that segregates modeling tasks into different categories uses the categories of hard-surface and creature (character) modelers.

If modeling tasks are split between hard-surfaces and character modelers, organic models will generally be split between these two groups. Organic models are models of objects that are not man-made, but are not characters either. Some examples of objects that would fall into the category of organic models include trees, mountains, rocks, and plants. Which group of modelers that would be assigned to these models would be determined by the intended use of the model in production. If the model is going to be animated in such a way that the model deforms and has to go through character rigging (animation setup), then the model would be done by the creature modelers. If the model does not deform, then the hard-surface modelers would do the model. Figures 6.54 and 6.55 are examples of organic

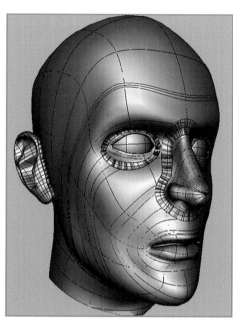

**Figure 6.52**
A patch model maintains a uniform distribution of geometry. Model courtesy of Max Ancar.

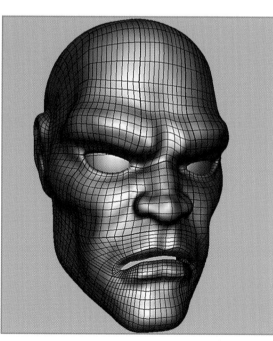

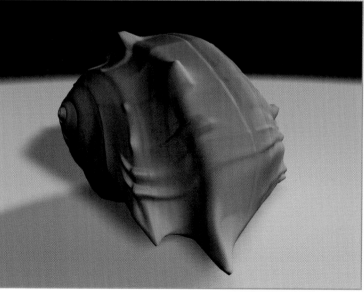

**Figures 6.54, 6.55**
This Sphinx (top) and the sea shell (bottom) are organic models, which would probably be modeled by the hard surface modeling department.

**Figure 6.53**
A single surface head requires fewer surfaces.

**6. Modeling Specialties**

113

models. These models do not animate like a character. The hard-surface modelers will do this kind of model.

Another example of an organic model is a prop that has an organic look and feel, but does act like a character. An excellent example of this is the talking hat in the film *Harry Potter and the Sorcerer's Stone* (2001). This hat in Figure 6.56 is probably one of the most entertaining characters in the entire film, but is simply a prop that was digitally recreated and animated. This hat definitely required character setup and character animation. Despite the fact that this hat is simply a prop, a character modeler would model this hat.

There are no concrete barriers between the departments that specialized modelers are working in. Environment modelers create some hard-surface models from time to time. Some hard-surface modelers model objects that get turned into characters. The lines get really fuzzy at times. When a modeler is working in a specialized environment like this, they know as much as possible about what do, but they also stay aware of the current processes and techniques in the other departments as well.

**Figure 6.56**
The sorting hat in *Harry Potter* is a prop that becomes a character. HARRY POTTER AND THE SORCERER'S STONE
© 2001 Warner Bros., a division of Time Warner Entertainment Company, L.P. All Rights Reserved.

# chapter 7
# Character Modeling Tutorial

I n this tutorial, the model is the character Dino from *Flintstones in Viva Rock Vegas*. Most production facilities use maquettes. If the model will be produced using model sheets or orthographic views, a maquette built in an action pose is created before the model sheets are drawn up. Building a sculpture in real life 3-D ensures that the proportions of the model will appear correctly in the virtual 3-D world in the computer. When a production facility has millions of dollars invested in the success of a 3-D character, building a maquette is a small price to pay to make sure it looks good before it is built.

The CG character used in this tutorial was intended to seamlessly integrate into shots where the animatronic puppet was used. This animatronic Dino was created by Jim Henson's Creature Shop. Rhythm & Hues was provided a model fabricated from urethane foam (Figure 7.1) that was used for reference. The foam maquette was poured from the exact mold that was used to make the puppet. The model that was constructed from this reference maquette was supposed to match the foam property exactly.

## Model Sheets

These drawings are normally used to define the look of the character in orthographic views used for modeling. Because the model had to be animated using digital character controls, the legs had to be straightened and spread apart. The face was changed a little bit to allow for nostril animation and easier eye animation (Figure 7.2).

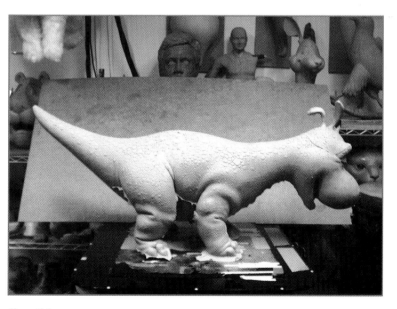

**Figure 7.1**
The maquette supplied by Jim Henson's Creature Shop.

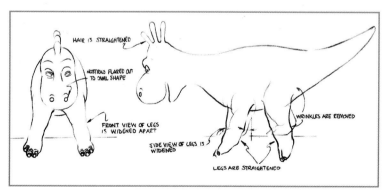

**Figure 7.2**
The model sheet used for modeling the final 3-D model.

## Digitized Maquette

The foam prop was digitized using a 3-D digitizer, resulting in data that was not as accurate as data that is digitized from a maquette constructed from sturdier materials. The actual model was available for reference, and the puppet maquette data had to be changed to accommodate the requirements for animation setup. Digitizing provided only enough data to begin modeling; looking at the actual 3-D sculpture provided the information that was required for the final model.

### Curve Network

The network for the construction curves is conceived before the digitizing begins. The way the surfaces will flow along the curvature of the eyes, mouth, and nostrils are all laid out on the face. The difficult transitions where the arms attach to the body and the legs attach to the hips are planned out at this time as well. Two important aspects of patch layout for modeling are explained. The first aspect is to enable the easy and efficient layout for surfaces on a model. The second, more important reason, is to lay out surfaces so that the final geometry will move along the surface the same way that skin moves when muscles move beneath the skin. The radial sections around the eyes, mouth, nostrils, arm intersections, and leg transitions, allow the geometry to move the way the actual parts of the body move. The muscles around the mouth move in directions that flow along the perimeter of the mouth. The muscles that lie beneath the lips travel radially around the mouth. The muscles around the eye that open and shut the eyelids are also laid out radially around the eye socket. These surfaces, if laid out in the way shown here, will move in a realistic manner because they match the musculature of the face.

### Network Strategy

Use as few surfaces as possible. When you are texture mapping a model, you will have to deal with each surface as a separate map. Keep all the surfaces close to the same size as the other surfaces. This enables you to maintain equal texture map sizes between surfaces, as well as maintain uniform distribution of geometry for animation and rendering purposes.

Never create a triangle. In nature, there are many places where the natural flow lines of the contours of the face seem to come to a point. Figure 7.3 shows improper surfacing strategies. The triangular region in the corner of the eye will never surface correctly. The detailed areas at the corner of the eye are bad places to try to maintain tangency between surfaces.

Try to keep exactly four surfaces at each intersection between surfaces, which allows for simple stitching of surfaces to be applied, keeping all surfaces tangent all the time throughout the animation. When it is impossible to maintain four surfaces at each surface intersection, use five-cornered intersections. The surfacing pattern shown in this eye diagram (Figure 7.4) can be used at eye, arm, hip, mouth, and any other locations.

The intersection shown in Figure 7.4 has five surfaces coming together at one point. Using this technique allows multiple surfaces to be introduced into a regular grid of surfaces without introducing triangular patches. When you align surfaces later, you will need to use special techniques to maintain tangency across this special condition (Figure 7.5).

Do not introduce patch boundaries in areas of detail. When you are trying to maintain tangency across surfaces in areas of detail, you do not have as much control as you need to keep detail and maintain tangency. Try to create detail from the surface and introduce patch boundaries across areas of the least detail (Figure 7.6). Detail can be added by adjusting CVs or by increasing isoparms if necessary.

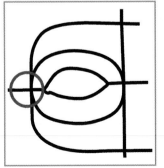
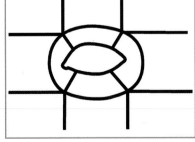
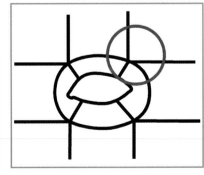
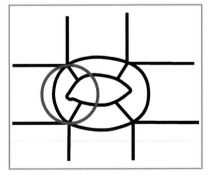

**Figure 7.3**
Improper surfacing strategy diagram.

**Figure 7.4**
Surfacing strategy diagram for transitioning round objects into larger, smooth areas.

**Figure 7.5**
The five-cornered intersection.

**Figure 7.6**
Do not add patch boundaries in small tight areas.

The lines that were digitized are set up so the lines can easily be used to create surfaces. Note how the lines radiate from the eyes and mouth so they can create radial surfaces around those parts of the face. Whenever possible, try to determine ahead of time how the surfaces will be built, then digitize accordingly. The lines shown on Figure 7.7 indicate the construction of the final surfaces.

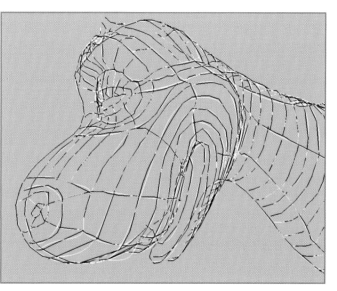

**Figure 7.8**
Convert degree-1 curves into degree-3 curves using Fit B-Spline.

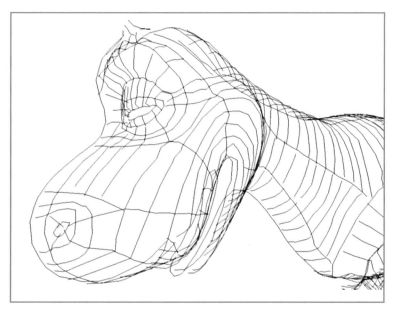

**Figure 7.7**
The foam sculpture was digitized using lines used in the construction of the actual surfaces.

The data can be imported as .obj or .dxf if you have polyline data to start with. Maya does not actually support polylines. When the data is imported into Maya, the polylines are converted into degree-1 NURBS curves.

Convert the lines into B-splines. If you digitized NURBS curves from inside Maya or imported B-spline digitized data, this next step is not necessary. Select the degree-1 NURBS curves in the file. When all of the lines are highlighted, use Object, Edit, Fit B-Spline to create degree-3 NURBS splines where the original digitized lines were (Figure 7.8).

## Drawing the Curves

Starting with the lines created in the previous steps, new curves are constructed. These curves can be created by manipulating, detaching, attaching and rebuilding the converted B-splines that were created earlier or by tracing over existing curves. The first step is to create flow lines that go across the entire head. Starting from the mouth and eyes, draw NURBS curves from the edges of the radial mouth and eye regions toward the back of the head. These lines will be used later during the construction of the initial surfaces. In Figure 7.9, the curves shown in red were created by tracing over the existing data. These lines were constructed as long, continuous curves to create large surfaces over the head.

Here are some additional tips on creating usable splines for a curve network:

◆ Use edit points to draw splines wherever possible. While you draw splines across other splines, you will need to connect splines to each other. Only edit points can guarantee that the splines will intersect.

◆ Draw continuous splines across the entire model whenever possible so that you can visualize the changes in the surface while maintaining smoothness across the model. If you create short splines that meet in the middle of the model, there will be a break in the continuity of the surfaces.

◆ Next, create radial curves to define surface boundaries. Using the flow lines created in the previous step, radial lines are created that begin to define the areas that are to be turned into individual patches. Edit point curves were used to create the radial curves. The points where the curves come together are certain to intersect. In Figure 7.10, radial curves around the mouth, eyes, and nostrils allow surfaces to be constructed correctly.

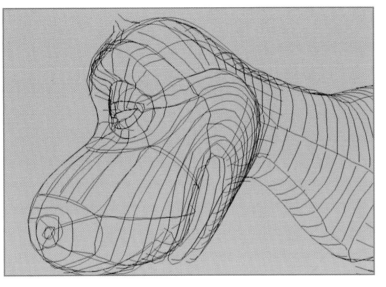

**Figure 7.9**
Trace over the B-splines to make new even curves.

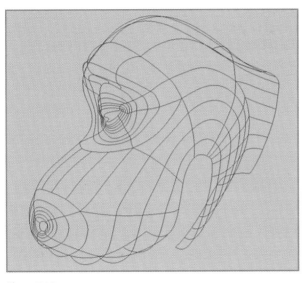

**Figure 7.10**
Use radial curves around the eyes, nose, and mouth to define surface boundaries.

## Patch Modeling the Head

Surfaces for this model were created in two steps. The first step was creating surfaces that cover the head. I called these "initial surfaces." The last surfaces are called "final surfaces," which are the initial surfaces broken up into surfaces that have all of the isoparms aligned. The term *patch modeling* was derived from these smaller surfaces. The smaller surfaces are all "stitched" together in a patchwork of surfaces that make up the 3-D character.

### Initial Surfaces

The head is the focus of the first part of the tutorial because the face has the hardest transitions for modeling. No effort was made to get the "initial surfaces" to have isoparms that align; the plan was to do this later. The most important focus of the initial surfacing phase was to have the surfaces have tangential continuity and smoothness.

Bi-rail surfaces were used almost exclusively to create the surfaces on the side of the head because they allowed me to make large patches that covered the majority of the head quickly. The larger surfaces would be broken up into smaller regions later. Using smooth curves that sweep across the entire face create a smooth surface network without using tangency tools (Figure 7.11). These initial surfaces of

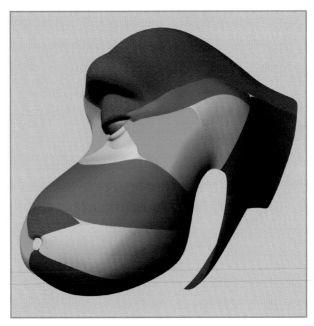

**Figure 7.11**
Initial surfaces across the head

the head are constructed so the surfaces are smooth, but the alignment of isoparms is not considered until later.

## Initial Surface Alignment Tools

The alignment tools discussed here were used to create the initial surfaces. These tools take advantage of curve construction to create and maintain tangency when building surfaces from curves.

### Align Curve

Align curve can be used to make existing curves have common end points, and have the end of the curves have continuity. The continuity options include positional, tangential, or curvature continuity.

### Project Tangent

Use project tangent to create smooth curve transitions where curves meet existing surfaces. Project tangent creates a tangency condition at the point where a curve coincides with the edge of a surface. First select a curve then the isoparm on the adjacent surface that you want the curve to line up with. Project tangent will also line up a curve with two adjacent curves to create a tangency condition. You cannot use project tangent to align a single curve to a single curve. The Align tool, which will be discussed later, will work for this.

### Surface Tangency Options

The square surface and the bi-rail surface provide options for tangency between surfaces that have been built and surfaces that are being built. These options operate on the surface boundaries. The square surface simply has one option that turns tangency construction on for all boundaries. The bi-rail surface has options that turn tangency on for the first profile, the last profile, or both first and last profiles.

## Separate Initial Surfaces into Patches

The surfaces that you created in the initial surfaces step were only partially ready to be aligned. In order to have a surface network that is ready to create a uniform mesh from, you need to detach the surfaces that were created across the boundaries or adjoining surfaces.

### Detach Surfaces

The initial surfaces have to be separated into smaller regions that allow the boundaries of the adjacent surfaces to line up with each other.

### Rebuild Surfaces

When a model made of different patches has uniform meshes, all surfaces have the same number and placement of isoparms as the surfaces next to them. If one sur-

face has four subdivisions that are equally spaced throughout the surface, the adjacent surface has to have four subdivisions that are equally spaced throughout the surface. Figure 7.12 shows initial surfaces broken into smaller patch surfaces that have common boundaries with the adjacent patches. The surfaces have been rebuilt so all the surfaces have the same number of spans, and the isoparms all align.

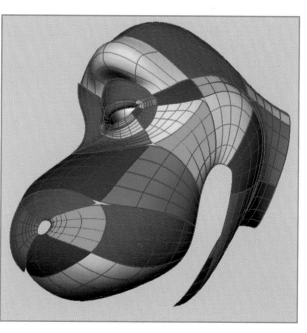

**Figure 7.12**
Patch surfaces created by splitting and rebuilding initial surfaces.

### Reverse Surfaces

By using a file-based texture map that defines the direction of UV parameterization, the surfaces that have been created can be reoriented so the UV coordinate space matches all surfaces, and the surfaces are facing the correct direction. Figure 7.13 shows a texture map that can be used to identify the direction of UV coordinates in a patch model. Figure 7.14 shows the surfaces of the model after the map has been applied. The goal is to get all of the surfaces to line up in a similar way and have the surface normals facing away from the model. This kind of texture map will show reversed surfaces quickly because the text will appear reversed. The U and V directions can also be quickly detected because the colors of the arrows indicate if the directions align between surfaces.

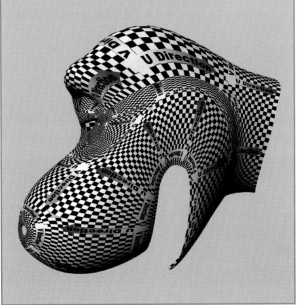

**Figures 7.13, 7.14**
A simple texture map (top), shows the direction of the surfaces on a patch model (bottom).

## Patch Surface Alignment Tools

Certain tools in Maya and other modeling packages as well, are specifically designed to assist in creating and maintaining tangency between surfaces after the surfaces have been built. These tools are used after the initial surfaces have been setup and separated into smaller patches.

### Align Surface

The purpose of the align surface tool is to modify two existing surfaces by creating positional, tangential, or curvature continuity between them. Try to tweak the values in the option boxes before you finish the align operation. At first pass, the results given from the align surface tool can seem somewhat disappointing. But by adjusting the different values, you can get different results for the align operation.

### Stitch Edge

Stitch edge aligns two adjacent surfaces and works much like align surface, but stitch edges allow the user to stitch partial surface edges to adjacent surfaces using a control along the stitched edge that adjusts the amount of the surface that aligns along the edge.

### Global Stitch

Global stitch works very differently than align surface. The process is very simple. Pick all of the surfaces you want to have aligned, then use global stitch. The problem with global stitch is that the surfaces do not behave the way they should all of the time. Global stitch does not maintain tangency between surfaces during animation setup and animation. If the settings are working, this tool will do a great job of keeping the surfaces tangent throughout production. Getting the tool applied correctly, however, can be tricky. Following are some rules for using global stitch:

◆ Always save before using global stitch. Maya allows for undo operations, but saving is still a good idea. Initial results appear satisfactory, but sometimes problems are discovered after it is too late to undo the operation.

◆ Use global stitch with the Keep Originals button off.

◆ Use global stitch only after the majority of the surfaces have been aligned using other alignment tools. Global stitch is the glue that holds the model together after it is animated. It is not the best tool for getting the surfaces to become tangent.

### Attach and Detach

When you have four adjacent surfaces that have been rebuilt to the proper subdivisions, you may have a condition where they cannot be easily aligned using the align or stitch tools. A simple solution is to use the attach tool to align the surface. The technique used here is to find a place where four surfaces come together, attach two adjacent surfaces (on the U side of the surface, for example), then detach at the isoparm where the surfaces attached, attach the surface on the other side (on the V side), then detach. Continue until you have attached and detached all four surfaces on all four borders. Figures 7.15–7.18 show the progression of attach and detach around a surface.

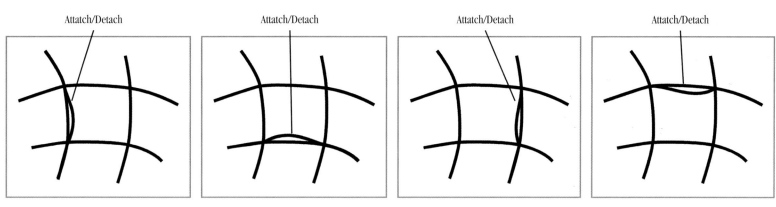

Attatch/Detach          Attatch/Detach          Attatch/Detach          Attatch/Detach

**Figures 7.15–7.18**
Attaching and detaching the four borders surrounding a surface

## Attach-Sculpt Surface-Detach

Attach-sculpt surface-detach is a variation of attach and detach. Often when you attach a surface, a ridge occurs where the surfaces come together. One way to get rid of this ridge is to smooth the surfaces that are attached before detaching them. The easiest way to edit these surfaces is to use the sculpt surface tool. This tool has a NURBS smoothing option that averages out the values of the CVs in the current selection.

Individual surfaces can be selected for editing with the sculpt surface tool, or individual vertices can be edited as well, using the Mask Unselected Vertices option before editing. The area that needs smoothing can be edited using the sculpt surface interactive brush, or an overall value can be set in the Max Displacement option box. Alternatively, the area can be smoothed using the Flood button. When you finish smoothing the points, detach the surface to restore the even surface layout.

## Pulling Points

Until now, the major reason for having a grid of surfaces that align has not been obvious. When you manipulate points on a surface to align with other points on adjacent surfaces, you can see why I use this approach.

The only points on a NURBS surface where you have direct control on the position of the surface is at the edges. Any other place on the surface will have CVs and hulls that pull away from the surface. You can easily change the shape of a surface in the middle of a surface by pulling points. But, unlike the vertices at the edges, pulling points in the middle of the surface provides less direct control of where exactly the surface will fall in 3-D space.

An additional row of hulls are inside the boundaries of each NURBS surface. If you look at a NURBS surface, you can determine the number of hulls by counting the number of spans in the surface, and adding 2. Because I am creating a grid where edges of surfaces line up with the adjacent edges of surfaces, I can snap points from one surface exactly to points of the adjacent surface.

The alignment tools do not completely fix alignment on a five-cornered intersection. Attach-detach provides most of the alignment along the surface edges, but to get the last little bit, you just gotta pull points.

In Figure 7.19, a five-corner intersection is shown where the vertices have to come together. By using a "mel" script, these vertices can be selected and snapped to their common center point (Figure 7.20). Further point snapping of points next to the corner points and simple point pulling results in a five-corner intersection with the surfaces that align (Figure 7.21). (The script used to snap these points is called JSnapCVsToCentre, written by Julian Mann, 1999, and can be downloaded from http://www.highend3d.com/maya/mel/.)

## Modeling the Body

The head of this model required strict adherence to digitized reference because it had to match a puppet exactly from shot to shot. The body had to be modeled differently from the puppet to accommodate animation requirements, and the body did not have to look exactly like the puppet because the body of the puppet was not shown very often in the movie. Rhythm & Hues was commissioned to do the character because the film needed a digital version of Dino for shots that showed the body. Therefore, a more natural approach to modeling the body was taken. The steps that were used to model the body are similar to the steps used to model

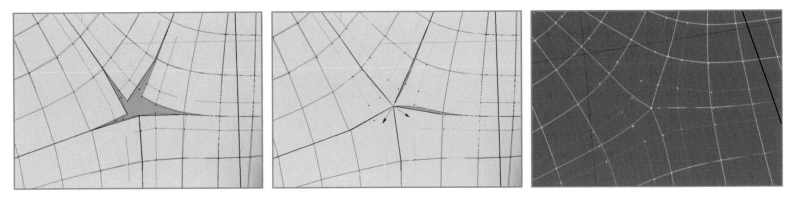

**Figures 7.19–7.21**
Snapping points together at a five-corner intersection.

the head, but an important difference is the way the model was started. The digitized reference was used in a much looser way for the body than the head, as outlined in the following steps.

1. The digitized reference data was used as a starting point (Figure 7.22).

2. Instead of copying and rebuilding curves from digitized data, rough NURBS primitives were used to approximate the position and layout of the reference data (Figure 7.23). NURBS sculpting of the primitive as a free-form shape was used to get the shapes of the legs and body. The transitions between the body and legs were also roughed-in. Using this technique, the NURBS primitives became the initial surfaces in the patch modeling process.

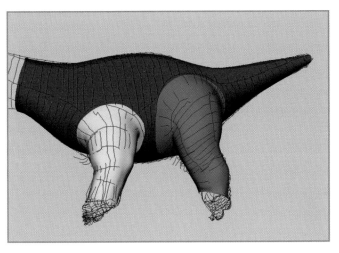

**Figure 7.23**
NURBS primitive cylinders were used to approximate the shapes.

3. Once the surfaces were the correct size and shape, the surfaces were rebuilt to get an approximate alignment between isoparms for the legs and body. The intent was to get the spans in the legs and body to be about the same size, not to get the isoparms lined up (Figure 7.24).

4. The surfaces were modified to get the isoparms to flow in the same direction. The majority of the work was done on the body to get the flow of the isoparms to go around the shoulders and hips of the character (Figure 7.25).

**Figure 7.22**
The digitized reference data.

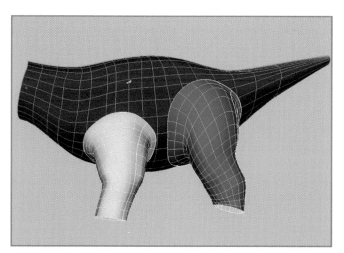

**Figure 7.24**
The cylinder surfaces were rebuilt to have matching span sizes.

**Figure 7.26**
The surfaces were detached to create a network.

6. Patch surface alignment tools and techniques were used to get the surface network created in the previous step to become the final surfaces shown in Figure 7.27. To create and maintain isoparm alignment and tangency, attach, detach, and rebuild surface tools were used extensively. While this part of the process is taking place, it is important to keep looking at the reference material. While using attach and detach, it is very easy to stray away from the actual shape of the reference material.

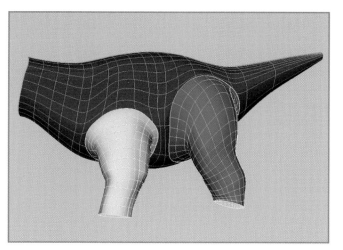

**Figure 7.25**
The surfaces were modified to match isoparm direction.

5. Once the surfaces had the approximate flow of geometry going in the right direction and position, the surfaces were detached to create a network of surfaces (Figure 7.26). From this point, the model can be approached as a patch model.

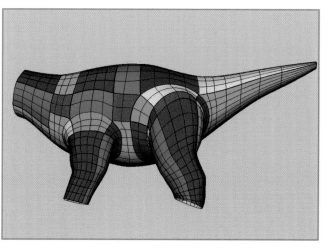

**Figure 7.27**
The final surfaces were created from the patch network.

7. Character Modeling Tutorial

123

7. The surfaces were aligned and smoothed. Any gaps between surfaces, and non-tangent conditions were cleaned up (Figure 7.28). Detail in the hips and shoulders were added to match the detail in the maquette.

8. The final surfaces for the body, shown in Figure 7.29, show the addition of the feet. The detail in the hips and shoulders was smoothed out due to issues that arose during animation setup. These wrinkles were added later during animation when the scene called for wrinkles.

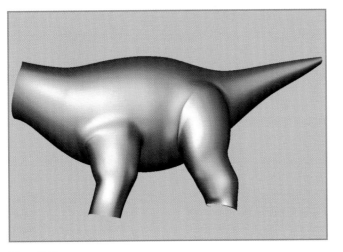

**Figure 7.28**
The surfaces were cleaned up.

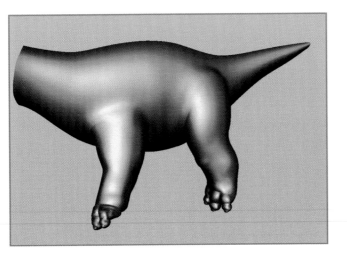

**Figure 7.29**
The final body model for Dino

## Surface Settings

Because we have used surfaces that align on all sides, and have all of the isoparms that align, the surface to polygon conversion is very straightforward. You should, however, make all the surfaces single-sided, and make sure all of the surfaces are facing the right direction.

### Low-Resolution Polygon Settings

There are two ways to control polygon conversion for creating polygon models from NURBS surfaces. One is to modify the settings in the Convert NURBS to Polygon option box. Start with General settings and select the Per Span # of Isoparms in 3D option. For a low-resolution model, the best setting would be one polygon per span. A mesh this low can be used for a wrap deformer as well.

Another way to control the resolution of a low polygon mesh created from a NURBS model is to copy all of the surfaces into another group, then rebuild all of the new surfaces to a lower resolution. Once this new lower resolution model is created, the same NURBS to Polygon settings described above can be used to create an even lower resolution mesh.

Sometimes NURBS models are used to create low-resolution "proxy" models that are later turned into subdivision models. The process to create a detailed character using this process for subdivision modeling is described in Chapter 13. These settings could also be used to create a low-resolution model for animation and to create a wrap deformer.

### Low-Resolution Model

It is common practice in all 3-D animation production to create a low-resolution model that accurately represents the high-resolution model. These models are used for creating fast animation. The manipulation speed is really quick and the playback speed is must faster too. Figure 7.30 shows a low-resolution model created from the NURBS surfaces that could be used for animation.

### Wrap Deformer

A wrap deformer is commonly used for complex character setup for animation. A model created for this kind of deformer is a low-resolution polygonal mesh or a low-resolution NURBS shape that accurately describes the high-resolution model. The common practice is to bind the skeleton of the character to the wrap deformer, and then bind the high-resolution mesh to the wrap deformer. The wrap deformer can be weighted easily, so the binding to the skeleton is efficient and accurate. Because the wrap deformer is created from the surfaces of the high resolution mesh, the points along the adjacent surfaces where the mesh usually falls apart is

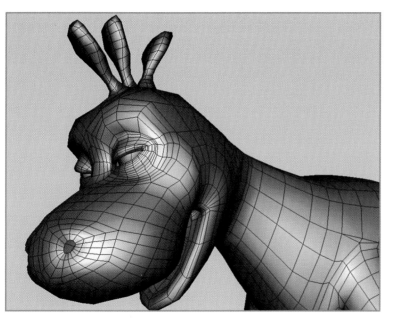

**Figure 7.30**
The low-resolution model created from the NURBS surfaces.

**Figure 7.31**
The final high-resolution polygonal model used for rendering.

bound by a common series of points that fall precisely where the points on the surface meet, ensuring that the mesh stays together at the correct places.

## High-Resolution Polygon Settings

Using the exact setting options described previously, but filling in the number of subdivisions per span to a higher number, such as 3 or 4, creates a high density mesh for rendering as polygons. This is the process that was used to render this model, because the rendering pipeline at Rhythm & Hues only supports polygons, not NURBS surfaces.

The NURBS surface construction allowed for the proper placement of polygonal geometry for animation, texturing and setup. The resultant model was extremely clean and was fast to build because, of the NURBS controls. Figure 7.31 shows a shaded view of the final model.

## Tessellation Settings

When rendering using Maya, pay careful attention to tessellation settings. The best way to adjust settings is to use the Attribute Spread Sheet.

The settings that work best for patch models is the explicit tessellation option, which sets a specific number of tessellated polygons to be generated at render time based on the spans in the surface being rendered. When the spread sheet is opened, the column under explicit tessellation attributes should be highlighted then turned to on. It will then be necessary to scroll over the Number Per Span U column and Number Per Span V column and adjust the explicit settings to appropriate values for that scene.

For models that are not built with patch modeling techniques, adjusting the tessellation parameters for the entire model is a bad idea. However, surfaces in patch models usually have spans that are relatively equal in size across the model, which allows the tessellation settings to be set using the Number Per Span options for the entire model. It may be necessary to adjust the tessellation settings differently for different surfaces if the spans for those surfaces get unusually large or small compared to the rest of the model.

**7. Character Modeling Tutorial**

125

# chapter 8
# Texture Mapping

Texture mapping falls between modeling and lighting. The texture mapping artist needs to be versed in technical issues related to the components of the geometry supplied for lighting and rendering, as well as the way that the geometry will behave when rendered.

Texture mapping, like modeling, is equally important to the creation of rendered images for film and television, as well as real-time video game production. The texture map on a model is the color component of geometry. The lighting and compositing trick used downstream in the production pipeline uses the texture map as a primary factor, just like the model that the map is applied to.

## Types of Texture Mapping

Many applications of computer graphics would not be possible without image-based texture maps. Texture mapping literally replaces detailed modeling and many applications. Some examples of how image-based mapping is helping different industries is using satellite photographs to create simulated flyovers of planets that have yet to be explored by humans, forensic autopsy photos to create moving images of living internal human anatomy, and architectural photography to create 3-D representations of entire city blocks and campuses. Emerging technologies, such as the creation of digital sets for broadcast and the use of low-resolution models for 3-D Internet content, would not be possible without texture mapping.

In the infancy of computer graphics, the majority of the technical innovations in the entertainment application of computer graphics were derived through military and industrial applications. As the technological achievements of computer graphics in entertainment become more and more advanced, industrial and military applications of computer graphics are following the lead of the entertainment industry.

## Texture Mapping for Entertainment

Texture mapping in the entertainment industry can be broken down into two major areas of interest. One is film and broadcast graphics, and the other is video game development. The main criteria that separates these two fields is that film and broadcast texture maps are created to be rendered in software and then played back image by image to create an animated sequence. Video games, on the other hand, are played in real time. The textures that are displayed in a video game must be optimized for real-time playback.

Image maps for surface texturing are normally created in a paint package. Different methods exist for creating maps. Some workflows allow the textures to be fully realized using a 2-D paint package, such as Photoshop. Other times, a 3-D paint package will be used. The images created from these programs can be a noise texture that is simply used to create a layer of visual complexity on a surface or a very realistic image that is used to enhance the visual appearance of a model.

Whether a texture map is being rendered in software or displayed in real-time, certain things about the way the computer treats texture maps are the same. Texture maps are computed as digital arrays that are read into memory by powers of 2. Each pixel of an image-based map represents one piece of digital information. The best way to optimize the way an image is read into the computer's memory is to keep the pixel depth of a texture image at a number that is a power of 2. The mathematical representation of this kind of number is the numeral 2 raised to a given exponential power. For example, 2 raised to the power of 3 would be $2 \times 2 \times 2 = 8$. Some default image sizes for texture maps would be 256 x 256 pixels or 512 x 512 pixels. Most computer systems have memory tiling to accommodate large data files, such as image maps. These tiles are broken down into smaller, more manageable power of 2 sized chunks. If a texture map is not created at an image size that corresponds to an exponent of 2, the computer will read the image into memory and allocates the memory so that the image is taking up the memory corresponding to the next highest power of 2 number available. For example, if a texture map is created at the resolution of 120 x 84 pixels, the computer allocates memory for that texture as if the texture were created at 128 x 128 pixels. That is not to say that all images will load in at exactly the dimension size allocated to the same power of 2 in both dimensions. Because of memory tiling, a map that is created at a resolution of 128 x 64 pixels will read into two tiles of 64 x 64 efficiently.

## Texture Mapping for Video Games

Texture mapping for video games, like texture mapping for film, also requires that careful attention be paid to getting the maps to look great. However, because most maps are created for video games for real-time playback, the maps must be optimized in size and in color space to be compatible with the intended game platform.

Color space can be defined as the number of colors that are found within any given color map. Color space, like the memory allocation issues related to image size, is defined using numbers that are of a power of 2. Video games commonly have a reduced color space available. In earlier game systems, the color palette consisted of no more than 256 total colors available per pixel. This type of image is referred to as an 8-bit image. Many earlier game systems employed a color look-up table to access these colors. This allowed the artist to customize the color palette to suit the design of the game instead of taking a default set of values for each color channel. The decrease in color complexity allowed the game hardware to map texture memory more efficiently in the system. The game consoles available today support a much higher degree of color space.

Image sizes for textures used in video games and other real-time applications tend to be small. Game consoles often have a limit on texture image size in the range of 256 x 256 pixels. A game console usually has a fixed amount of texture memory that can be easily described in terms of how many textures of this fixed resolution will load into the game. You must understand what this limit is prior to creating any textures for the game. A texture artist should lay out the size and number of texture maps to be created for the game based on this memory allocation limit and the requirements of the game. You must also understand which objects will be seen close up and which ones will be off in the distance. With this knowledge of the game design and an understanding of the hardware limitations for texture memory, the artist can lay out which textures need to be detailed and large and which ones can be small. In Figure 8.1, a texture map created for a video game character shows the way the artist must allocate the texture budget between what is

important, or what needs detail, and what is not important. Notice how every part of the character is texture mapped using this one map, even the plain color regions, which are defined by just a few pixels of color on the map.

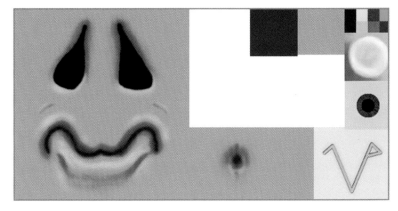

**Figure 8.1**
A texture map created for a video game character.

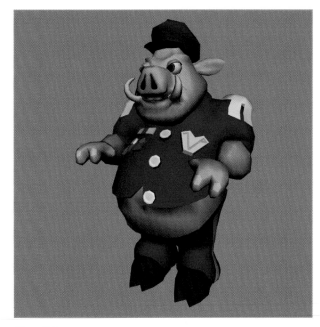

**Figure 8.2**
The character with the texture on it. *Character courtesy of Jef Shears and Dane Shears.*

In this planning stage, the artist can also determine which textures can be tiled. *Tiling textures* is repeating a single texture many times over a surface to increase surface detail without loading more textures into memory. When textures are repeated, the edges of one side of the texture must line up exactly with the corresponding edge of the image on the other side of the texture. The artist can use several tricks to paint textures that will line up in this way. One method is to use the offset filter in Photoshop. By offsetting the image and cloning parts of the image to blend the edges together, the artist can create a seamless texture.

Using tiled textures in a video game allows a large surface to be mapped from one small image without any degradation in resolution. An obvious example of how tiling can be used in a video game would be a section of road in a driving game. The road itself is basically made of the same material and the same relative surface detail for very long distances. In creating one map that describes one section of the road, and repeating that image indefinitely, an artist can create a road at very little computational overhead.

The visual style of a video game can be very graphic. In many character-based video games, the textures are commonly painted without the use of any photographic reference material. This gives the texture artist a lot of creative freedom in the creation of the look and feel of the game.

Some other video game types depend heavily on photographic textures. Examples of games of this nature include sports games that have celebrity sports figures in them and driving games that use recognizable vehicles. In the case of sports games, a celebrity athlete will often be photographed for surface textures, motion captured for animation, and scanned with a 3-D scanner for modeling purposes. If the game company is paying a premium price for the use of a celebrity athlete, it makes sense to spend extra time, money, and effort to ensure as close a likeness as possible.

Another aspect of creating textures for video games is the notion of prelighting. This is the process that allows light sources to be indicated within the maps themselves. This is a way to cheat by minimizing light sources in a video game. A video game with illuminated areas painted in where light would cast upon a surface can save lots of CPU cycles. The model in Figure 8.3 has a simple a white material with no additional lighting; the shading that is visible is because of the vertex colors applied by the "prelighting" of the polygons. Figure 8.4 shows the model after the prelit white material had texture maps applied to it.

This can be done using several methods. The simplest method is to paint the surface map so that the surface appears to be lit from a specific light or direction. This is a very effective way to create the illusion of lighting on a surface. The

**Figure 8.3**
A model after the lighting has been "baked" into the vertex colors.

**Figure 8.4**
The prelit model after the textures have been applied. *Character courtesy of Jef Shears and Dane Shears.*

problem with this method is that it is not a very flexible solution, and maps created this way must be tiled or used repeatedly in order to be efficient. Another way to create the illusion of lighting on a surface would be to use color assignments at the vertex level to adjust the light and dark values of a 3-D model and then layer textures on top of the shaded geometry. This technique allows the texture artist to use the same map over several different models and still achieve very different looking results. Another way to achieve this is to use layered textures. Layered textures are computationally expensive and not used very often in video games. But in some cases, like the case where a car is moving underneath clouds that are reflected in the surface of the car, the computational expense is well worth the overhead. In this case, the texture of the car serves the base texture, and reflected clouds shown in the surface are serving to light the car to match the environment.

## Texture Mapping for Broadcast and Film

Artists creating texture maps that are intended to be rendered by a software program are more interested in realism than optimization. A model that is being texture mapped for rendering will generally have the individual parts of the model mapped separately using different images for each part of the model. For example, the texture map for a character's face will be on one image, the texture map for a hand will be on another image, and so on.

High-resolution textures created for film use often have pixel dimensions in the range of 2048 x 2048 or 4096 x 4096. For texture maps created to be rendered in software, the color maps will seldom have a color bit depth less than 32-bit (8 bits per channel multiplied by 4 channels: red, green, blue, and alpha). In many cases, large complex texture maps will have a bit depth of 64-bit (16 bits per channel). This increase in color range makes the texture maps compatible with the actual film images, which have a dynamic color range larger than 256 colors (8 bits) per channel.

These images that are created for texture mapping objects for film can be very complex and detailed. In the field of visual effects for film, photographic reference from background photography and from other reference photography is used extensively. In the field of feature-length animation, photography can also be used as a basis on which to start painting a stylistic texture map for a character, a prop, or an environment. The end product for a texture map that is created for visual effects and feature animation will appear very different, but in many cases, the reference data for both is derived from photography.

This extensive use of high-resolution reference photography to create texture maps is why it is essential for texture mapping artists to do a great deal of research before sitting down to paint textures. Finding just the right image to create a texture from can save an artist hours or days of painting.

A texture artist involved with film work must become familiar enough with modeling to understand how the geometry that is built will affect them. A texture artist must also understand how the object will move during the animation to be able to compensate by adding resolution where it will be necessary and cheating resolution to optimize rendering whenever possible. The texture map artist must also become familiar with the lighting conditions they will have their maps rendered in. The texture mapper should usually have a complete scene available, set up for animation and rendering. When the maps are to be tested, the artist will simply render the scene with the new maps in the actual animation and lighting conditions used for production.

When creating textures for film, the texture artist usually must be careful not to include imagery that is already showing evidence of a light source. The scene from which the object is textured within is already lit from lights that have their own direction and value. Adding additional light sources shown within the map itself can cause problems in the final render, creating confusion between the direction and placement of the lights that control the scene lighting and the lights that appear on the textures.

Figure 8.5 is a picture of a stone wall that was taken in direct light. This kind of map may be suitable for video games, but is not suitable for film production. The rendered lights in the scene would conflict with the predefined lighting in this texture map. Figure 8.6 shows a map of a stone wall that is suitable for scenes where

**Figure 8.5**
A texture map that was taken in bright direct sunlight.

**Figure 8.6**
A texture map that has been created to reflect a neutral lighting environment.

extensive digital lighting will take place. This map was photographed in neutral light, such as an overcast day, or was painted to match a neutral lighting situation.

A texture artist will only rarely tile textures for film production. If an image is tiled over a surface that is to be rendered, many times the object will have another layer of textures applied to the same surface to break up the obvious repeating that is caused by tiling. These additional layers can use an additional set of UV coordinates on the model or can simply tile at another increment in order to create enough visual complexity to break up the appearance of texture tiling.

In order to create organic realism, such as the visual complexity in the surface of a character's skin, this kind of layering is essential. Skin is translucent, and subconsciously, everyone can detect when a character is rendered with flat surface mapping. Layering several maps for color, specularity, vein maps with transparency, and subtle bump mapping creates the visual depth required for realistic skin rendering.

Image-based mapping in film goes beyond surface description. Image maps are also used to describe lighting in the environment. Image-based lighting is quickly becoming the primary method a computer-generated object can be integrated into a photographic background. The processes involved with image-based lighting range from the creation of reflection maps that are balanced into the scene lighting that enhance the realism, to the creation of light sources that sample the values of the background image to merge the computer-generated model into the scene.

In some films, the background image is the texture map that is used on the computer-generated model. In the case of a talking animal film, such as *Stuart Little*,

the animals are filmed doing fairly ordinary animal things (Figure 8.7). The heads of these animals are then carefully tracked and modeled to match the exact positions of the animals in the photographic background plates. When the 3-D geometry matches the exact shape and position of the animal head for every frame, the animal head is animated to act as if the animal is talking, and the background image of the original animal is mapped onto the geometry for every frame. Projecting the camera view onto the tracked animal head model before the model is animated generates the texture coordinates for the model. This allows

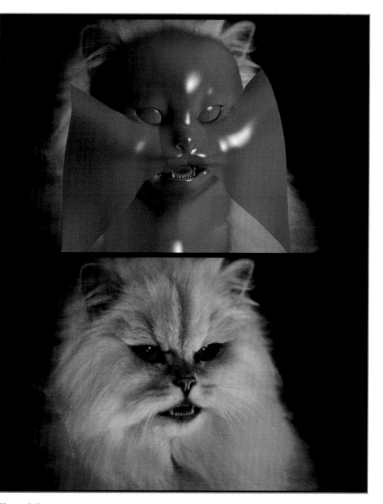

**Figure 8.7**
The digital production behind a talking animal film. "STUART LITTLE" © 2002 Columbia Pictures Industries, Inc. All Rights Reserved. Courtesy of Columbia Pictures.

the background image to animate along the surface of the model of the animal head after the model is animated.

In this instance, the lighter is basically a texture mapper, and the texture mapper, a lighter. Because the scene lighting for the exterior of the head is fully realized using textures projected from the background image onto the head, any stretching or discontinuities caused from the background image being projected onto the 3-D model of the animated animal head must be corrected using texture painting techniques. The corrected textures are layered on the 3-D model over the background image. By the time the finished animation is shown on film, many layers of corrected textures are usually used to complete the illusion of the animal talking. Note that the interior of the mouth is fully computer generated, and careful attention must be paid to get the lighting of the mouth to match the texture-mapped exterior of the animal head.

## Becoming a Texture Mapper

Texture mapping is a field, like 3-D modeling, where traditional art background can be very useful. Most texture mapping artists have a strong ability to create 2-D images. Traditional illustrators will commonly become texture mapping artists. This ability to create illustrations can be used in the field of texture mapping.

*Matte painting* is the process of creating an artificial background for a film or video production. A matte painting must be entirely convincing in its realism. One process for creating matte paintings is to take a low-resolution 3-D model and texture map the model so that it appears to be a completely realistic background. Creating a matte painting allows the production to create a limited sense of a full 3-D scene. When the camera is moved in front of a background that is created this way, the background shows evidence of its 3-D construction.

When a texture painter creates a matte painting using this technique, the texture artist must be very skilled to pull off the illusion of a completely realistic background.

Photographers are also likely candidates to become texture mapping artists. Photography and manipulating of photographic images is used extensively in visual effects texture mapping. Advances in digital technology in the areas of photography and scanning have streamlined the process of gathering photographic reference for texture mapping.

If a person were to apply for a job as a texture mapping artist, it would be important to emphasize the ability to create 2-D images. It would not necessarily be important to show every single texture map that the artist has painted, rendered, and animated on a demo reel. In some cases it is better to show high-resolution

still images of texture mapped objects, as well as still images of artwork that was created by hand. Most large studios will see hundreds of demo reels. Although it is true that the demo video is still the main way that a studio will review your work, sometimes the best way to stand out is to submit very high-quality 2-D images as well.

## Texture Mapping Opportunities

Texture mapping is considered a necessary and vital part of creating 3-D computer graphic images. All production facilities involved with digital production require texture mapping at some level. The places where texture mapping occurs are a primary concern to any artist that desires to create texture maps professionally. Video game studios are one place where texture mapping artists have become indispensable. Another venue for texture mapping talent is in film and video production. The issues associated with these different places where texture mapping takes place will be discussed in the following sections. Another concern to the texture mapping artist should also be: "Where in the production process does texture mapping happen?" Before the model is built, the modeler must understand what will be textured and what will be built as geometry. When the shots are being animated and rendered the texture maps are already in place and ready to go. Although it is clear that the texture mapping generally occurs after modeling and before the final rendering, the question remains about whether texture mapping is part of production or pre-production. Pre-production is sometimes a more prestigious part of film work because that is where the conceptual decisions are made about a film before the individual shots are being worked on. Problems are associated with being categorized as pre-production, however. Sometimes there are instances where texture mapping will be part of delivering every shot, making texture mapping part of the actual shot production. This will be discussed as well.

### Game Production

The texture artist in game production has a larger role in the look and feel of the final game than the texture artist in film. Game teams are generally smaller than film crews. Because fewer people are involved in creating a project equal in scope to a visual effects film project, more tasks have to be accomplished per person.

Texture mapping on a 3-D model into a video game contributes a great deal to the look of the model. Models generated for video games are generally lower resolution and have less detail than models created for film and video. Also, video game tends to be more graphic than a film or video production. The only way this graphic look is conveyed is through texture mapping. During the time that a video game is being played, the user sees nothing except geometry that is texture mapped. There are no photographic backgrounds like the ones that would be seen in film or video. If there is a panoramic landscape, it is because a texture mapper has painted a panorama on a polygonal surface that is displayed in the scene. In cases where a texture mapper is responsible for the look and feel of the final game, the texture artist should have a keen sense of the design of the game.

It never hurts to know more than one skill. This is especially true when working for a video game production studio. Most people in video game production will be asked to do more than one thing during the production of a complex video game. If the company is required to turn out several hundred more animated sequences and there's no additional time or budget to hire more animators, every person involved with the production of that game will end up animating at least a couple of those sequences. This is why it is important not only to be a highly skilled artist, designer, and technician but also to be a good person to work with. The ability to be flexible and to change things without taking these changes personally are necessary skills in any production job. There will be many times when it is more important for an employee to be a good employee than a good artist.

## Film and Video Production

The key to being successful in the film studio as a texture artist is the ability to easily understand the direction given by supervisors and translate that direction into beautiful images that are mapped onto the 3-D models. Film studios are much more demanding when it comes to high-quality work than video game production studios, or even television production studios, for that matter.

In any film production environment, communication is critical. During the daily reviews, artists are expected to understand explicitly what is being said. If the artist understands the direction being put forth by the supervisor, but does not know exactly how to implement that direction, the artist must take on the responsibility to communicate that to the right people.

It never hurts to ask questions, especially if you know the right people who have the correct answers to those questions. If you spend five minutes communicating your concerns to someone who can help you solve your problems, you can save yourself hours of work.

In film production, artists must remain open to comments about their work and keep a positive attitude whenever possible. As unfair as it may seem, the people who are your supervisors are being paid to criticize your work. If you understand that it is just their job, you will find it easier to accept the criticism and simply move on. Eventually the artist will understand what the supervisor expects and will deliver it without receiving any criticism.

## Production and Pre-production

Many people wonder if texture mapping is part of the film production, or is completed before production begins? If computer graphics production is defined by the animation, lighting, rendering, and compositing of shots that are going to be in the film, then texture mapping would be considered pre-production.

Many companies will establish a pipeline based on this paradigm. One reason that this fits easily into the business plan of many companies is because the production that is being worked on is being financed on a per-shot basis. Since the shots cannot be produced until texture maps are on the 3-D models, the modeling and texture mapping aspect of the production must be considered an additional pre-production cost. Sometimes these pre-production costs will not be financed by the production but rolled into general overhead.

Most extensive productions will have a budget allocated for pre-production and research. It is from this budget that the texture maps are created. In many small productions, such as commercials and small film jobs, no budget is in place for pre-production. The production costs, which generally barely cover the amount of money it will take to deliver the shots, must be stretched to cover modeling and texture mapping.

The one instance that was mentioned before where texture mapping is clearly part of the production process is the example where texture mapping was used to create the illusion of talking animals. In this case, extensive texture mapping is used to deliver each shot, and texture mapping is clearly a production cost.

# chapter 9
# Texture Mapping Tools

This chapter explores the concepts and tools used for texture mapping. The process used to texture map an object depends a lot on the 3-D model that is being texture mapped. The way the 3-D model will eventually be displayed has a lot to do with the way it should be texture mapped. If the model will appear in a scene that is rendered for film, the texture mapping techniques used will be very different than if the model will be used for a video game.

## Mapping Coordinate Systems

Placing an image on a 3-D model can be done either by wrapping the image onto the model, like putting wallpaper up on a wall, or by projecting it onto the model, like projecting a slide onto a wall. These two main methods of applying images to objects use different processes for mapping. Putting up wallpaper is an example of 2-D texture mapping (Figure 9.1). Projecting a slide onto a wall is an example of 3-D texture mapping (Figure 9.2).

In the cases where images are applied to geometry using 2-D texture mapping techniques, the 3-D model must have a coordinate system that corresponds to the texture maps that are being applied. This coordinate system is the mechanism by which the texture maps align themselves to specific parts of the model. This relationship between the texture and the model is part of the geometry definition. The modeling entities that are responsible for placing a 2-D texture onto a model are called *UVs*.

If 3-D texture mapping techniques are used like image projection (Figure 9.2) and image reflection, the coordinate system exists outside of the model. 3-D texture coordinate indicators for 3-D textures usually appear as icons in the modeling interface. Different types of 3-D texture placement techniques will usually have different icons. Planar projection will usually have some kind of plane in the icon, spherical will usually appear as a sphere, and so on.

### 2-D Mapping Placement Controls

Different software packages handle the 2-D placement of textures in different ways. Maya controls the placement of 2-D textures using an

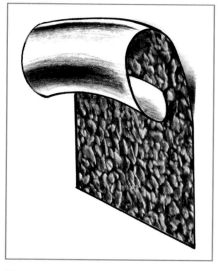

**Figure 9.1**
2-D texture mapping can be thought of as wallpaper being applied to a wall.

**Figure 9.2**
A photographic slide projected against a wall illustrates 3-D texture mapping.

9. Texture Mapping Tools

entity called the *2-D placement node* (Figure 9.3). Once a texture map is assigned to a model using 2-D placement, the controls that determine the number of times the texture will repeat and the direction it will rotate will be in the 2-D placement node attribute window.

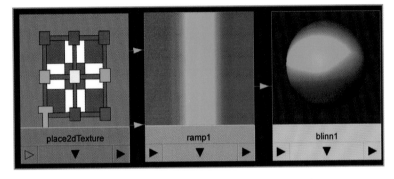

**Figure 9.3**
The 2-D placement utility in Maya controls the way 2-D textures are positioned on texture-mapped geometry.

The controls in the 2-D placement node window are fairly self-explanatory, but the default settings in this window are set up for texture tiling, meaning that UV wrapping is turned on. For custom texture mapping, such as the painting of high-resolution detailed textures for a character, turn off UV wrapping in this window. When rendering an object with UV wrapping on, artifacts related to UV wrapping may appear on the model. These artifacts will show up on the model as lines that appear at the edges of the surface that is being mapped. These lines are small slivers of repeating texture being displayed in the wrong place.

Maya uses two main types of 2-D textures: file-based textures in which the user creates a file that is mapped onto an object, and a 2-D procedural texture in which the user will use one of the algorithmically created 2-D images available for mapping the object using the 2-D placement node.

One procedural image that is worth mentioning is the *ramp*. The ramp is the workhorse of all procedural textures available in Maya. The ramp is a mathematically simple concept when compared to other procedural textures. The controls in the ramp texture, such as noise, ramp type, and noise frequency, make this texture valuable. In production, the simple ramp is used everywhere. In many cases where a light falls in the wrong way on one part of an object but looks great everywhere else, the ramp is used to make the light fall off in a very controlled way by simply mapping a dark colored ramp onto an object with transparency. This is done a lot more often than you would expect.

It was mentioned earlier that the ramp is a one-dimensional image. Mathematically, a simple ramp is a one-dimensional image. This definition falls apart, however, when the notion of noise along both dimensions is introduced, or when the ramp is converted to a file-based texture, the ramp becomes, by definition, a 2-D image (Figure 9.4). Think of the ramp as a 2-D image that uses all of the rules that apply to all other 2-D images.

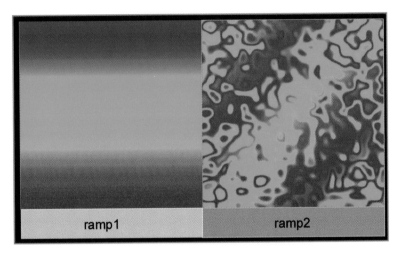

**Figure 9.4**
The ramp on the left is a simple ramp that can be described as a one-dimensional texture. The ramp on the right is the same ramp with noise and UV wave applied to it.

## 3-D Mapping Placement Controls

Several different types of 3-D textures are available in most modeling and animation packages. These 3-D texture options include image projection mapping, reflection mapping, and the placement of 3-D images, or what are commonly called *3-D procedural textures*. Each one of these placement types has its own icon. This icon appears in the workspace and can be manipulated like every other object in the scene. This icon serves as the coordinate system related to 3-D texture.

### Projection Mapping

*Image projection mapping* is a technique where an image is projected onto a 3-D object. These images can be one-dimensional (like a ramp) or 2-D. 2-D images include file-based textures, such as scanned-in photographs and drawings, or procedural 2-D images like fractals.

The 3-D placement icon for a planar projection texture (Figure 9.5) appears in most 3-D modeling software packages as some kind of flat surface that indicates the position of the image that is being projected and a directional indicator like an arrow that indicates the direction in which the image is being projected. This icon needs to be scaled, rotated, and moved into the correct place before the texture is applied correctly.

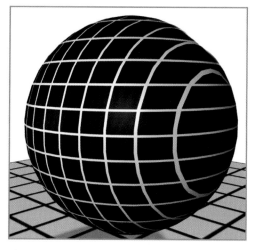

**Figure 9.5**
Planar mapping.

Planar projections are an easy way to place a picture on an object quickly using one direction vector. The problem with this method is that when you place a 2-D image onto a 3-D object in this way, the edges of the 2-D image stretch across the top of the 3-D object creating streaks along the top and bottom of the object.

Projection textures do not view correctly when textures are turned on in the display. Unlike 2-D file-based textures, 3-D textures are not processed through the OpenGL graphics hardware, and the display must be updated through software. For this reason, any time a projection texture needs to be checked for accuracy and visual placement, the best way to check it is by test rendering the map on the object.

Perspective texture projection occurs through a pyramidal-shaped projection node. A perspective texture allows a map to be projected onto an object the way a camera sees it. This is the drawback when dealing with a perspective projection icon. It is not a camera, it is an icon. Even when the Look through Selected button is pushed, an error message appears indicating that the icon is the wrong entity type for viewing through. In order to view the texture through a camera, a new camera must be created to view through. The best way to do this is to create the perspective texture placement icon and allow it to remain in the default creation position. Then create a new camera without moving it at all. Parent the icon to the

camera. Now, when the viewport is switched to the new camera, a clear view of where the perspective projection is being projected can be seen.

In Figure 9.6, a 3-D model of a woman's head has been perspective texture mapped using a photograph of a pretty girl's face. This trick can make a 3-D model that is pretty good look fantastic. Many 3-D models that use this technique will look great until the model is animated, then the problems associated with this mapping technique will show up.

**Figure 9.6**
In perspective mapping, a camera shows an icon projecting onto a model of a woman's head, using a picture of a woman to map the head.

The reason it is important to see through the camera that is being used for projecting texture is because if the object is viewed through any viewport other than the point of view from which the texture is being projected, obvious streaks will occur outside of the viewpoint of the projection. Because a perspective projection only works correctly from one viewpoint, it seems like an unnecessary workaround to have to parent a camera to the projection icon in order to use it (Figure 9.7).

Other 3-D placement types include spherical (Figure 9.8), cylindrical (Figure 9.9), ball (Figure 9.10), cubic (Figure 9.11), triplanar (Figure 9.12), and concentric (Figure 9.13). All of these placement types behave in much the same ways you

**9. Texture Mapping Tools**

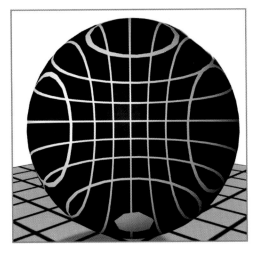

**Figure 9.8**
Spherical mapping.

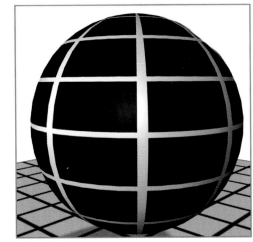

**Figure 9.9**
Cylindrical mapping.

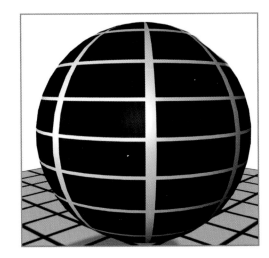

**Figure 9.10**
Ball mapping.

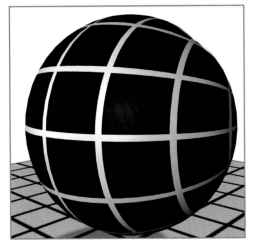

**Figure 9.11**
Cubic mapping.

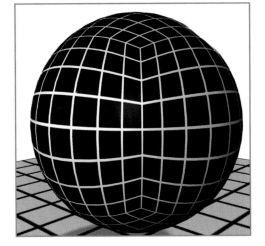

**Figure 9.12**
Triplanar mapping.

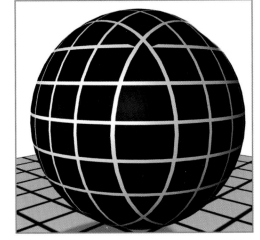

**Figure 9.13**
Concentric mapping.

expect them to based on the shapes of their projection icons. Some interesting things about these 3-D projection types can be noted. For example, a spherical projection appears very different than a ball projection. Ball projection mapping tends to simulate the way the world would reflect back onto an object, whereas spherical projection mapping wraps the object the way the panels on the beach ball are spherically wrapped. Ball projection mapping requires the use of an image that appears like the desired texture photographed on a highly reflective ball.

Spherical mapping will map a square image but will pinch the image at the top and bottom poles.

Two methods exist for mapping a single image onto a complex object that attempt to correct the stretching that occurs when an object is mapped using a projection vector. These two types are the triplanar and the cubic mapping types. The inclusion of additional planar projections at different angles minimizes the stretching artifacts caused by planar projection. Unfortunately, the planes that are used for these additional planar projections can be difficult to control for complex objects. It is best to test these projection types by rendering them before accepting the results. If the object being mapped is a box or building, a cubic projection map should work easily. The triplanar projection map, on the other hand, is a little more difficult to please easily in the scene unless the object being mapped is so organic that the seams between the planar projections are obscured by the detail of the model.

The easiest projection types to control out of all the 3-D projection map types available are the planar projection, the spherical projection, and the cylindrical projection. These projection types will generally serve most of the time.

## 3-D Procedural Textures

The controls that apply to *3-D procedural textures* can fill a book by themselves. Procedural textures are useful when you are trying to create images very quickly using easy-to-use materials.

The problems with these textures is they are good at some things, but they never seem to be good at the things they are supposed to be used for. For example, the procedural wood texture is not good for wood, but using this texture as a bump map is a really good way to create that distinct pattern found in automobile taillights. Another great bump map for automobile taillights is the bulge map (Figure 9.14).

The leather procedural texture does not look at all like leather, but it looks a lot like ground that has small balls of dirt randomly strewn about the place (Figure 9.15). And the water texture, admittedly, can look like water with enough sweat

**Figure 9.15**
The ground uses a leather color and bump map to create soil.

and hard work but can easily create a fairly decent color and bump map for hair when the map is stretched way beyond what would be normally acceptable for this procedural map.

The real thing about procedural textures is to keep your mind open to new possibilities about how to use them and be ready to try something new if the procedural textures are not working.

## Placing 2-D Texture Maps on NURBS Models

Textures for NURBS surfaces are mapped according to the parameterization of the surface. The construction of the surface dictates how the map will be applied. Each surface will have its own texture map. If an artist is texture mapping the face of a character, and the model of the face has 40 individual surfaces, there will be 40 texture maps associated with that model.

After being given a particular model for which to create texture maps, an artist should first examine the model. If the model is to have image-based maps applied to it, the geometry should be clean and continuous along the areas where the textures will be applied.

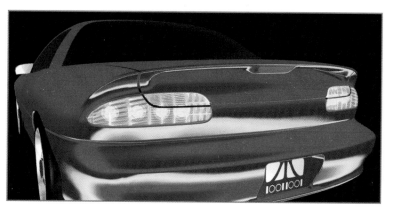

**Figure 9.14**
The reflection in the paint of this car is simply a ramp used as a reflection map; the taillights use a bulge map for the bump.

The texture artist should examine the parameterization of the surfaces that they are expected to apply textures to. When building a spline-based model, the modeler, for purposes of accurate construction, will often use surface parameterization of 0 to N number of spans. What this means is, the number of times a map will be repeated throughout a given surface can be determined by counting the number of spaces in between the surface isoparms. Needless to say, this does not make it easy to map a single image onto a surface that is parameterized in this way. Prior to submitting the model for texturing, the surfaces should be rebuilt to a parameterization of 0 to 1. This will force the bottom of the texture to be at the bottom of the surface and the top of the texture to be at the top of the surface.

One way to test the suitability of a model for texturing is to apply a generic map like a grid or checkerboard pattern to the model (Figure 9.16). Note that this map should be file based. This means that a real picture of a grid or checkerboard should exist and should be used to generate this texture. Maps that are generated using procedural grids and textures will not use the hardware acceleration to make the textured display fast and clean. The fuzzy appearance of the procedural texture in hardware display mode will not help you see where the problem areas are. Using this map will show any areas along the surface that will cause problems when the model is to be textured. Another good idea is to try to correct any orientation issues associated with the surfaces as well. The modeler should work with the texture mapper to get the model prepared for texturing. To get each surface oriented correctly and cleaned up for texturing, use an image of a grid or checkerboard pattern that also has some indication of U and V direction in the map. By viewing the model with this map applied to it, the modeler can go over the entire model checking for surfaces that are oriented correctly or for surfaces that can have their parameterization cleaned up for texturing.

The U and V wrapping must be turned off for mapping images onto surfaces. U and V wrapping will leave traces of wrapping at the edges of the surface unless it is explicitly turned off.

One way to ensure that a surface will accept a texture map that fits cleanly within the length of the surface, regardless of the parameterization of the surface, is to make sure that the surface texture mapping attributes has Fix Texture Warp turned on (Figure 9.17). The simplest way to accomplish this is to pick every surface in the scene and use the attribute spreadsheet to adjust the render parameters. In the render parameters, the Fix Texture Warp column should be turned on before mapping the surfaces.

This button is adjusting the difference between uniform surface parameterization and chord length parameterization. When a surface is mapped without the Fix Texture Warp option, the texture follows the parameterization of the surface. This

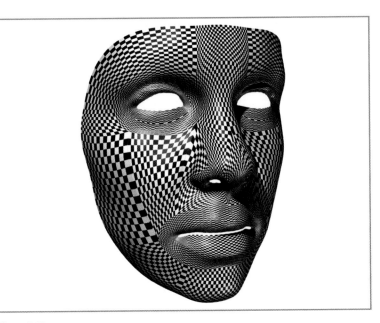

**Figure 9.16**
NURBS models should have surfaces tested for warping and discontinuities using texture maps.

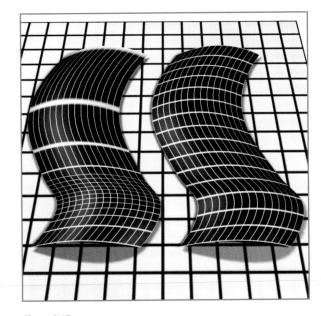

**Figure 9.17**
These two surfaces are identical except that the one on the right has the Fix Texture Warp toggle turned on.

is called *uniform parameterization*. The texture is following the parameterization of the surface uniformly along each span of the surface.

If a surface is mapped and the textures flow along the distance of the surface evenly from top to bottom, regardless of the interior parameterization of the surface, this is called *chord length*. The texture is following the surface along the chord length of the U and V distances along the edges.

When Fix Texture Warp is turned on, it applies the chord length option to the texture mapping along that surface by wrapping the texture according to the length of the U and V of the surface edges instead of the interior parameterization of the isoparms.

## Placing 2-D Texture Maps on Polygonal Models

If the geometry to be textured is a polygonal model, the texture map artist should examine the model checking for discontinuities in the surfaces and for areas where mapping may be difficult. Unlike NURBS models, a polygonal model can consolidate many large areas into one texture map. Generally each major section of a model will have its own map. In the case of a character model, the head will have its own map, the hand will have its own map, and so on. Sometimes, especially in the field of video game development, the entire character or even several characters will use a single texture map for all the surfaces.

The primary thing to look for is the existence of texture coordinates. Like the texture coordinates found in NURBS surfaces mentioned earlier, the texture coordinates and polygonal surfaces are known as UVs as well. By default, UVs do not occur on polygonal surfaces. They must be applied in some way. The position of each pixel in a texture map is determined by the UV coordinate system applied to the polygonal geometry.

The value for each individual UV texture coordinate is assigned to the vertices of the polygonal geometry itself. In this way the assignment of texture coordinates to polygonal geometry is similar to the parameterization of NURBS surfaces. If there is insufficient geometry to apply textures to, or the model itself is messed up in some way, the textures will not be applied correctly.

However, unlike spline-based surfaces, UV coordinates in polygonal models can be applied in many different ways and can be edited after they are applied. They can be modified and customized to fit the specific model to which they are applied. The process of applying customized UV coordinates to a model is very much like constructing the model itself. In essence, the artist is modeling the UV coordinate system, providing much more control over the placement of textures than is possible using the parameterization of NURBS surfaces.

These UV coordinates should be checked prior to accepting the model for texturing. When testing the model for texture coordinates, the artist should use one or more test maps that allow the UVs to be visualized (Figure 9.18). It may not be enough to simply use a map of a grid or checkerboard. Sometimes a uniform noise map will show more discontinuities and stretching along the surfaces. Again, this should be a file-based map instead of a procedural grid or checkerboard.

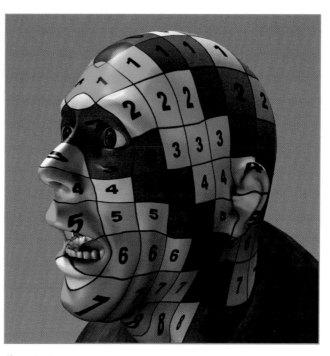

**Figure 9.18**
Polygonal models should use test maps to ensure that the model has UVs and the UVs are suitable for texture mapping.

One goal for correct UV coordinate application is to have a fairly uniform distribution of UVs along the surface of the model. The distance between individual UV coordinates should be relatively the same. The best and easiest way to ensure that this happens is to build the actual model with this in mind. If the model is built with a uniform distribution of points, it will be much easier to have the UVs equidistant.

Another goal of correct UV placement is to ensure that the UV coordinates themselves stay within the range of 0 to 1. The UV coordinates are set up to indicate where a rectangular image will be mapped on a 3-D model. The exterior range of these UV coordinates should remain rectangular as well. The lower corner of the

UV range should line up with the lower corner of the texture map; the upper corner of the UV range should line up with the upper corner of the texture map.

The rectangular texture map itself cannot have a parameter range outside of 0 and 1. If the UV coordinates for any given texture map exceed these values, the texture will repeat itself.

When laying out UV coordinates on complex models, you can use blocks of space that range from 0 to 1 per block. If UV coordinates are arranged in this way, the artist can avoid layering many of the sets of UV coordinates on top of each other. An example of this is a model that has two different parts that need to be mapped. One part could have the texture coordinates take up the UV space that exists from 0 to 1 for both the U and V directions. The other set of UVs can rest in the space that ranges from *1 to 2* in the U direction, and 0 to 1 in the V direction. Both sets of UVs get the texture maps applied to them correctly, and the UVs will not overlap.

If the artist chooses to use this technique, the UV space that is used for each object's texture map should be explicitly called out in the 2-D placement node for each UV set used. If UV wrapping is turned off, and the UV's exist outside of the range of zero to one in U and V, no textures will appear at all.

## UV Projection Methods

The most common way that UVs are applied is to project the UV coordinate system onto the polygonal model. You must usually project UV coordinates onto a model using a simple projection method even if the UVs are later going to be edited manually. The workflow for placing UVs using the projection method requires the user to create the UVs first, usually based on the world space of the current entities having the UVs applied to them. Then the projection manipulator is placed using the graphic user interface controls or by changing the values in the Channel Box.

This process does not really show what the UVs look like. During the process of applying UVs, the UV texture editor should be open so the final UVs are visible while the UVs are being placed on the object.

The planar projection method uses a flat surface to project UVs onto an object. As with other planar projection tools, this technique will cause stretching of the texture at the outer edges of a 3-D shape.

The cylindrical projection method projects UVs onto the object using a cylindrical shape. This will give much more even distribution around the circumference of a complex form but will also cause stretching of the texture at the top and bottom of the model.

The spherical projection method uses a sphere to project UVs onto the model. The spherical shape will compensate somewhat for the stretching that occurs at the top and bottom of the model. However, there will be pinching at the upper and lower poles of the sphere that will cause problems.

One very useful projection method is to project UVs based on camera view. This allows the user to get the exact view that is needed before applying the UVs to a model. This is a more intuitive process than moving a planar projection icon around a model to get the UVs in the correct location.

One thing that all of these methods have in common is that they project a rectangular set of coordinates to 3-D shapes. The rectangular shape of the UV space corresponds to the 0 to 1 parameterization found in NURBS surfaces and the rectangular shape of the texture maps themselves.

All of these projection methods are very useful, but for complex texturing applications, they must be used in combination with each other and with other texture coordinate application methods. The application of texture vertices would be simple if the only models that needed to be textured were planes, cylinders, and spheres. Certain problems are inherent in projecting texture coordinates onto a model. None of these projection methods by themselves can address these problems.

One problem that occurs on a consistent basis when applying UV coordinates to a model is the problem of UV overlap. UV overlap is a condition where UV coordinates will be projected in such a way that one piece of 3-D geometry will fall and line directly over another piece of 3-D geometry relative to the vector that is used for projecting the UV coordinates onto the model. This forces one layer of UV data to be on top of another layer of UV data, causing portions of a texture image to repeat in these areas.

Another problem is the issue of uniform size and distribution of UV data across the model. Each of these projection methods will create some type of distortion or stretching along the vectors used to project the UVs. Try to maintain some correlation between the size and shape of the UV information and the original polygonal geometry. When UVs are projected onto a model, a distortion often occurs because the projection does not conform to the 3-D topology of the model.

This type of distortion is similar to the problem encountered by mapmakers during the era when navigators were unable to accurately account for the differences in distance between what visually was correct when viewing what was newly discovered as a round earth and what the actual distance would be along its surface. Earlier maps straightened out the longitude lines of a globe to create a flattened view of the round earth. The lines of latitude were represented as the horizontal lines of a perfect grid, creating what is known as the *cylindrical equidistant global projection*.

This type of projection is similar to the type of mapping coordinates applied using cylindrical texture mapping techniques. The problems of distortion are similar as well.

In 1568, the Flemish mathematician Gerardus Mercator developed a method of redistributing the distances between the latitude lines in a global (orthographic) view of a globe, creating what visually appears to be more space between the latitudes toward the poles and visually compressing the lines of latitude near the equator. This redistribution accounted for the actual distances found on the round planet and represented those distances on a flat map. Although this particular map projection suffers from making the North and South Poles vastly larger than they are, it does offer sailors the practical opportunity to chart an accurate course by drawing straight lines on a map (Figure 9.19).

The logic employed by the Mercator projection is the same theory behind accurately applying texture coordinates to a complex 3-D model. The Mercator

projection can only serve as a philosophical milestone for applying UVs to an object—not many models that need to be texture mapped will be as simple as a round planet. And even the Mercator map itself is not useful for navigating the poles of the earth.

The philosophical lesson that can be applied to texture mapping is that texture coordinates should adjust to create an even distribution of pixels in the texture map along a geometric surface that may not have a uniform distribution of geometry.

Another lesson would be the way that Mercator adjusted the map to suit the geometry, moving the lines of the map (the texture coordinates) closer together where there is more surface area and farther apart where there is less surface area. This is the same type of compensation that needs to take place when adjusting UV coordinates along the surface of a model.

## Other UV Projection Techniques

The techniques described here are not the standard methods in a software package. These techniques are really tricks that have been used in production that have proven to be useful.

Some recent technologies and methods to project UV coordinates onto a model have rendered some older techniques somewhat obsolete. An example is the 3-D morphing technique used to project texture coordinates onto a model. This painstaking method started by copying a finished polygonal model and then carefully flattening the model into a 2-D shape (Figure 9.20). The flattening process was done using mostly manual pulling of points to ensure that there was no overlap and to ensure that there was a uniform distribution of geometry. The final result was a model shaped like a flat square or rectangle.

This model had the texture coordinates projected onto it using the planar mapping method (Figure 9.21). The planar projection icon would line up with the perimeter of the flattened model (Figure 9.22). Once the UVs were applied to this flattened model, a 3-D morph would then be set up (Figure 9.23). The flattened model would be animated to become the original 3-D model (Figure 9.24). Once this animation was complete, the result would be the original 3-D model with perfectly uniform UVs applied to it (Figure 9.25).

The advantage in having a model that has UVs applied to it in this way is that the texture map associated with this model can be painted using a 2-D paint system or a 3-D paint system. Because the texture coordinates occur in one continuous surface, textures can be painted on without any concern about painting across different UV patch definitions or overlapping UVs.

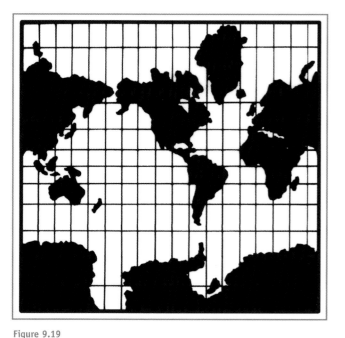

**Figure 9.19**
The Mercator map fits the geography of the world onto a flat grid, but like the unwrapping of UVs on a model, stretching occurs toward the top and bottom of the map.

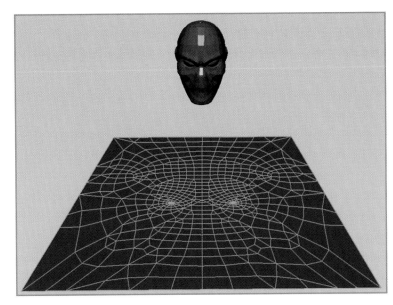

**Figure 9.20**
When you use the flattened morph target technique, first flatten a copy of the model.

**Figure 9.22**
Then a text texture is applied to the model.

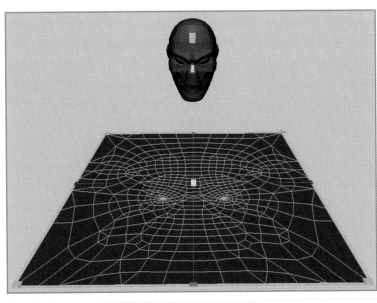

**Figure 9.21**
The next step is to apply UVs to the flattened model.

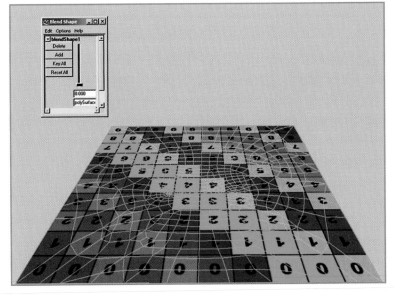

**Figure 9.23**
The flattened model is then turned into a blend shape, and the original head is the designated target.

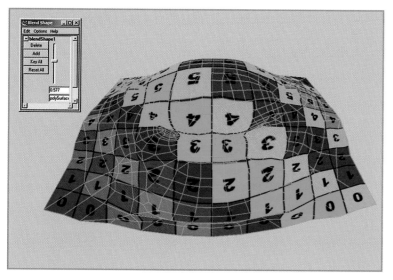

**Figure 9.24**
The model is morphed.

This method requires the modeler to copy the original model and use a smoothing tool to eradicate surface detail. This can be done using Maya's sculpt polygon tool, the *average vertices tool*, or any other smoothing tool used in other packages. The goal is to get any areas that create UV overlap smoothed out into one continuous surface (Figure 9.26). Once this is accomplished, the duplicate model has UVs applied to it using a spherical or cylindrical projection method (Figure 9.27). Because the goal is to avoid overlapping UVs, choose which method was most appropriate for this and to use the UV texture window to ensure that the position of the placement was correct.

Once the UVs are applied (Figure 9.28), the UVs could be transferred to the original model by using a morph, as described earlier. Another way to transfer UVs would be to use the Maya transfer UV tool available in the UV texture window (Figure 9.29). This feature allows the transfer of one UV set onto another model. The criteria of the model must be identical in polygon number, orientation, and topology. This is the same criteria for creating a morph target where the 3-D morph creation checks for topology. If the models can morph by using identical topologies, the transfer UV option can work as well.

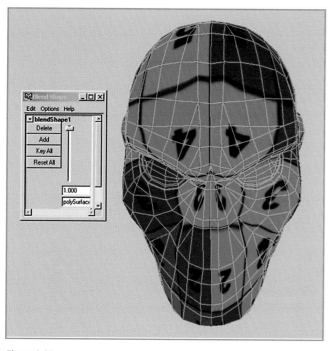

**Figure 9.25**
The finished model.

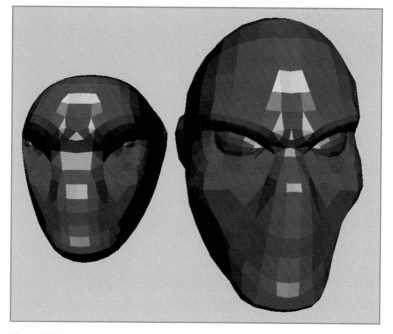

**Figure 9.26**
When you use a copy of the original model, vertices on the copied model are smoothed out using the average vertices tool or the smoothing function in the sculpt polygon tool.

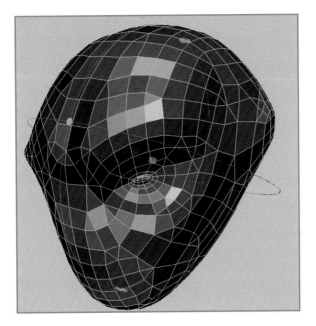

**Figure 9.27**
UVs are applied using a basic mapping scheme, like cylindrical or spherical mapping.

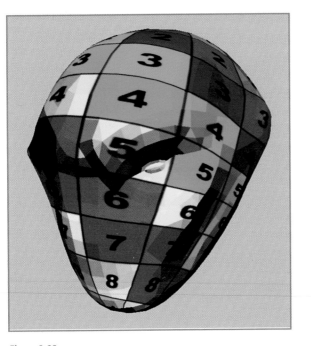

**Figure 9.28**
UVs on the copied model are tested using a test map.

**Figure 9.29**
UVs are transferred onto the original model using the polygon transfer function.

More recent technologies have proved to be efficient in creating uniformly distributed texture coordinates but have not addressed the issue of minimizing the number of the UV patch definitions. These methods fall into the category of *automatic mapping*. This projection type breaks down a complex model into smaller parts based on a specific angular range of surface normals in that area. These smaller areas are then planar mapped one at a time, and their resultant UVs are arranged in a UV space of 0 to 1 along with the rest of the parts of the model. This process is all automated and can save hours of time, unless you must have one continuous surface for painting UVs, in which case it does not work very well (Figure 9.30, 9.31).

This technique works best for complex mechanical shapes, like a military vehicle, that have distinct angular differences making up each surface.

It also makes the use of a 3-D paint system that supports projection painting a virtual necessity. The ability to manually paint across two different UV sets is very time consuming and difficult. In most cases, it is not practical to try to even begin doing this. It makes more sense to use a projection paint system, or a projection mapping system to texture the object after using this mapping scheme.

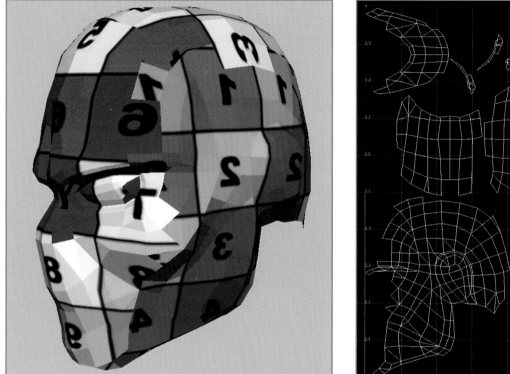

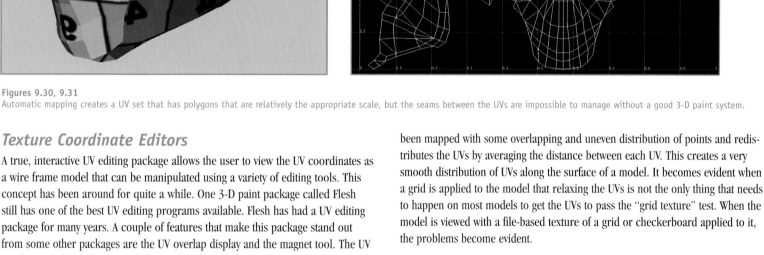

**Figures 9.30, 9.31**
Automatic mapping creates a UV set that has polygons that are relatively the appropriate scale, but the seams between the UVs are impossible to manage without a good 3-D paint system.

## Texture Coordinate Editors

A true, interactive UV editing package allows the user to view the UV coordinates as a wire frame model that can be manipulated using a variety of editing tools. This concept has been around for quite a while. One 3-D paint package called Flesh still has one of the best UV editing programs available. Flesh has had a UV editing package for many years. A couple of features that make this package stand out from some other packages are the UV overlap display and the magnet tool. The UV overlap tool shows the user a bold display of where the UV coordinates are overlapping. The magnet tool uses a falloff region around a single UV or a group of UVs to unravel a problem area of UVs that are tangled together.

Maya has taken many lessons from the Flesh UV editor and has created a UV editing tool that is very robust and usable. One feature that has been borrowed from other texture editors is the relax feature. This feature takes a set of UVs that have been mapped with some overlapping and uneven distribution of points and redistributes the UVs by averaging the distance between each UV. This creates a very smooth distribution of UVs along the surface of a model. It becomes evident when a grid is applied to the model that relaxing the UVs is not the only thing that needs to happen on most models to get the UVs to pass the "grid texture" test. When the model is viewed with a file-based texture of a grid or checkerboard applied to it, the problems become evident.

One thing that makes the Maya editor easy to use is that it uses virtually the same tool set that is used for modeling in the UV editing package. When the artist is going from modeling into UV editing, it is helpful to be able to pick an object in one window the exact same way it would be picked in the other window.

The way to take advantage of the texture editor's interactivity is to work with the modeling window open, with textures turned on in hardware display mode, and have the texture editor open at the same time. While the UVs are moved, the modeling window updates the textures in real time. When you are using a grid, the goal is to get the squares on the grid to appear as square as possible, or at least as uniform as possible.

The first step in using the Maya interactive UV editor is to apply a set of UVs that can be edited. The UV set should be chosen based on which mapping scheme will get the model closest to the final UV pattern. Spherical mapping was used for the model shown Figure 9.32. This mapping scheme handles most of the model well, but, as shown, the front and back of the model need attention.

Using the UV texture editor, the UVs are moved and scaled to the center of the UV space. This allows a lot of room at the edges to work. The edges are then straightened out along the border (Figure 9.33). Getting an even distribution of space between UVs along all of the edges helps maintain an even distribution of space between the UVs during later stages.

The relax tool is then applied to the UVs inside the border. This redistributes the interior UVs in a uniform and clean way (Figure 9.34) The model created from

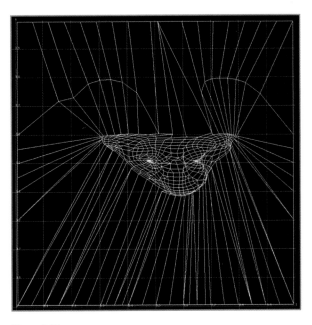

**Figure 9.33**
The border of the UVs is edited to get the outside of the UV set to line up along the outside of the UV space evenly.

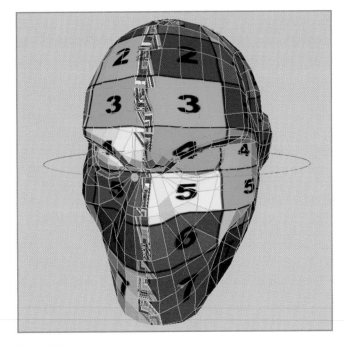

**Figure 9.32**
Spherical UV coordinates are applied to the model.

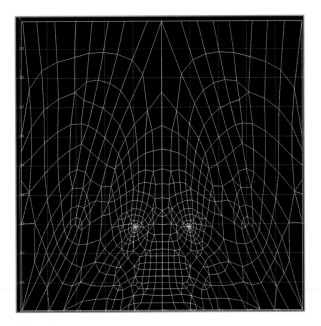

**Figure 9.34**
Once the UV border is mapped, the rest of the UVs can be easily placed using the UV relax tool.

this process is easy to apply textures to and very suitable for painting in a 3-D paint program (Figure 9.35).

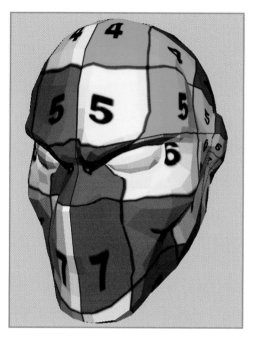

**Figure 9.35**
The result shows that the front and back of the model are cleaned up, and the rest of the model has evenly parameterized UVs.

Other texture tools are available. Several methods exist for dealing with UVs in packages, such as Lightwave and 3D Studio Max. Deep Paint, a paint package produced by Right Hemisphere, makes a product called Deep UV, which handles many complex UV mapping problems. Products, such as Deep Paint and Flesh, which have UV editing and 3-D paint in one package, help the user take advantage of the power of UV editing capabilities.

## Subdivision Interpolation

*Subdivision modeling* is the process of creating models from low-resolution polygonal cages and using these low-resolution models for creating new subdivision surface models, or using polygon-smoothing algorithms to create a higher-resolution model. This type of model creation has dramatically increased over the last few years.

This type of modeling takes full advantage of the creation of smooth and uniform UV texture coordinates on a polygonal model. The higher-resolution model inherits the texture coordinates created by any of the methods listed earlier. This really creates an amazingly fast workflow. The application of UV coordinates to a low-resolution model leads to a dramatically faster process of UV editing.

The problem associated with using these types of models when texture mapping is that the low-resolution model will have the UV coordinates interpolated differently in the high-resolution model. This interpolation can be subtle or dramatic. The best way to minimize the impact of this interpolation is to do the task of texture mapping on the high-resolution model. Painting on higher-resolution geometry may take more time, but it will eliminate the possibility that the UV coordinates will not be correct after the model changes resolution.

### Bubbles in the Wallpaper

During the process of editing UV coordinates, it may be impossible to eliminate all of the stretching and discontinuity associated when the model is being textured. Chasing these problem areas during the process of editing UV coordinates is much like flattening out the air pockets while trying to put up wallpaper. You can easily move these problems from place to place, but they usually end up having to be somewhere. Your best choice is to put these problem areas in places where they will not be seen. In cases like this, the discontinuities in the UV coordinate system should be hidden. This can be accomplished by modifying the UV coordinates so that the discontinuities occur in some place where they will not be visible when the model is rendered or displayed on the screen.

For example, when you are applying UV coordinates to a character's face, one of the best places to hide UV discontinuities is under the character's hair. Places where another layer of geometry covers the problems are always good solutions. Other places could be the interiors of the nose and ear. These are places with little surface detail in the texture but enough irregularity in the model to hide some irregularities in the UV coordinates.

Another strategy that is commonly used to hide discontinuities in UV coordinates is to put the discontinuities in a place where there is very little texture complexity. Smooth areas can be found in many places along a model if you know where to look. In the example of the character's hand, it is common to split the textures along the perimeter of the character's palm. If you examine the side of a hand, you will notice very little surface texture when compared to the palm or the back of the hand.

## Texture Map Creation Processes

This section explains the process of painting 2-D texture maps. The techniques shown here begin with very basic methods that require very little extra software or effort, and range to specialized tricks that require different software.

## 2-D Texture Map Techniques

The process of creating the actual image that will be used as the texture map is more complex and demanding than any chapter in a book can spell out. It comes down to the ability to convey 3-D detail in two dimensions. No one technique works best for every scenario when it comes to texture mapping. Since so many types of models need to be textured, you will need to approach every model with the particular needs of that model in mind. Several workflows will assist in quickly allowing a texture artist to get the job done effectively.

*Reference mapping* starts by mapping the model with a map that can be referenced easily in 2-D (Figure 9.36). These maps, like the grids or checkerboards mentioned earlier, can be used to visually determine where detail would occur along a surface. These simple maps are fine when you are examining parameterization of an area that will be covered by a single texture map. When you are determining the placement of texture maps along areas with more than one surface, or with a closed surface that may have seam problems, the reference map should also include some indication of where the edges of the texture map would be (Figure 9.37). Several maps are available on the Internet that would provide this kind of visualization cue, and making one from scratch is quite easy to do as well. Using a

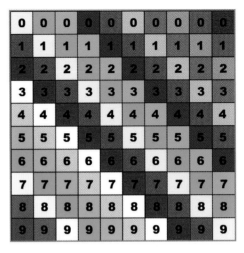

**Figure 9.37**
The actual map can be used as a background layer to begin painting in a 2-D paint package.

map that allows the visualization of where specific areas of detail would fall in a specific area on a model can be a fast and easy way to quickly get an idea where to begin painting a texture map on a model.

Several utilities are available that allow the UVs seen in the UV texture editor to be captured as an image file. Maya has a UV snapshot option available in the texture editor window. This resultant image can serve as a template for painting texture maps that are specifically tailored for the model.

When you are painting an image based on a snapshot of the original UV coordinates (Figure 9.38), the UV image should be used as a layer that can be diminished in opacity while painting. Creating the textured image on the same layer as the UV image will allow artifacts of the UV image to appear in the texture and will erase your reference while you paint.

Some 3-D paint packages are simply better than others. Some artists never get used to anything except the tool they started out with. Many gifted artists use nothing but Adobe Photoshop. There really is nothing wrong with this. If the same person was a painter who could create masterpieces using only one brush, there would be no discussion about whether this was a good thing or not. The problem is that people who do not have access to excellent 3-D paint systems, or people who do not want to use 3-D paint systems for the final image, lose all the advantages of 3-D paint.

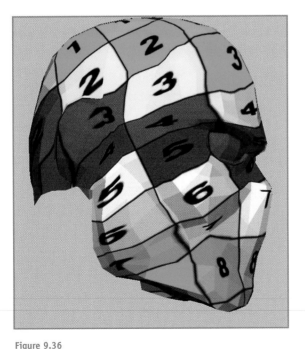

**Figure 9.36**
This diagram shows how a reference map can be used to strategically look at the model to determine where to paint the maps.

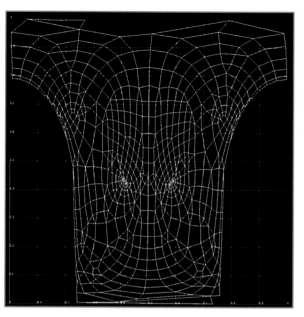

**Figure 9.38**
A UV snapshot can serve as a road map for painting textures.

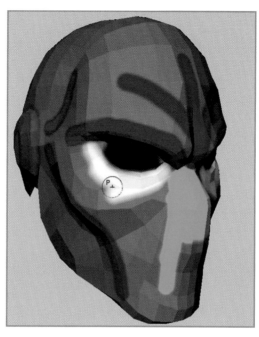

**Figure 9.39**
Using simple 3-D paint tools, you can create markup images that can serve as a template for painting textures in a 2-D paint program.

Maya has a 3-D paint system called, simply, 3-D Paint Tool. This tool is not a natural evolution of the Alias|Wavefront product called Studio Paint, which is arguably the best 3-D paint system available anywhere. The tools in Studio Paint are not anywhere to be found in Maya. Instead, the 3-D Paint Tool has a very limited tool set, and the control available through the drawing tablet is nothing like Studio Paint. The one thing 3-D Paint Tool does have going for it is that it is 3-D.

One workflow that would create really great reference images for creating textures in a paint package, such as Adobe Photoshop, would be to use Maya to create markup images (Figure 9.39), then transfer those images into Photoshop for final painting (Figure 9.40). Markup images are simple textures that outline areas on the model where details are to be drawn. If the texture that was to be drawn was a character's face, then the markup image would have lines indicating the areas of the eye opening, the nostrils, the mouth opening, the eyebrows, the ears, and so on. These basic shapes could be fleshed out in a 2-D paint package using the much more sophisticated tool set available there.

Many texture painters will begin with photographic reference material whenever possible. This creates realistic detail and gives the correct color range to a surface that is to be painted. The painter will add any additional detail by cloning parts of

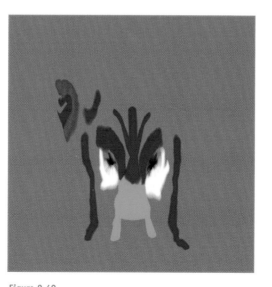

**Figure 9.40**
The markup image will need to be used as a layer, and the results will need to be checked several times to get the alignment of the textures correct.

the original photograph. This keeps the final texture in the realm of the realistic image but changes it using values and details gathered from the photograph.

Photographs, for the most part, do not look anything at all like the UVs that are being painted. They are laid out very differently. Although the basic details are oriented to each other the same way, their position and relative scale are usually way off. This creates a real challenge for the artist. Only so much can be accomplished by cloning parts of an image. Completely reconstructing the image to match the proportions of the UVs is usually out of the question.

One tool that has come to the rescue of many texture painters is a 2-D morph package Elastic Reality. By creating a 2-D morph of the photographic reference from the original photo to an image of the photo that has been stretched and deformed to match the UV layout, the artist can save hours of time painting the same result. Any remaining discontinuities can be painted manually to fix the texture after morphing. For the reference, or target, image the texture artist can use either a UV snapshot or a markup image, as previously mentioned.

Figures 9.41–9.45 illustrate the process used to modify an image using elastic reality to create a texture map.

**Figure 9.42**
This is the original image before morphing. The image is a montage of a face and ear pasted into one image.

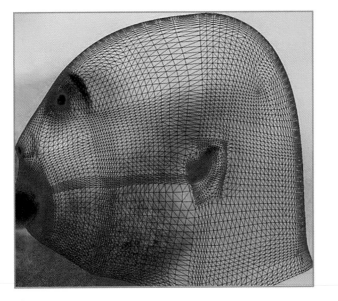

**Figure 9.41**
Using Elastic Reality to modify an existing image to create a new image can save many hours of work. In order to know what the image needs to be morphed into, the UVs for the model need to be unmeshed first.

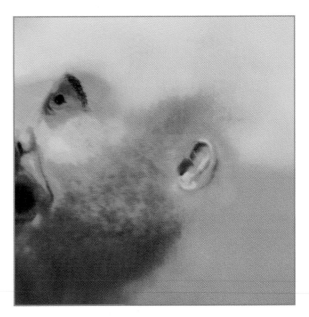

**Figure 9.43**
This is the image after morphing in Elastic Reality. This image has been dramatically changed to match the UVs.

152

9. Texture Mapping Tools

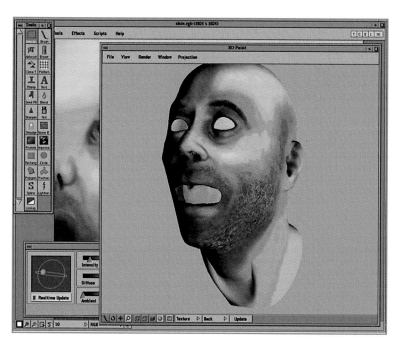

**Figure 9.44**
The map will not be perfect and will need to be fixed in a paint package. This map was edited in Amazon Paint.

**Figure 9.45**
The finished render.

## 3-D Texture Map Techniques

3-D texture mapping is almost always mentioned only in terms of mapping NURBS models. 3-D mapping tools, like projection textures, override the UVs that are applied to a texture. They do not eradicate the UVs on the model—they just do not use them.

The goal for creating great textures that can be deformed and do not stretch on the model is to have file-based texture maps that fit the parameterization of the NURBS surface, or the UVs of a polygonal surface, cleanly and without distortion. Projection mapping tools do not deform at all and do create wild stretching when applied at the edge of a model.

Surprisingly, however, one tool that can be used for creating excellent textures on NURBS models as well as polygonal models is 3-D projection.

Transforming layered 3-D projection texture to file-based texture is accomplished by creating several projection maps. For example, a decent side view, top view, and front view of the object that is to be textured would be a good start. These views are developed using the orthographic projection methods mentioned in the modeling chapters of this book. The details of these maps must line up in 2-D so they can line up in 3-D. Photographic reference is a great starting point for these images. If you can possibly get orthographic views of the object that is to be textured, that would be great. You could use more textures, or fewer textures, but the use of three textures illustrates the point pretty well.

These images are then loaded into a layered texture. A special texture is available in Maya. The layered texture is used instead of the Maya layered shader because the layered shader "bakes in" the lighting at a later stage of this process. Baked-in lighting works for some video game applications but is not used for anything else.

This layered texture has three projection textures, and each one has an orthographic image loaded into it, projecting onto the model from the appropriate directions. Transparency maps are then created based on the image maps. These maps serve as a mask that softly erases the areas toward the edge of each map where the stretching would occur along the edge of that map. The perimeter of the map is masked away, leaving the center, the area that would have the best detail based on the projection.

Once all of these layers are projected simultaneously onto the model, the model should appear as if the textures are nearly complete. Projecting textures will almost always leave some evidence of stretching, but that can be cleaned up later. The goal is to minimize the stretching by creating the masks for the texture edges (Figure 9.46).

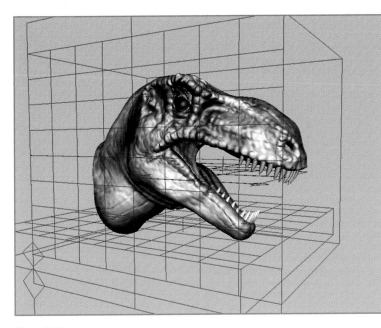

**Figure 9.46**
Using a layered texture to cover the entire surface of the model.

**Figure 9.47**
Using the file-based textures on the model.

The model is then selected in the modeling window, and the texture is selected in the texture window. Using the editing menus in the texture window, the artist will use the Convert to File Texture button to convert the solid textures to one or more file-based textures. The result is one or more images that are "rendered" from the projection texture that follow the parameterization of the NURBS surface, or the UVs on a polygonal model. This amazing trick can take three images of the model projected in the correct way and texture a complete patch NURBS model with hundreds of textures in minutes (Figure 9.47).

A variation of the projected texture method is to create a procedural texture that looks pretty good (Figure 9.48) and, by implementing the same steps mentioned earlier, create one or more file-based textures from that (Figure 9.49).

If an artist could create a fantastic skin shader using a 3-D procedural texture, but needed to paint additional details on top of that, this process could be used in combination with other techniques to create a file-based texture map that could be layered in a 2-D paint program with a 2-D texture that is being painted for a model from a UV snapshot. By using this as a layer, the artist can achieve excellent surface detail that is already specifically suited to the exact geometry that is being textured.

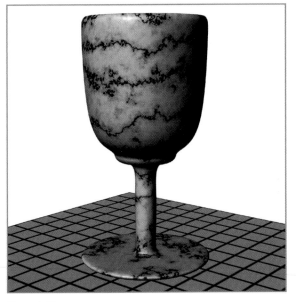

**Figure 9.48**
A model using a 3-D procedural marble shader.

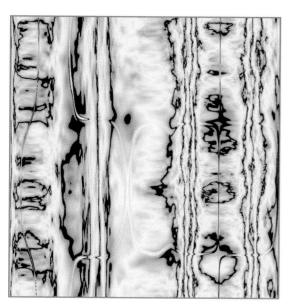

**Figure 9.49**
The 3-D procedural shader can be converted to a file-based texture using the resultant marble image file shown here.

The artist must adjust various aspects of this texture, such as opacity, hue, and saturation, to suit the surface being textured. For example, if the procedural texture that represents age spots is being layered into the painted texture of a hand, the artist should make sure there are no age spots on the palm.

Some procedural textures that may be good candidates for this process would be a leather texture or a granite texture. These textures will require quite a bit of parameter adjustment before a decent organic shader can be developed, but with a little effort, a really nice surface shader can be worked out.

Texture mapping can be a complicated process. Thankfully, there are many tools available for the texture map artist to use when preparing 3-D models for mapping, and creating maps for 3-D models. As the artist begins to use these techniques, the artists will find more techniques and may even begin to invent a few themselves.

# chapter 10
# Texture Specialties

The field of texture mapping, like the field of modeling, has many areas of specialization. People who enter the field with different backgrounds take their own approach to solving various problems and are able to use these approaches to master a specific area of texture mapping. Texture mapping includes a wide range of applications, but these can be broken down into three major areas of specialization: organic texture mapping, hard-surface texture mapping, and matte painting. Organic and hard-surface texture mapping cover the majority of circumstances where a texture painter has to map a 3-D model in a scene. At times, the scene will have to be extended artificially, and the texture painter will have to know about the rules of matte painting. Matte painting is a field of endeavor unto itself, but texture painters often find themselves in situations where they must deal with the rigorous demands of painting environments. A category of texture-painting that does not fall into any is animated talking animals.

## Organic Textures

Organic texture mapping usually refers to the texture maps found on things that are not manufactured, such as textures on trees, rocks, and animals. Texture mapping a character or human is also organic texture mapping. The key to successfully creating organic textures is to create visual complexity within the surface. Objects that occur in nature do not usually have flat areas of color; they will usually have discolorations, imperfections, and patterns.

Texture painters will take advantage of all of the tricks they can to create this kind of detail in the surface. Creating this surface detail usually requires several layers of detail to be created. Part of this layering is achieved by creating different maps to describe the different aspects of the surface, such as the color, specularity, bump, and displacement of the surface. Layers of complex imagery are also used to create organic realism within each individual map. A detailed example of this process is shown in the tutorial in Chapter 11.

## Hard Surface Textures

Hard surface texture maps describe the surfaces on objects that are manufactured from metal, plastic, or even wood. The colors and mechanical details of these objects can be applied using texture maps. But the thing that makes hard surface texture mapping successful is the ability to blend a manufactured object into the real world—in a sense, making an inorganic object more organic.

This tutorial shows how to apply color and detail to a hard surface model and shows the process of showing how to apply dirt and grime to the object, making it more realistic. This tutorial is designed to walk the user through the process of creating texture maps on a medium- to high-resolution hard surface model.

Each scene or prop has differences that will require special handling, with time usually being the biggest factor. The amount of work that will go into most projects will usually be determined by how much time is available.

The first step is to familiarize yourself with all the parts of the model, and if possible, find out how the model will appear in the shot or scene. This helps determine the level of detail required and how much time to assign to each area. Many times equal detail must be applied to an entire model because production doesn't yet know what angles and how close it will appear. After getting acquainted with the model, test grids or checker patterns are applied to examine the UVs of the model (Figure 10.1). The fuselage texture map of the jet created for this tutorial is a 2048 x 2048 pixel file (2K), and the engine texture map is 1024 x 1024 (1K), which allows finer detail in a smaller space.

Figure 10.1 shows some distortion in different areas along the fuselage. This indicates that the UVs need to be adjusted in the areas of distorted texture. When the UVs are adjusted the textures wrap evenly throughout the fuselage.

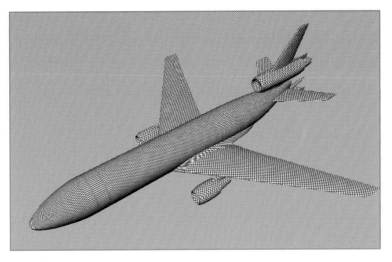

**Figure 10.1**
The fuselage of the airplane without the UV fix.

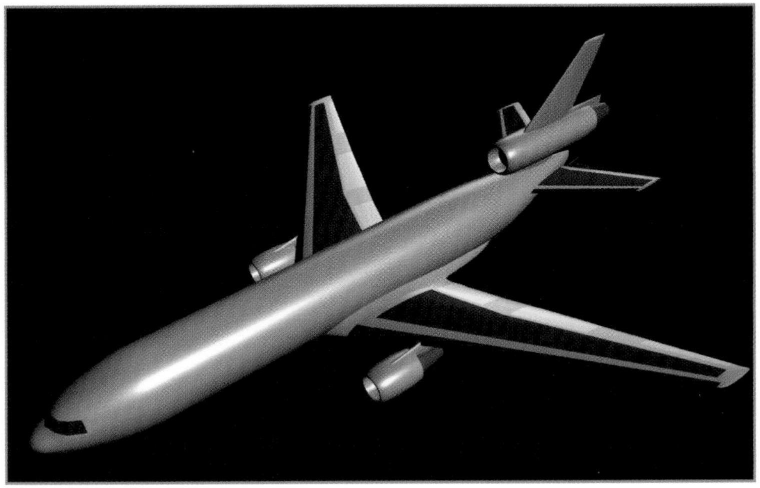

**Figure 10.2**
The basic maps applied to the objects with appropriate map resolutions.

After applying the test patterns, the maps will be resized. Different maps may be included at this time that help describe different attributes of the materials being used (Figure 10.2). These will help define the amount of roughness, shininess, or reflectivity the material has. These details will sometimes get overly detailed in the texture maps because the rendering process will degrade the textures by motion blurring the final image, or by applying depth of field. If this detail was not included in the initial textures, the lack of detail that would appear in the final image would make the object appear computer generated.

Now that the basic model is set up, the basic colors are blocked out and patterns are applied to the model, which gives you a good overall look at the color and design. At this point the texture mapping artist would then get feedback from the lighting or art department.

It is important to keep these color maps in different layers at this stage because things can change a lot throughout the process. Isolating different parts of the texture maps in different layers allows the artist to remain flexible. In most VFX (visual effects) projects, staying flexible is crucial.

At this point, graphics and other details are added to complete the look (Figure 10.3), such as decals, vents, rivet, peeling paint, and so on. These details are also kept on separate Photoshop layers. Again, keeping the details of these maps separate allows the artist to stay flexible.

**Figure 10.3**
The color maps in place on the airplane.

File management is a problem associated with working with texture maps for film. Using massive image files can lead to a time management problem. Some texture maps for film production can get as big as 700Mb. These files take a long time to open and close, not to mention the time spent working in them. It is a compromise between system requirements, production time, and level of detail required.

Having said that, the goal of this process is to create a "Photoshop project file." This file will include all the material maps on separate layers. I use the detail in one layer in this file to edit another layer. For example, I can use the detail in the color map to edit the specular and bump maps as well.

With the preliminary changes completed, the next step is to block in the values for the other material maps. During this process I do many test renders to adjust these material maps until I have the desired result. The most laborious part of the process is adding the minute detail that makes the model come to life. This can be approached in several ways. One requires accurate photographic reference of the object or prop or photographs of *noise maps*, which are usually pictures of concrete (Figure 10.4), oil smudges, or rust. This can be any photographic reference of organic noise. These are used by overlaying the map on top of the blocked-out initial texture painting.

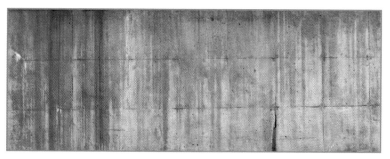

**Figure 10.4**
The map used for creating the dirt layer.

The noise or reference images are applied over the blocked-out maps. Many refinement passes are made, each one adding more detail to the model.

Before sending the textures off to the lighter, one additional refinement pass should be made. All the different surfaces should be brought up to the same level of detail and refinement. Figure 10.5 shows the texture used for the body of the jet before and after this refinement pass. The lighter section shows the more basic texture, whereas the darker, more detailed section, shows the additional refinement.

The finished render shown in Figure 10.6 shows the edited color maps applied to the model. Now the textures are done!

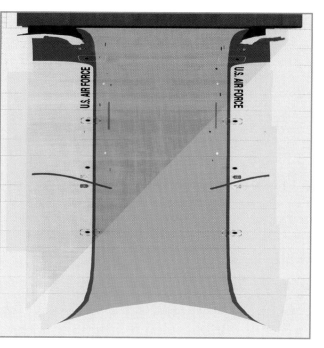

**Figure 10.5**
The dirt layer is applied to half of the map, and the other half is without.

**Figure 10.6**
The final render, with edited color maps applied to the model.

**10. Texture Specialties**

159

## Matte Painting

A matte painting is when a background, or large portions of a background, is replaced with a 2-D image. Matte painting that is done in studios today uses scanned-in photographs to begin the painting process. Matte paintings used to be painted by hand. A typical scenario would be where a matte painter would paint the top of a skyscraper on a piece of glass. The glass would be positioned so the camera would see the bottom of a two-story building, and the glass would be placed so the skyscraper image looked like it was the top part of the smaller building.

This kind of camera trickery has been replaced with an entirely new set of digital tricks.

Many times, images of a portion of a scene will be placed on a flat plane placed in 3-D space and rendered as a texture map, in a sense, replacing the glass painting used in earlier film production with a digital backdrop. When this process is used, it is sometimes called a *set extension*. This can be thought of as a texture mapping situation, because the texture painter is being asked to map a 3-D model. But because the model is very primitive, and the textures are very complex, it is really a gray area between texture painting and matte painting.

Matte painting has some striking similarities to texture painting. The 3-D detail in a model is completely substituted by the images that are painted by the painter. The control of color, highlight, bump, and reflection are all controlled by the images created by the painter. And the dependency on excellent reference information is critical to texture paining and matte painting.

However, there are some differences between texture painting and matte painting:

◆ Texture painters usually create maps for 3-D objects in the scene.

◆ Matte painters create images that replace 3-D objects in the scene.

◆ Texture painters spend a lot of time trying to get reference images to appear orthographic.

◆ Matte painters spend a lot of time trying to add perspective to match the scene.

◆ Texture painters try to get the lighting of the textures to be neutral so the light added by the digital lighters will not be affected by the textures.

◆ Matte painters painstakingly create lighting to match the lighting in the scene.

During the production of *Flintstones in Viva Rock Vegas*, Alison Yerxa, a designer and artist at Rhythm & Hues, was asked to take an image of a river gorge (Figure 10.7) and enhance the image to create a large river.

**Figure 10.7**
The original photograph of the river gorge.

**Figure 10.8**
The finished matte painting.

The ground on the bottom of the river bed was raised up to allow the image of the dinosaur that would be composited in later to appear as if it were standing in the river. New ground had to be created at the banks of the river, as well as the shadows that were cast over the ground.

The original image of the river was copied, raised up in the image, and widened to fill the new space between the river banks (Figure 10.8).

One key to successful matte painting is finding and using good reference photos. These photos are scanned and transformed so the color and lighting match the original background plate.

Although photographic reference is a critical benefit, the time-honored techniques of painting images by hand are the most useful for creating the matte image. The ability to match perspective, lighting, and color comes from the ability to paint, and are the elements that create the successful final image (Figure 10.9).

**Figure 10.9**
The final image with the 3-D dinosaur composited in. Copyright © Universal Studios. Courtesy of Universal Studios Publishing Rights, a Division of Universal Studios Licensing, Inc. All rights reserved.

10. Texture Specialties

# Talking Animals

Many films use cats, dogs, pigs, and babies as actors who deliver many lines of dialog. These films are categorized as *talking animal films* in film production studios. Texture mapping is the one thing that makes talking animal movies work.

Talking animal films have their own production process, which is different than the process used to create most 3-D characters. The process begins with the filming of the animals on the movie set, where the visual effects supervisor will be present to make sure that the animals move naturally while the filming is taking place. Excessive blinking, twitching, and shaking in the animals will require another take. The VFX supervisor makes sure that animals do not move their mouths too much. This may sound odd because the digital artists will be working to get the animal's mouth to move, but when the background film has the animal's mouth moving, it causes many problems.

Once the film is delivered to the visual effects studio, the digital pipeline follows the following steps:

1. The film is scanned to create digital background images.

2. Carefully constructed models are created of the animals that talk in the film. Figures 10.10–10.12 show the model built for the character Monty in the film

*Stuart Little*. Talking animal models must be exact. A lot of time was spent simply matching the whiskers. The ears were modeled to be objects that would be tracked, and not rendered, which accounts for the lack of detail in the ears.

3. The models are carefully tracked to match the background images. In the 3-D animation program, the tracking animator will place the model of the animal head in the exact position and pose of the animal that is filmed.

4. The camera position is used as a point at which UVs will be projected, and UVs are applied to the model for each frame. New UVs are used for each frame based on the positions of the camera, and the model guarantees that the background image will map perfectly to the model of the animal head. At this point, the model should be able to be rendered in the scene, and the model should not appear at all. The model should blend seamlessly.

5. The animal head is animated to match the dialog for the scene.

6. Now the head can be rendered, and the head should appear to talk, except for areas that will stretch and twist due to animation and texture stretching.

7. The areas that are distorted need to be adjusted using new texture maps that are superimposed on top of the background images projected on the model of the head. These images are created by using masks applied to the 3-D model that allow painted replacement textures to be used in problem areas without affecting the rest of the textured head. Typically, the lips and the sides

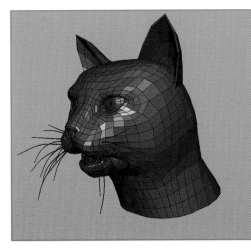

**Figure 10.10**
The medium-resolution wireframe model.

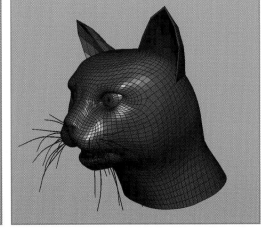

**Figure 10.11**
The high-resolution wireframe model.

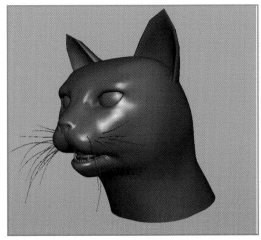

**Figure 10.12**
The high-resolution 3-D shaded model.

of the mouth will be replaced throughout the scene using this technique. Other areas will be replaced as required.

8. The whiskers are removed from the background image using digital painting techniques.

9. The head is rendered with 3-D geometry used for the whiskers. This rendered image is composited over the background plate (Figure 10.13).

The applications of texture mapping vary from production to production. In some cases, texture maps will simply create a subtle change in surface texture in a model; in other cases, the texture maps will replace the model. The texture painter should be ready to deal with these different scenarios by being aware of the specialties of texture mapping.

**Figure 10.13**
The top image shows the original cat before digital altering; the bottom image shows the character Monty talking in the film *Stuart Little*. "STUART LITTLE" © 2002 Columbia Pictures Industries, Inc. All Rights Reserved. Courtesy of Columbia Pictures.

**10. Texture Specialties**

163

# chapter 11
# Organic Texture Mapping Tutorial

In this chapter, I explain the process of applying organic textures to models, using a model of a bird. Lopsie Schwartz, a texture painter who has worked on several films, including *Dr. Dolittle 2* (2001) and *The Lord of the Rings: The Two Towers* (2003), created the textures on the owls for *Harry Potter and the Sorcerer's Stone (2001)*, and the techniques she used are explained in this chapter.

The most common question asked by people trying to learn the process is, "How do you attack a project?" Although there is no one right way, this tutorial presents detailed steps on how textures are created and applied in a production environment, in which the model is usually already designed and modeled for you. In addition, the animation setup technical directors and the animators may be working concurrently on the same model as you paint the textures. As a result, you often do not have the luxury of being able to change the model to fit your needs. You must adapt to the model. This tutorial walks you through the same steps taken when texturing the digital owls for *Harry Potter and the Sorcerer's Stone*, using a model of an owl and aiming for a "photo-real" style of textures. Usually, the model is built before any texture mapping is done. The model shown in Figure 11.1 is a different model than the one used in the actual film, but is similar enough to be used in this tutorial.

For the Harry Potter movie, the textures were created using Rhythm & Hues' proprietary software and Alias|Wavefront's Studio Paint, but for this tutorial, Maya, Photoshop, and Deep Paint will be used.

The key to making something seem photo-real is to get photographic reference material. For this project, the first step is to determine what type of owl this is supposed to be. For the purposes of this tutorial, the model shown in Figure 11.1 has the textures of a barn owl.

**Figure 11.1**
The base model before textures were applied.

First, check the UVs on the object. Sometimes the modeler will apply a checkerboard pattern to get approval of the UV's on a model. Using a simple checkerboard pattern may not provide enough information about the UVs.

The map illustrated in Figure 11.2 provides more information about the UVs than a simple checkerboard. Using this illustration as a guide, this map can be replicated. This map can be helpful in many different situations, and a map like this one should be kept handy so it can be used on a regular basis. A map helps you identify problems quickly during the approval process. When the UVs have been

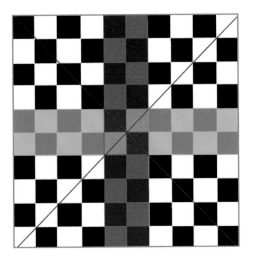

**Figure 11.2**
This checkerboard pattern was used to inspect the model for proper UV placement.

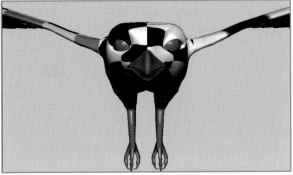

**Figures 11.3, 11.4**
These images show the model being checked in Maya for discontinuities and stretching.

**Figure 11.5**
Using the color in the test map to examine the wing.

checked, the modeler can be informed of changes that need to be made to the UVs, or the changes that can be made by the texture-mapping artist.

This modified checkerboard pattern gives much more information than the simple black-and-white checkers. This checkerboard technique gives you a quick visual cue on the UVs and can easily solve 80 percent of your texturing problems by catching them before it is too late. Some of the things that are being checked when inspecting UVs using this technique are strange non-square patterns, overall map placement, the number of pixels allocated to high-definition areas, and how much of the map is actually being used.

By checking the model with this texture map, the seam where the two symmetrical halves of the model were joined is visible. This seam is nothing to worry about. It is also possible to see something that would not be apparent with the black-and-white checkerboard. There are different groupings of feathers, and they have different UV coordinates. This condition makes it impossible to create a single texture map that can be used on all the feathers.

After examining the model with the map applied to it, the UVs on the model can now be approved, and the actual texture mapping can begin.

The first things needed to begin texture mapping are a few high-resolution rendered images of the bird. The images need to be higher resolution than the maps that will be created later. For the purposes of this tutorial, the rendered images are 2K, or 2048 x 1536 pixels.

The side view, a top view, and a bottom view need to be rendered. These images should include the full view of the bird (Figures 11.6–11.8). The front view is required to texture map the face, so the face should be larger in the frame for this image (Figure 11.9). These images will be used as templates for placing photographic images.

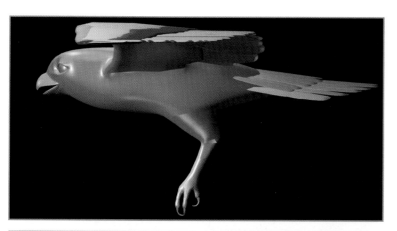

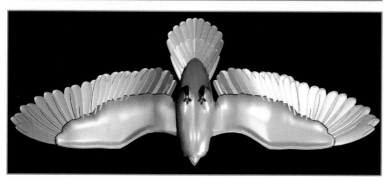

**Figures 11.6–11.8**
Orthographic views of the entire model were rendered.

**Figure 11.9**
An orthographic view of the face was rendered.

## Creating the Look with Scans

The next step in the process is to acquire photographic reference and begin scanning it to create texture maps. At this point many novices will ask: "What is the challenge in that? Anyone can scan and drop." Well, yes and no. Anyone can do it, but very few do it well. In film and television, you are commonly creating something that has to match a live or existing subject. At the very least, you are matching a background plate, and starting with photos or scans is more efficient. The more photographic reference you can get, the more realistic the finished product will be.

Anything that is scanned from print material, such as books and magazines, will need to be de-screened. De-screening is a setting that is available in most scanning software packages. Also, if copyrighted material is used, it should be used according to the laws regarding such material.

In production, images, such as photos taken on the set, conceptual paintings, and inspirational photos, will often be supplied for texture reference. It may be necessary to take additional photographs. The texture mapper should be ready and able to take reference photographs when needed. It is part of the job and is cleaner in all ways over print and Internet material.

Figures 11.10–11.13 are examples of photographs taken explicitly for production. Pauline Ts'o, the visual effects art director, took these photographs. These images display the way owls look in the real world. Many subtleties about the way an object behaves in the real world can only be determined by using photographs.

**11. Organic Texture Mapping Tutorial**

**167**

**Figure 11.10–11.13**
These reference images from *Harry Potter and the Sorcerer's Stone*, taken by the visual effects art director at Rhythm & Hues, Pauline Ts'o.

When the person who has taken the photographs is working on the project, that is an added bonus. There is even more information about the way something looks that can only be derived from seeing the owl oneself.

Once the reference images have been gathered, they need to be color corrected to be in the same color space. Use specific color information sampled from the owl itself to match the color values in the other images. One way to accomplish this is to use the color eyedropper tool in Photoshop to sample color values of a specific part of the bird, and match those values for the same part of the bird in another image.

When gathering photographic reference, it will be nearly impossible to get a photograph of the bird in the exact pose that will match the rendered images that were created in Figures 11.6–11.9. That is part of the challenge. Advanced scanning manipulation skills need to be used to create source images that are more useful.

The next series of steps take the images created in Figures 11.6–11.9 and adapt scanned images to fit these rendered images. The intent is to create ideal texture images that match the rendered images from scanned images that do not match the rendered images. The eventual goal is to place the images that are created in the steps that follow directly on the 3-D model. Without ideal texture images, the details of the image and the model will not line up.

## The Face

Throughout the following steps, several images will be created for 3-D projection in a 3-D paint package. The face of the owl will be the first texture image that will be created using this process.

1. Open the paint program of your choice. This tutorial will use Photoshop. Bring in the render of the face (refer to Figure 11.9), and bring in a front face picture of a barn owl. As you can see in Figure 11.14, the proportions are completely different.

2. Next, get the outer face ring to fit the model. Transform or deform the image until it fits the head outer size (Figure 11.15).

3. Notice that the eyes do not fit at all. The first step for correcting this is copying the region of an eye and pasting it to a different layer (Figure 11.16).

**Figure 11.14**
The rendered image of the owl face and the scanned image of the owl are shown.

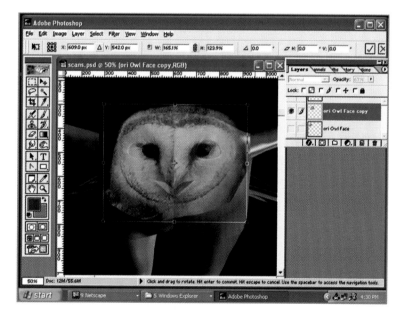

**Figure 11.15**
The scanned image is transformed over the face.

11. Organic Texture Mapping Tutorial

**Figure 11.16**
The eye is copied and pasted for scaling.

**Figure 11.17**
The image of the eye is scaled over the eye in the model.

4. By reducing the opacity of both the new layer and the head, the shape and size of the model's eye can be seen below. Next, the eye is resized to fit, using the same transformation method used for the head (Figure 11.17).

5. The head and eye layers are merged together after transforming the eye, and increasing the opacity for both layers back to 100 percent (Figure 11.18).

6. The same copying and transforming steps are repeated for the other eye. After merging the second eye onto the face, any visible pasting artifacts should be blended away. The clone tool and smudge tool used in combination work well for blending these artifacts (Figure 11.19).

7. Save this work as a single flattened image. This process has generated an image that can be directly placed on the model in a 3-D paint program.

**Figure 11.18**
The opacity is restored, and the head and eye images are merged.

**Figure 11.19**
The other eye is transformed to make the head image symmetrical.

## *The Top View*

The top of the bird will be textured now. Beginning with the top view of the owl produced earlier (Figure 11.20), scanned images of bird feathers will be positioned on the wings of the owl until the entire top side of the bird is mapped.

1. A barn owl has a brown and gray mottled look on its back and top sides of the wings. Set the clone tool to 100 percent to shape a wing, using the top view as a template.

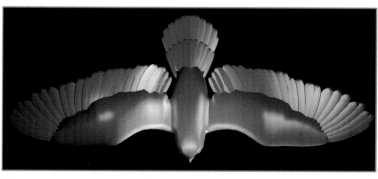

**Figure 11.20**
The top view of the model.

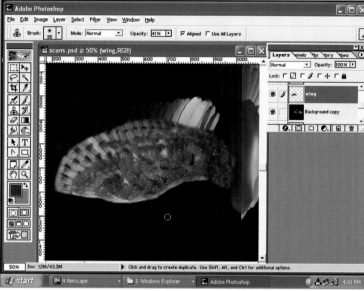

**Figure 11.21**
The entire wing of the bird with textures.

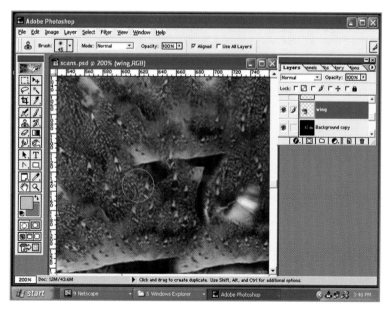

**Figure 11.22**
The clone tool is used to copy the feathers to fill in the top of the wing.

Once this is done, duplicate and flip the wing texture image horizontally (Figure 11.23).

2. Position the flipped wing to the other side to form the other wing. You could make one wing and apply the same texture to the other wing later (Figure 11.24).

If this owl will receive any close attention, however, the textures should not be too symmetrical. Part of getting a photo-realistic look is to not have anything too perfect. The model is already perfectly symmetrical, so it will be necessary to add some variation to the final image by adjusting the textures.

3. Fill in the body and top of the head, blending in the wings. Keeping different parts of the image on different layers allows for added flexibility and control. For example, despite previous color correcting, there will still be image layers that don't match up. In Figure 11.25, the pattern used on the head was too bright and of a slightly pinker hue than the rest of the bird.

4. By adjusting the hue, saturation, brightness, and contrast, the head layer blends in with the rest of the owl texture. Keeping it on a different layer helps simplify the color correction. Once the wings and body and head all look good, merge the layers (Figure 11.26).

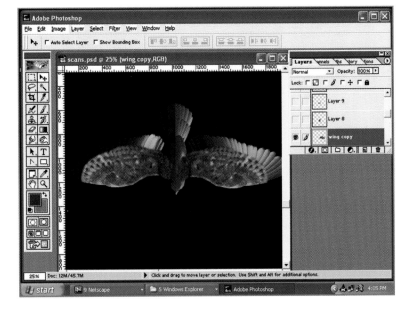

**Figure 11.24**
Forming the other wing.

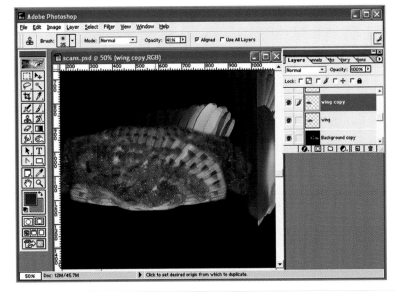

**Figure 11.23**
Flipping the wing horizontally.

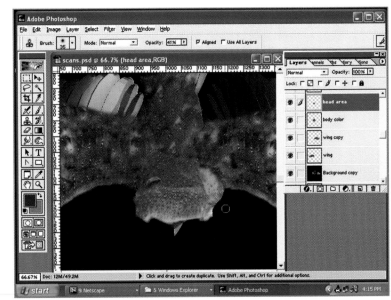

**Figure 11.25**
Color correction on the head that no longer matches the rest of the bird.

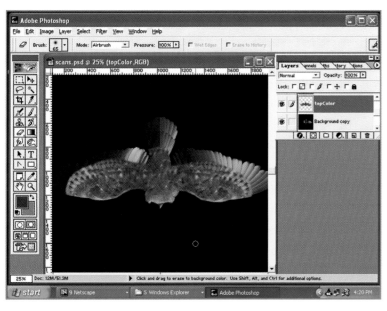

**Figure 11.26**
The top projection view of the bird with textures.

The edges of the texture image extend beyond the edges of the model image. Because this is going to be used as a projection, it is better to give some leeway beyond the model. Any image that extends beyond the model in the 3-D paint package will simply fall outside the boundaries of the model and will not be used. Also, Deep Paint will allow the parts of the image that should not be used in the projection to be erased before the image is projected on the model. It is simpler to create data that will be thrown away later than to add that additional detail later on.

## The Side View

The side view (Figure 11.27) shows different challenges than the face and top views. In this section, the legs of the bird need to be addressed, as well as the side of the body.

1. The barn owl has a light spotted underbelly—a very different color than its top side. An area of this lighter underside can be cloned from one of the photographic reference images and used to fill in the underside (Figure 11.28).

2. Next, texture the feet. The feet on this owl are a yellowish color that blended about halfway down the owl's white spotted feathers. Using a close-up image of a hawk's feet, the feet of the owl are created using the photographic reference of the owl as a guide for color and placement (Figure 11.29).

**Figure 11.27**
The side view of the bird.

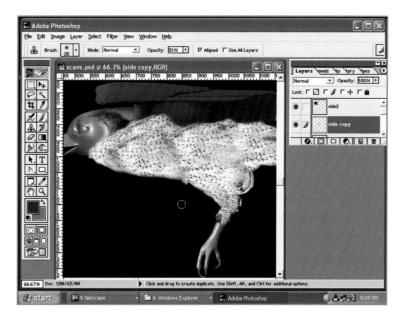

**Figure 11.28**
The side projection view of the bird with cloned textures.

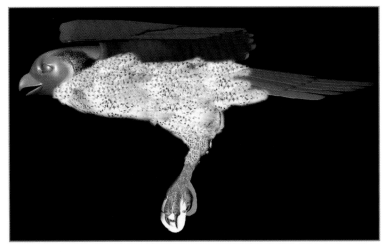

**Figure 11.29**
A hawk's feet being used for the owl's feet.

The hawk's feet are color corrected to the right color and then cloned to create the shape of the model. This is all that needs to be done from this side. Normally, the side of the face would be done at this time also. However, lots of blending will be done on the face using the image created for the front projection of the face; no additional work will be needed in the side view.

Creating these images using this technique may seem like a lot of trouble to go through if there is a 3-D paint program available. However, if these images are accurately and cleanly created in 2-D using Photoshop before projecting them as 3-D textures, this process should save time in the long run. The blending and painting done in most 3-D paint programs do not give the textures the kind of color and detail consistency that can be achieved using this technique.

The model will be imported into Deep Paint for 3-D texture projection. There are options available for importing the model into Deep Paint from Maya. Deep Paint has a great plug-in that can be used to import the model and textures from Maya into Deep Paint. This plug-in creates a special texture node that loads multiple image-based texture files into a single texture node. The process of loading many image-based texture images with very cryptic names into Maya for rendering is made easy and seamless. But, if there is a need to access the individual texture images, these complex texture nodes created by Deep Paint are difficult to extract specific data from. This process can either save a lot of time or cause confusion depending on the final requirement. For the purposes of this tutorial, the Maya plug-in for Deep Paint will not be used.

# Import the Model into Deep Paint

Deep Paint has many high quality paint options and can create high-resolution images that conform cleanly to the UVs assigned to the model. It is capable of creating professional quality work for projects like this one.

1. First project the face. The face is done first because there will be a lot of stretching down the body after projection which can be fixed by layering the body textures over the stretched areas. The model is scaled and rotated face forward. The Deep Paint projection options should be set to "first surface only" so the face image is not projected all the way back to the tail feathers. The "face photo" created earlier is imported and aligned with the model (Figure 11.30).

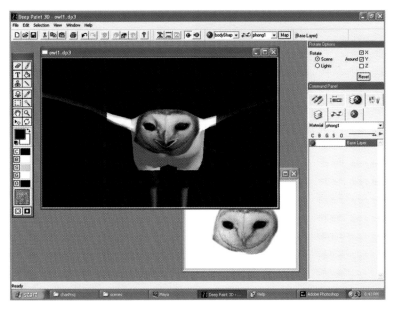

**Figure 11.30**
The front view of the owl is shown being textured in Deep Paint.

2. When the image of the face is projected on the model, the white part of the image stretches across the body. The white area outside the face will be covered with other projections later on. The model should be rotated into the model in top view. The "top photo" that was created in earlier steps is imported as a 2-D image in Deep Paint.

3. Make sure that the head part of the top view image is erased in projection mode before the image is projected onto the model. If the previous projection is accidentally projected over, the face will have to be projected again. Once the top view is aligned and properly edited, project the image onto the model. As with the face projection, the projection mode should be set to "first surface only" (Figure 11.31).

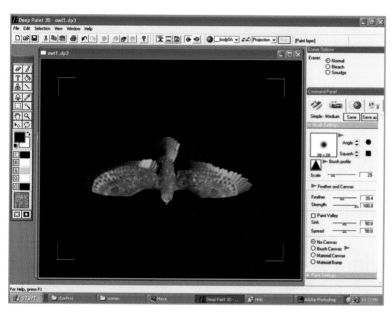

**Figure 11.31**
The top view of the owl textured in Deep Paint.

4. Rotate the model to the side view. Make sure that the projection mode is set to "project both sides" because the side view of the model will be projected through the model to create symmetrical textures on both sides of the model. Import the image created earlier for the side texture.

5. Before projecting the side image onto the model, the face and wings should be erased from the image while it is in projection mode. If this step is skipped, the projections on the face and the top will have to be redone (Figure 11.32).

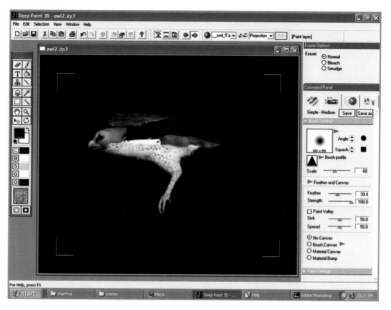

**Figure 11.32**
The side view of the owl is textured in Deep Paint.

## Import the Textures into Photoshop

Deep Paint can create high-quality 2-D image maps by interpolating the 2-D orthographic texture images that were created earlier onto a 3-D model. This would be very time consuming to do in a 2-D paint program. But the 2-D editing tools in Deep Paint are not as stable and reliable as the tools in Photoshop; therefore, Deep Paint has a plug-in that facilitates the import and export of 2-D images to Photoshop.

The texture maps that were created in Deep Paint are imported back into Photoshop for final clean-up using the Deep Paint plug-in. This process is not only efficient and fast, but it also creates an image of the UVs that appears as a layer in Photoshop that helps in the process of painting textures in 2-D.

### Wing

1. Open the wing texture in Photoshop. The bottom of the wing will be missing. The barn owl's wing has a light underside that matches the belly. Import the texture created for the side projection texture into Photoshop (Figure 11.33).

2. Cut and paste sections of the white spotted texture to the underside of the wing, making sure to keep it on a separate layer than the rest of the wing (Figure 11.34).

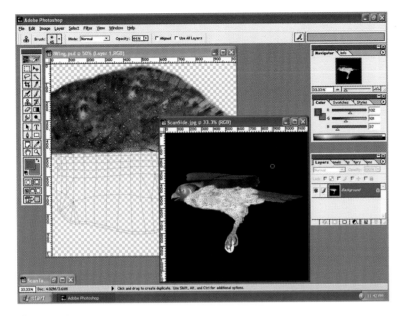

**Figure 11.33**
The wing texture is imported from Deep Paint.

3. Pay attention to the direction of the feathers; if necessary, rotate the feathers (Figure 11.35).

4. Clean up the white areas and merge with the gray-brown areas. Blend where the two colors meet (Figure 11.36).

### Toes

1. Export the color image layer only. Repeat the process for the other wing.

2. Next, texture map for the owl feet needs to be cleaned up. After importing the file from Deep Paint, just one toe needs to be filled in (Figure 11.37).

   By using the clone tool, the toe can be easily painted by copying one of the other toes (Figure 11.38).

### Body and Beak

1. Bring in the body file. A lot of stretching will occur through the middle of the belly of the owl and many blank areas will appear throughout the texture. To fill in the belly area, the same "side photo" (refer to Figure 11.29) created earlier will be used. Using the same cut and paste and clone methods used for the wings, the underside of the body can be filled in (Figure 11.39).

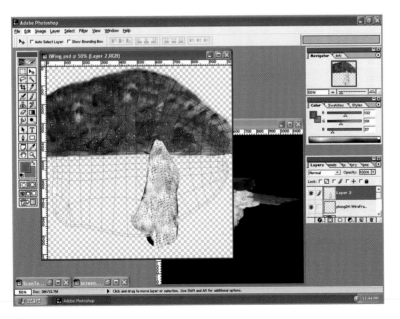

**Figure 11.34**
Texture from the side image is cloned on the wing texture.

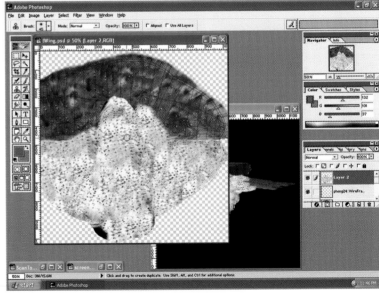

**Figure 11.35**
The rest of the wing underside is filled in.

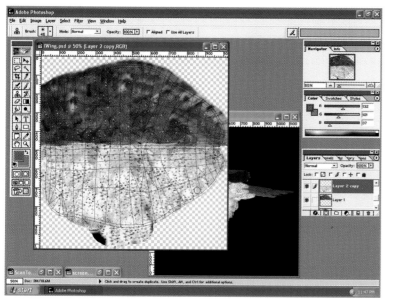

**Figure 11.36**
The wing texture is cleaned up.

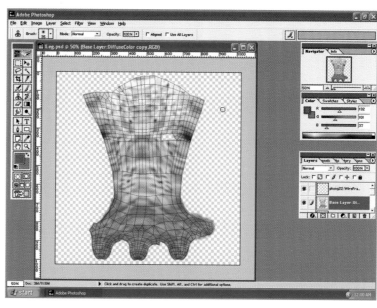

**Figures 11.38**
The toe map after the toe is added.

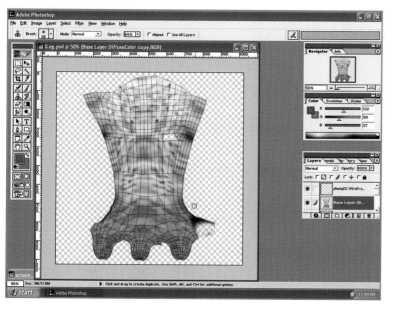

**Figure 11.37**
The foot UVs before an additional toe is added.

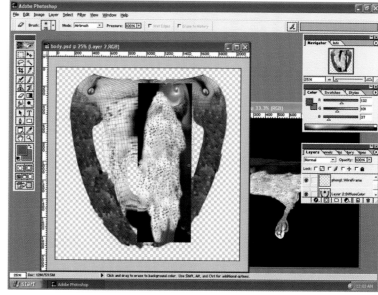

**Figure 11.39**
The body texture is shown being edited in Photoshop.

2. Zoom in close to the face and blend between the head area and the gray area. Clean up the areas around the eyes and then blend the gray top into to the white underside (Figure 11.40).

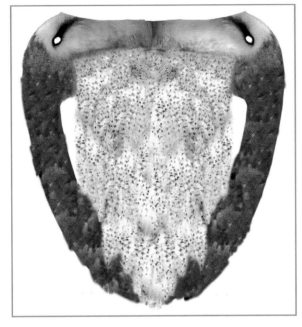

**Figure 11.40**
The cleaned up body texture map.

3. Save the body texture. Next edit the texture of the beak. Import the texture map for the beak from Deep Paint. The face projection should be mostly projected onto the top of the beak, leaving the underside blank. Use the clone tool in Photoshop to fill in the lower beak texture. With this model, a thinner, smaller beak is faked by manipulating the textures, so keep the sides of the beak looking like facial feathers (Figure 11.41).

## Details and Clean-up

Small details can push the realism into the realm of photorealism. These small items can make or break the final image.

1. Take the newly created texture maps and apply them to the color channel of the owl. The rendered image can be seen in Figure 11.42.

2. You will do final clean-up after you have created the rest of the color maps.

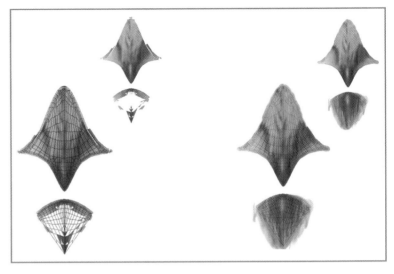

**Figure 11.41**
The bottom of the beak is filled in, and the top beak is cleaned up.

**Figure 11.42**
This is a test render of what the preliminary textures look like before clean-up.

3. Next, create the feather textures. Select one of the feathers of the model and export it out to Deep Paint. Create the striated pattern of the feather on the feather geometry. This is accomplished using a combination of photographic texture reference and hand painting. Once again, you have two different colors for the top and the bottom (Figure 11.43).

4. The individual feathers will require bump, specular, and transparency maps in addition to the color map created in the previous step. For the bump map, individual ridges on a feather should not be created, which would cause crawling or moiré in the finished rendered image. Simply draw a faint line for the stem of the feather (Figure 11.44).

5. For the specular map, it is only necessary to break up any specular hits and keep the values low. The Photoshop cloud render was used to create the specular map shown in Figure 11.45.

6. Because this model does not have the many layers of feathers that an owl has, a transparency map should be applied to the tips of the feathers. This will help give the illusion of depth and give a more realistic look to the owl in flight (Figure 11.46).

7. Now comes the big cheat. Remember the image of the checkerboard on the feathers and the UVs were not the same for all the feathers (Figures 11.3, 11.5)? This will now allow these feathers to be mapped very quickly. Rather than having to make variations of a feather, just one image will be used to map all the feathers. The slightly different UVs give the impression of variation (Figure 11.47).

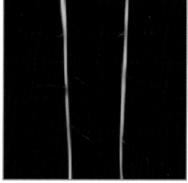

**Figure 11.43**
Feather color textures created in Deep Paint.

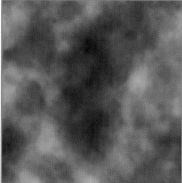

**Figure 11.44**
Simple bump maps for feathers.

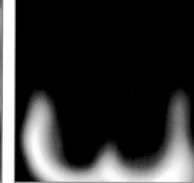

**Figure 11.45**
A cloud render used for a specular map.

**Figure 11.46**
The transparency map for the tips of the feathers.

**Figure 11.47**
This image shows the feather textures applied to the model.

11. Organic Texture Mapping Tutorial

Figure 11.48
Eye color and beak
interior color is applied.

8. Next assign color to the eyes. Color the eyes a shade of black, but avoid using 100 percent true black. Nothing that shoots on film will ever be 100 percent black. Also, give the interior of the beak a nonintrusive dark color (Figure 11.48).

9. Next, work on the bump maps. The first thing most people try to do to make a bump map is to convert the color maps to black and white, which would be inappropriate in this case. The bump is not based in any way on the color markings of the bird. Look for a white bird, and study the shading of it. That is what the bump map will try to emulate.

10. With such a colorful owl, the bump can be very simple. Also, because an owl's wings are quite smooth, you will forego bumping them. Either in Photoshop or in Deep Paint, create a soft, billowy bump map for the body and legs (Figure 11.49).

11. For the specularity maps of the body, legs, and wings, a simple noise map created in Photoshop will work perfectly well. (Figure 11.50).

12. Apply them all to the owl, and the textures are finished (Figures 11.51, 11.52)!

This process was used to create the textures on the owls in the film *Harry Potter and the Sorcerer's Stone*. The owls as they appear in the film have additional feathers added using Rhythm & Hues' proprietary software system, giving a heightened level of realism.

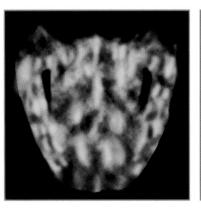

Figure 11.49
A simple bump map is applied to the body texture.

Figure 11.50
A simple specular map is applied to the model.

**Figure 11.51, 11.52**
The final model with
textures.

**Figure 11.53**
The owls from *Harry Potter and the Sorcerer's Stone*. HARRY POTTER AND THE SORCERER'S STONE © 2001 Warner Bros., a division of Time Warner Entertainment Company, L.P. All Rights Reserved.

inspired
3D MODELING AND TEXTURE MAPPING

# PART III

# Practical Application

# chapter 12
# Planning a 3-D Project

One of the goals of this book is for you to create a small animated story that can be used as an example of how models and textures are prepared for a real project. This chapter is an overview of the factors involved with planning work on a project. This chapter provides information about the various aspects of modeling and texture mapping that come into play before work begins on a project.

## Project Background

Sometimes the most important part of a project is not what the project is but the circumstances that surround the project. Many factors dictate the extenuating circumstances that surround any given project. For example, a project that has been taken from one studio and awarded to another will have a certain amount of baggage associated with it, would cause the new studio to work long hours and produce high-quality results in less time. The studio's producers and directors, and the people working downstream from the producers and directors will all be under pressure. Any digital artists assigned to a project like this must be aware of these extenuating circumstances.

### Producers and Directors

On a large project, such as a feature film being produced by a visual effects firm or film studio, several production personnel and other people with director status of some kind or another will be assigned to the job. The work that is produced for this film will have to be approved by all of these people. Becoming familiar with the film's primary director is often not possible or practical if the immediate task that needs to be done is simply modeling a character for the film.

The primary director will eventually have to approve the model, but usually the artistic director will present the model to the film's director after the art depart-

ment gets a chance to approve it. As a person working on a production, a modeler or texture map artist needs to be familiar with the art director, the lighting supervisor, the animation supervisor, and the visual effects producer.

Try to learn about the projects these people have been previously involved with and get an understanding of what they would like to see on the project. Sometimes the one thing that will save more time on a project than any other factor is the ability to know what the supervisor wants before he or she asks for it. Continue to try to apply this rule throughout the production, and the work will be approved much faster.

### High-Profile Projects

Expect a certain amount of pressure with every project. Sometimes the day-to-day activity on a project will seem fairly routine. And other times the entire project will seem like a frantic struggle just to get the project finished. Be prepared for the worst but hope for the best when it comes to this type of pressure. It will never be convenient to have to stay many extra hours to complete a task, but you should try to prepare yourself for this extra work.

High-profile projects usually require new technology or new techniques that have never been tested in production. The digital artist must be prepared to learn these new technologies and be willing to document problems and provide solutions to workflow issues, which requires patience and the ability to communicate easily with other people involved with the production.

### Reusable Resources

A reusable resource would be a model or even a complete scene that can be recycled from a previous project. Large studios have an advantage in this area. Many large studios have been producing high-quality work for many years. Because all of the data has been backed up and documented, restoring the data and reusing whatever may be appropriate is a fairly simple task.

This type of recycling saves many hours of work. Most people would be surprised to learn how many trucks and cars they see exploding in an action film were used for car commercials before they became stunt cars. This is true for many things that appear in scenes. Many people, animals, furniture, buildings, and vehicles have appeared before in other productions. If the studio has a record of a specific prop that was previously produced ready to throw into a scene, you will usually find it easier to throw that prop into the scene than to create it from scratch. Even

if a particular digital property does not specifically suit the scene that is being worked on at the time, an object can be restored and used as 3-D reference and still provide a great time savings in the long run.

In many cases, a studio will have a model or texture map library. Figure 12.1 shows examples of models from Viewpoint, a company that produces 3-D models that can be purchased. Many model and texture map suppliers will create models and textures that are sold in libraries, and will create custom models and textures as well.

**Figure 12.1**
These 3-D models were purchased from Viewpoint.

When planning for the production of a specific model or series of texture maps, try to find out if a project like this has been done before. If data for the type of project you are working on has already been created, it may be the best solution to try to salvage at least some of that previous data.

## Political History

Many projects have a history that goes beyond the straightforward documented series of events. Sometimes certain events happen that are not related to a professional work environment but can still affect the digital artist. As a digital artist, you usually will not understand the full ramifications of every event that takes place in a large studio. Some signals, however, can be interpreted as political warning signs. For example, anytime an artist receives a project that was started by somebody else, there is usually a reason why the person who started that project is no longer working on it. You should try to understand the reasons for this. The goal is not to become intimately acquainted with the sordid underbelly of office politics; instead, the goal is to make every attempt to avoid the pitfalls that other people have fallen into. By understanding the mistakes of others, a person can avoid making the mistakes themselves.

Try to find out who was originally on this project before you and who else is currently working on this project besides you. Get to know the people involved with the project, and speak to them about the history of the project. Try to understand what is expected, and solicit feedback from those working on the project. The best defense against political backlash is to do the best work that you possibly can.

# Character Design

Few stories can be told without the use of a character. In some cases, the main character can be an inanimate object that reflects the world around it. In most cases, the story proceeds by having people or anthropomorphic characters participating in it. In the case of animation, the characters are usually exaggerated in some way but remain appealing to the audience. This is a critical point and is the most difficult part of the design process.

Generating appeal is one of the trickiest things to accomplish when creating a 3-D character. Appeal is the thing that makes some of the classic cartoon characters timeless. It is also the thing that gets lost when those characters are turned from 2-D icons into 3-D characters. The most loved cartoon character can simply look odd and unnatural when seen from all angles.

Studios can take certain steps to ensure that the character development maintains a course that will be suitable for the production. By using these methods that combine traditional art and design with computer graphics production, the digital artist can develop a character that will have the appearance and functionality needed for the story.

During most real production experiences, there will be many people involved with the design of a character, especially the main character. This is a good thing. When a designer is creating a 3-D character, it will be important to have the opinions of novices and experts alike to determine whether a character will be believable or not. Unlike 2-D characters, three-dimensional characters have many visual cues that people will relate to real-life people and animals. In cases like this, if it looks weird, the audience will just "feel" it.

## Storyboards

The first consideration in the development of a character for a story is a story. Normally the story will be approved at least preliminarily before storyboarding begins and some initial character studies have been drawn up. The storyboard artist can make assumptions about the look of the character based on these initial sketches. If the design changes dramatically during the course of production, it will not be critical because the storyboards indicate action and timing and will not be heavily used for the overall look of the character.

Storyboards are important in designing a character because storyboards will identify the range of motion that will be required of the character during the project. Getting an idea of what the character will be expected to do throughout the story is critical in designing the final character. This information is essential for identifying the way a character will be modeled and set up and is also useful in determining the final appearance as well. Although the actual specifics of the appearance of the character are not fleshed out during the storyboard phase, what the character is expected to do is important when designing the look of the character.

Figure 12.2 shows the storyboards that James van der Keyl created for the character and animation described for this book. These storyboards were used to determine the range of motion that the character would need and how to model the character to accommodate this range of motion.

**Figure 12.2**
Storyboards are one source of valuable information for the modeler.

**Figure 12.2**
(continued)

## Character Sketches

The process of sketching the character to determine the look is probably the most important part of the design process. Much of the way the character will look and feel is determined from these initial sketches. The first character sketches normally occur before storyboarding takes place, allowing the storyboard artist to have an idea of what the character will look like before putting the character into the action of the story. Character development sketching can happen concurrently with the storyboarding process. As the storyboards become final, the final character sketches are usually generated.

Certain things about the character are determined while the sketching is taking place. These are critical things, such as the overall height, the color palette, the proportions, and some technical considerations related to fabricating the character as well.

Initial character sketches will usually be perspective drawings of the character in an action pose. This will allow those involved with making decisions about the design of the character to see how the character will appear during the animation. These poses should convey the personality of the character as well. If the character

is low-key and passive, the shoulders may appear to slope down, and the back will be hunched over a bit. If the character is bold and proud, the chest of the character could be out, and the head held high.

The pose should also convey what the character would be expected to do during the animation. If the character is an action hero, the pose will convey speed and dynamic movement. If the character is slow and methodical, the pose should be stationary while also conveying the thoughts of the character.

Figure 12.3 shows some facial poses for the character shown in the storyboards shown in Figure 12.2. These poses show the range of expressiveness required for the character's face.

## Model Sheets

The poses in the character sketches will provide a lot of information about what the character will look like, but these sketches cannot be used to fabricate the model for the character. The final model of the character must be built in a neutral pose.

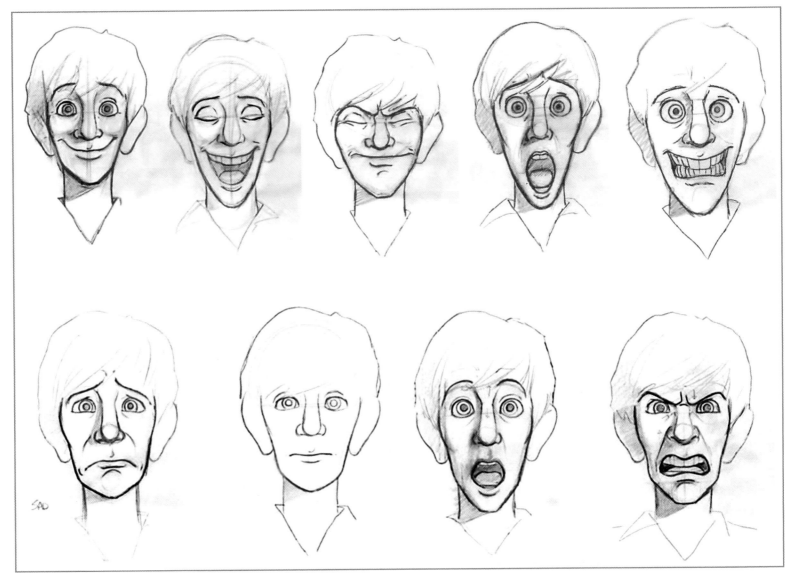

**Figure 12.3**
These character sketches from James van der Keyl show some facial poses for the character in the animation storyboarded in Figure 12.2.

In order for the model to be constructed in a neutral pose, *model sheets*, which are orthographic drawings of the final design, must be created.

For many reasons, the character that will be used in the animation cannot be modeled in an action pose. During the setup of a character for animation, the character's joints should be positioned so the character setup person can easily access the various parts of the body and head, taking advantage of symmetrical construction and world space coordinate systems whenever appropriate.

During the texture mapping process, the extremities of the character's body must be fairly accessible for positioning various UV mapping tools and 3-D paint tools.

## Neutral Poses

A common way that characters are positioned is called the *Christ pose* (Figure 12.4). Unlike the pose of Christ on the cross, the palms of the character in this pose are generally facing down toward the ground. This pose makes setup easy to do. The legs are nearly vertical and straight, the arms are positioned straight out perpendicular to the spine, and the hands are flat, with the fingers extending

directly in line with the line of the arm. This facilitates fast and easy construction of skeletons and positioning of deformers and textures.

Unfortunately, this pose makes for pretty lousy animation. When inverse kinematics (IK) are applied to a model, the joints will develop a tendency to fall back into the position where they were first bound to the model. This position for the joint is called the *preferred angle*. If the joints of a character are posed straight out, the tendency of the joints will be to pop into straight lines while moving. Also, because the joints have no preference whether to move forward or backward, they will oftentimes move in directions opposite to the intended motion. Neither moving forward or moving backward is preferred over the other because the joints were set up in a straight position.

The pose used by most studios now can be thought of as a *modified Christ pose* (Figure 12.5). This pose demands that the joints be slightly bent in positions that facilitate ease of movement. The knees should be built in such a way that they inherit a bend out toward the front of the character. The joints at the hips have a slight rotation of the thigh projecting toward the front of the body. The arms are

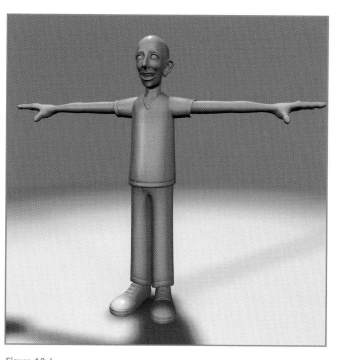

**Figure 12.4**
The Christ pose is easy to set up and model because everything is at 90 degrees to world space.

**Figure 12.5**
This modified Christ pose has the arms in a more relaxed position, the hands in a neutral position, and the legs slightly apart and bent at the knees.

positioned in such a way that they will naturally bend at the elbows, and the shoulders rotate toward the front. The hands are slightly cupped in a position one would expect to see if the character was simply having his hands rest naturally. The spine and neck should have a natural curve.

If taken to the next logical step, the pose will almost be similar to the pose of a character riding a cruiser motorcycle (the Harley pose) as in Figure 12.6. The top of the body will be bent forward, giving the joints of the spine a preferred angle forward. The arms and hands will be positioned comfortably out in front of the body, and the legs will be bent up into the body and not extended with the feet on the floor.

This position sets every joint at a preferred angle but is seen as too difficult to work with by most people doing animation setup or texture mapping. The spine, unlike the arms and legs, does move backward, though it moves forward more than backward. The same can be said of the joints at the hips, shoulders, and neck. For this reason, the Harley pose is seen as an unnecessary step.

All of these poses address issues that are fundamental to the successful setup of an animated character. In each pose, the limbs are constructed so the joints along each limb fall within a theoretical plane. In the leg, for example, the rotation of the knee will occur only in one plane, like the hinge on a door. To simplify the setup of the leg, the plane of knee rotation is extended along the entire leg. Starting at the hip, moving down to the knee and ankle, all the joints in the leg exist within a single theoretical plane. The foot is extended out in the direction of the plane created by the alignment of the hip, knee, and ankle. This approach to positioning the joints allows each limb to have a single local coordinate system. This makes the animation setup of the limbs more efficient. The same is true of the rotation of the elbow. The elbow will rotate in only one direction, the entire arm rests within a single plane that aligns with the rotation of the elbow. This planar approach to neutral pose creation allows the character setup technical director to create setups that are flexible and easy to maintain. Figure 12.7 illustrates the planes along the arm and the leg.

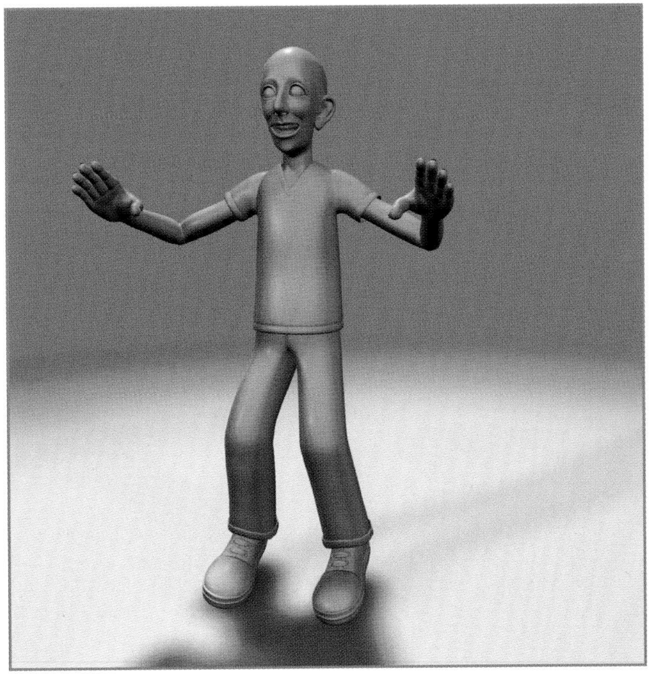

**Figure 12.6**
This Harley pose has every limb in its most relaxed position, at 50 percent of its range of motion.

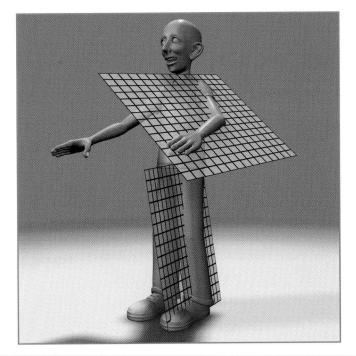

**Figure 12.7**
The arms and legs are bent along a single plane each.

## Orthographic Drawings

Once the character designer has established a neutral pose that will be appropriate for the animation setup pipeline, the designer should work with the modeler to create orthographic drawings that represent the approved character. Orthographic drawings are needed to construct the final character for two main reasons. The first reason is that orthographic drawings represent the neutral pose that is required for animation without any perspective distortion. The second reason is that orthographic drawings can be easily used for reference by loading them into the modeling software as image planes. This ensures that whatever is drawn by the designer in orthographic views will be correctly conveyed in the 3-D model. Having this reference available directly within the model program allows the modeler to easily get the model approved based on the orthographic drawings provided.

However, simply because the model matches the drawings does not mean that the model will always appear correct. It was mentioned earlier that a 2-D character does not always translate easily into a 3-D character. Once the character can be represented with surfaces that have volume and shading, it takes on a brand-new appearance. Oftentimes this appearance looks different from the intention of the 2-D sketch.

## Maquettes

To keep from having to remodel the character many times for it to look correct, many studios will build a 3-D model of the character using clay. A character that is represented using 2-D drawings can look great from one side. But a sculpture has to look good from all sides and will be a much better indication of what the 3-D model will look like.

Different studios have different standards for building these sculptures. Some studios will use oil-based clay, some studios will make molds and pour permanent sculptures, and some studios will use clay that hardens and becomes semipermanent. The method used for sculpting the maquettes is determined by how the studio intends to use the sculpture after it is created.

Some productions require that the sculpture be used for reference only, and the orthographic drawings are used for final approval of the model. In cases like this, the maquette can be sculpted in an action pose that reflects the movement and personality of the character. If the sculpture is used for visual reference only, the maquette does not need to be constructed from permanent materials. Oil-based clay can be used easily for maquettes intended for visual reference only.

Some productions use the final maquette for digitizing and creating 3-D data from the sculpture. In cases where 3-D data is derived from the sculpture, the sculpture must be constructed in a neutral pose. If a sculpture is going to be digitized, it must be constructed from permanent materials. Hardening clay, like Sculpey, is generally used in these circumstances. After the maquette is hardened in an oven, pencil lines are drawn on the surface of the sculpture indicating where the digitized points will be sampled. The flow of these points represents lines through which the final surfaces will be constructed. Digitizing data along the lines of the final construction makes the job of constructing surfaces much easier and saves a lot of time.

Figure 12.8 is the foam casting that served as a maquette for creating the character Dino in the film *The Flintstones in Viva Rock Vegas*. This was an actual cast from the mold used by Jim Henson Studios to make the puppet of Dino. The goal was to match the foam model exactly because there would be scenes where the puppet would be cut with computer generated scenes. The foam used to make professional quality puppets is made from *urethane* rubber and remains dimensionally stable compared to other types of flexible casting compounds.

**Figure 12.8**
The urethane foam maquette used to create a digital character.

The modeler must also consider how the model will be created. Will it be constructed from napkin sketches? Will it be constructed from orthographic model sheets? Will a maquette be digitized or scanned with a 3-D scanner?

A modeler should try to establish a single source of reference as the one thing that will be looked at as the final criteria for approving the model for two reasons. First, using a single source of reference will make the job of the modeler easier by establishing a single source of data that can be used to construct surfaces from. Second, different sources of finalized data can be different from each other, making it impossible to establish which source of information is correct unless established before any modeling takes place.

## Planning the Modeling Process

Each studio will have different standards for modeling based on the production requirements for that studio. The final models for a video game will be different from the models delivered for a feature film. Resolution, rendering, animation setup, and production schedules will all need to be taken into consideration before any modeling takes place.

### Construction Requirements

For the modeler, the primary consideration for modeling construction is the requirements of the animation department. Animation setup and the demands that the animator will have for the model will determine a lot about how the model will be built. To be successful in any given studio environment, a modeler should become as familiar with the requirements of the animation department as with the requirements of the modeling department.

Just as the animation of a model will dictate the way it is constructed, the studio will also have its own requirements as well. The studio itself, due to rendering software requirements as well as other production tools, will impose requirements on the model. These requirements can change from production to production and can even change throughout the course of a production.

### Surface Types

Construction standards vary greatly from studio to studio. A modeler should fully understand the requirements of the studio before constructing any models. These requirements include the kinds of surfaces that are used to construct the final models. NURBS, polygons, B-splines, and subdivision surfaces are some of the possible options that different studios use when delivering final geometry for rendering. Most studios will allow some latitude regarding which type of geometry can be used during the construction of a model. But the final model must fit within the production pipeline or it is useless.

### Studio Standards

Beyond determining the geometry type used for final production, the studio will often impose other standards as well. These standards include naming conventions for file names, directory structures, naming conventions for nodes and groups within the model itself, naming conventions for shaders and textures, and standards for file names and types used for texture image files.

To a person who has little experience with a structured studio environment, having so many standards will be perceived as unnecessary and excessive. But these standards are put in place for a reason. All it takes is a couple times where a digital artist cannot find a file because he or she did not follow procedure, or the file the artist used cannot be used by production because it was not named correctly, and the artist begins to see the beauty of this fanatical organization.

Every file that is turned in should have every possible node named with a name that follows studio procedure. In the case where no established procedure exists, the file should have node names assigned that are short, are descriptive, and consistently follow some internal naming convention. For example, if the right arm on a model is called "R_arm," the right leg should not be called "legRight." If the studio does not have a convention in place, the artists should create their own convention.

When the model is submitted for setup and rendering, this will pay off many times over. The people who use those models will be happy you took a little extra time.

### Model Size and Scale

*Model size* relates to the memory footprint of the model, and *model scale* relates to the geometric scale of the model within the computer. Both of these issues will have a profound effect on the production and should have careful attention paid to them before submitting a model for final setup.

The memory that is used to load most models is usually small when compared to the amount of memory required to render an image. Some models, however, can take up huge amounts of memory. A detailed environment model, for example, can be memory intensive.

The memory footprint of a model is dependent upon the geometric complexity of the surfaces used to create the model. Every additional surface, every additional row of vertices, and every additional smoothing pass will add to the amount of memory the model will require to load, move, and render. Several factors determine the geometric complexity of a model. Although making a model larger than necessary is never a good idea, there will be cases where the model will require additional optimization based upon production requirements.

A large production will usually have a memory "budget" set up for a typical render. This budget is split among the things in the scene that need to be rendered. If there are large amounts of motion blur, atmospheric effects, raytracing, or radiosity involved with rendering a scene, the budget left over for the model will be slim. The model will have to be optimized to get the render done efficiently.

Modeling for video games has even tighter requirements for model optimization. Often the model will have a strict limit placed upon the number of polygons allowed per model. Every part of the geometry will weigh down the real-time playback speed of the model. Each additional vertex, vertex normal, and vertex color has to be within the allowable limit when dealing with real-time playback.

Another factor that controls geometric complexity includes the distance the model will be seen from the camera. If the model is a complex shape but will only be seen from far away, the model can be optimized dramatically. When many complex models need to be seen small, or far away, the model can be prerendered and applied to a series of cards that are animated in the scene. This will provide huge memory and time savings.

Rendering and mapping considerations will also be important when determining model complexity. If there are extensive displacement maps and realistic color maps on a fairly simple shape, the model can be made from extremely light geometry. Many detailed landscape models are made from low-resolution models and are mapped with highly realistic texture maps.

Model scale, on the other hand, is usually determined by scene setup. At the stage in which initial camera motion is roughed out is usually called layout stage. The global scale for the models is determined there. If the scale is not determined and the scale is left up to the modeler, it is usually a good rule to make the scale small. Maya defaults to 1 unit equals 1 centimeter. This is a decent size for many personal-sized objects like a telephone, or maybe even an entire single character. But for a fairly large scene, like the action taking place in a room, 1 unit equals 10 centimeters would be better. For a large room or a large building, 1 unit equals 100 centimeters would be better still. On the flip side, some studios will even think of the unit in terms of imperial measurements, such as feet and inches. Many productions have adopted a paradigm that 1 unit equals 1 foot but still leave the units in the software set to a metric scale to avoid conversions.

## Blend Shapes

Facial animation can be accomplished by creating blend shapes, by controlling the face using animation controls, or a combination of both techniques. In studios where the animation of the character's face is controlled using animation controls, the modeler will have a little bit of extra time after the model is submitted for setup and animation.

Usually many things will require a modeler's attention after a model is submitted for setup, so the modeler should not really go on vacation until the final renders are being cranked out. But as far as additional modeling is concerned, much of the task is complete.

In some studios, however, a large percentage of what the modeler will be doing after the initial construction of the approved model is working on face shapes for facial animation. This task should be planned for ahead of time, and the time required for building these additional models should be accounted for in the budget and in the schedule. The final number of these additional models will vary from production to production. The final result of this additional modeling is called a *face shape library*. It will be called different things by different studios, but these face shapes will be the basis of the facial animation for that character.

This face shape library will consist of localized face shape models that have the exact geometric topology as the model of the face that will be animated. A localized target will consist of a specific area of the face that is modeled in a specific way. For example, a smile will usually be broken into a left smile and a right smile, allowing the animator to adjust the two shapes independently. Different looks will be achieved by blending several shapes together. A left eyewink shape can be added to a left smile shape and a right eyebrow rise to get a knowing smirk. This additive approach to facial animation allows the animator to get hundreds of combinations from a fairly small face shape library.

Here is where looking at the storyboards will really pay off for a modeler. The requirements of the animation will dictate which shapes will be built. The modeler will want to work on creating shapes that have emotion and expression but are localized to the region they are specific to.

Part of this face library usually includes a series of *phonemes*. These are face shapes that are specific to speech. There are several opinions as to the exact number of phonemes required for adequate speech recognition. The general procedure is to use these shapes as base shapes for speech, and emotive blend shapes are added during that animation to achieve the performance.

For the character created for this book, many blend shapes were created. Figure 12.9 shows some of these shapes.

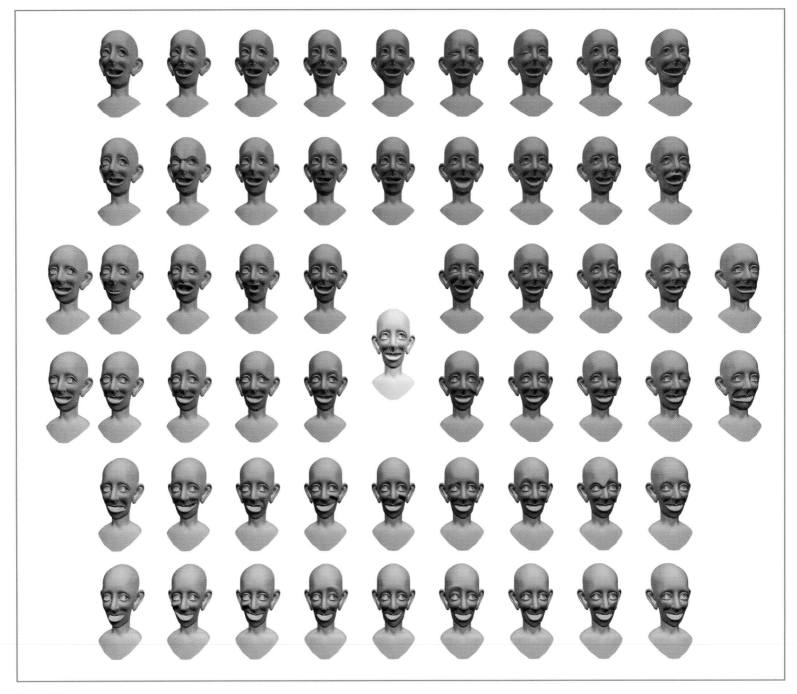

**Figure 12.9**
Some of the blend shapes created for the sample project.

## The Project Team

Within any studio environment are more unwritten rules than are in the employee handbook. A lot of people do not want to get involved with the political makeup of a company, especially if the political waters are treacherous. The good news is that a person can do certain nonpolitical things to avoid some of the "land mines" that are found when dealing with folks in any organization. These are simple rules that apply to every work situation, whether you are working in the deep halls of a major corporation or freelancing out of your living room.

The first rule is to find out who is involved with the project you are working on. Make a point of meeting them and try to be social with them. Once you associate a face with the job title, the intimidation factor will diminish. Once they see your face, they will be more eager to call you directly with problems associated with the model instead of handing the model back to your supervisor every time a node name is misspelled.

The second rule is to ask questions. Make sure you maintain an open channel of communication and use it whenever an important issue needs to be resolved. One computer graphics studio has a policy that is spelled out to everyone working in production: Do not spend more than 15 minutes trying to work out a problem on your own. This is not bad advice. Sometimes you will realize that you could have figured out the problem on your own after you get the answer, but the question is: when?

Get to know the way the model will move from department to department. These other departments—animation, animation setup, and lighting—are your clients. Their needs are your problem. Make sure that you know what their needs are and that they know that you care about their requirements.

### Animation

Speak to the lead animator about the sequence that the model will appear in. Make sure it is understood where the model will bend, what needs to move, and how much movement will be involved. Try to get sketches or notes from the animation department that document the motion and the range of motion required for the bending geometry. Try to get a name from the animation department that can be used as a contact person in case there are any questions.

The surfaces that are required to bend should be modeled with the parameterization lined up along the direction of the bend. The surfaces that are required to bend a lot should also have adequate resolution to allow the geometry to appear smooth after the surfaces are bent.

Blend shapes are another special concern for the animation department. Most studios that use blend shapes regularly will have a list of blend shapes that they use for every production. In addition to these, there will be specific blend shapes required for certain shots that animation should be able to provide to the modeler. In certain cases, the blend shapes will have to be sketched out in order to get the exact shape that the animator is looking for. Make sure that the animation department gets a chance to approve the blend shape before the model is passed off to production.

### Animation Setup

Animation setup will have requirements that need to be satisfied before finishing a model. The setup department will usually agree with the animation department when it comes to the required movement but will have additional things they need in order to get the movement to happen. Sometimes the modeling department will be asked to create low-resolution cages that will be used to deform the high-res model or will be asked to make special "icons" that will appear as 3-D wireframe elements in the animation window.

There will also be standards that are specific to the animation setup department that the modeler should become familiar with. These standards include naming conventions for geometry and specific placement of joints and limbs for skeleton setup. These conventions should be detailed and clarified before the model is started. As with any other department-specific issues, try to get a name of a person who can be contacted for questions regarding the model. Have the contact person look at the model before the model is passed off.

### Lighting

Modeling and texture mapping must work closely with the lighting department to get the model ready to render. For lighting, the most important thing for a modeler to get right is the UVs on the model. If the model consists of polygons, the UVs of the model should be even and distributed in such a way that no stretching and no twisting occur. If the model consists of NURBS surfaces, the surfaces should be rebuilt with a UV parameterization ranging from 0 to 1, not 0 to number of spans.

Another consideration is the assignment of materials or shaders. The assignment of materials usually falls into the domain of the model maker before passing it off for texturing. The modeler should ask the lighter which objects would fall into which material groups. Materials can be simple colors or simple grid or checkerboard textures. Before the model leaves the modeling department, the lighter and the texture mapping artist should approve the assignment of materials and the placement of UVs on the surface.

## Planning the Texture Mapping Process

Now that the model has moved from the modeling phase to the phase where textures are applied to it, the job of the texture mapper is to get the model ready for production. Several issues related to production are addressed at this stage. The UV coordinates must be checked to ensure that they will not twist, tear, or distort. The textures used to map the model have to adjust in size to ensure that the memory required to render the image will not be excessive. The file types and bit depths used in the texture files must be compatible for the current production standards. Along with everything else, the overall color palette used to create the textures must be compatible with the color palette used in the overall production.

### UV Coordinates

The model should have had UVs applied to it already from the modeling stage. The texture-mapping artist is responsible for ensuring that these coordinates are suitable for the project. The first step in this examination is to view the model with a file of a test pattern applied to all surfaces. This test pattern can be a grid, a uniform noise pattern, or a checkerboard. Many test patterns use colored squares to identify problem areas by color. This works exceptionally well for complex models.

Different patterns are used for different things. Sometimes it is a better idea to look at the UV coordinates of a model using a fine noise pattern if the maps that will be applied are organic and have fine detail, such as skin or animal hide. It is usually a good idea to examine the model closely in the modeling window and to create some test renders of the object using these testing maps.

The model should be examined for stretching UVs. There will always be a small amount of distortion in the mapping coordinates. But in areas where the maps are stretched enough to create long streaks in the maps, there will not be enough pixels in the actual texture map to support detail. By counting the squares in a checkered test pattern, you can determine the actual number of pixels that will be assigned to the area that is being stretched. By determining the percentage of the area being mapped by dividing the overall area by the number of grid squares being affected by the stretching, then applying that percentage to the number of pixels in the map, the actual number of stretched pixels in the map can be calculated. If one square of a 10 x 10 grid is being affected by stretching, then 25.6 x 25.6 pixels in a 256 x 256 texture map will be stretched. By using this estimation process, the texture mapping artist can make judgment calls about what stretching is excessive and what is acceptable.

The texture mapping artist should be familiar with the process of applying UVs to geometry. Artists familiar with this process will be able to speak intelligently with the person applying the UVs about how they will be applied. Also, in many studios the job of UV assignment will be left up to the texture mapping artist, and there may also be times when the UV assignment scheme may need to change and the texture artist needs to reapply them. In cases like these, it will be critical that the texture mapping artist thoroughly understands the process of applying UVs.

### Image Resolution and Bit Depth

Each production will have a standard for the average size for most texture maps that will be used in that production. If the production is a television show, the texture map size could range from 256 x 256 to 2048 x 2048 pixels. If the production is a feature film, the texture map size could range from 1024 x 1024 to 4096 x 4096 pixels. Texture maps that are larger than 4096 x 4096 pixels are fairly common for large areas that will be seen up close.

As a rule, texture mapping for software rendering will allow much more texture memory than texture mapping for real-time applications. For video games, the texture map size will tend to be much smaller. All of the textures of the entire scene often fit into one texture map that is no larger than 512 x 512 pixels. Video consoles today have more texture memory than the consoles in the past, but the amount of texture memory available is always limited.

The process of applying textures almost always necessitates that the texture artist prepares at least one render of the finished texture maps. A good way to test the appropriate resolution of the textures is to set the output format of the render of the image to the same size of the final render that will be produced. If the object that is being rendered looks fine with the resolution of the textures that are applied, then the texture resolution is probably fine as well.

In many cases, the object that is being rendered will be seen with many other objects that are being textured. If many objects are loaded into the scene, the memory consumption for the render begins to get high. At this time texture artists will have to consider lower-resolution images for the textures.

It is a good idea to try to get an estimation from the shot supervisor of what the available memory will be for the shot in which the object that is being textured will appear. The texture artist will never want to start with the lowest possible resolution. The initial texture size should be an image size that is approximately what would be considered the highest acceptable resolution for the texture on that object. If the object will have a texture size that is no larger than 1024 x 1024 pixels, then a map that is 4096 x 4096 pixels should not be applied to it. However, if the largest acceptable resolution is beginning to give memory problems during the final render, then reducing the resolution of the texture maps is always much simpler than it would be to increase the resolution of the texture maps if the initial texture map size was too small. Detail within a texture map can always be removed; putting it in is much more difficult.

Bit depth is a different type of resolution issue. Bit depth is the number of colors per channel that appears in the texture map. Most common paint packages support 8 bits per channel. If the production requires images that are 16 bits per channel, then it is important to make sure that the paint package being used supports these higher depth images. This decision must be made prior to any texture mapping. Once texture files are being saved at 8 bits per channel, it is impractical to try to increase the bit depth to 16 bits per channel. Again, losing definition is easier than increasing definition. In this case, this rule applies to the additional colors per channel in a 16-bit per channel image.

## Color Palette and Style

When planning a texture mapping job, the artist should get familiar with all the production artwork, the storyboards, and any existing work that is already in production. Make sure that the art director, along with the person who is in charge of approving the final lighting and texture mapping, has detailed any information regarding the look and feel of the final image. Because texture mapping contributes such a large part of the final rendered image, each map must be thought out carefully.

One easy way to make sure that the texture maps being created are compatible with the vision of the art director is to use approved artwork and any published color palette information as a source for defining colors in the maps that are being worked on. Opening the images in the same paint package that the texture maps are being painted in, and sampling colors and even small texture samples from those images, will ensure that the texture maps will be compatible with the approved artwork.

## Texture Reference

Gathering reference data for any texture mapping job is a critical step toward a successful project. Which kind of reference material is gathered will vary depending on the type of project that is being worked on. If the project is based on real life, then photographic reference is the easiest, most abundant, and most accurate reference data available.

However, if the project is super stylized, and the art director is going for a specific look, photographic reference may not be the best source of texture reference. If the project you are working on is an animation of a dream experience where the entire scene looks like a Van Gogh painting, then getting references of Van Gogh's paintings will clearly be the best place to start. The same would be true for many other stylized projects or projects that are based on illustrative styles like cartoons.

## Photographic Reference

Part of the time that will be required during the texture mapping job will be the process of gathering reference data. Make sure that this is understood up-front. If the texture mapping assignment requires that detailed maps of buildings be applied to simple geometry, then possibly most of the time spent on the job will be out on the street taking pictures of buildings. Supervisors must be aware of this before the project starts. Trips to the library, bookstores, and magazine racks should also be part of the time spent gathering information if it is required.

Figures 12.10 and 12.11 show an example of photographic reference for some fruit that will be texture mapped with photorealistic textures. Further reference would include getting scans directly from the fruit by placing it on the scanner, giving very accurate surface detail for realistic textures.

## Stylized Reference

Many texture painters will do nothing but paint. The maps that will be created for the project they are working on will include nothing but hand-drawn brush strokes. Generally projects that fall into this category will not be super realistic. That is not to say that there should not be reference data available for a project like this.

When dealing with an artistic project like the ones where there will be no cloning of photographic reference material, the artist must refer to other artistic material as reference. If the project requires a texture mapped 3-D environment in an animated feature where 2-D characters will interact in that environment, then detailed production artwork must be available as reference for the texture maps. Figures 12.12 and 12.13 show examples of stylized reference.

**Figures 12.10, 12.11**
These photographs are examples of texture reference gathered for photorealistic texture assignments.

**Figures 12.12, 12.13**
These images are examples of stylized reference.

12. Planning a 3-D Project

# chapter 13
# Constructing the *Inspired* Character

In this chapter the focus of the discussion will be the character and not the development of the environment. This is not to say that the environment is not important, but the process will be easier to detail if the focus is limited to one character.

James Van Der Kyle created the storyboards in Chapter 12 to produce an animated short film. This short animation was created for the tutorials in this book and other books in the "Inspired" series. The design for this character shown in these storyboards was not the original design. Figures 13.1 and 13.2 show the original designs.

## Process for Building the Character

The sketch shown in Figure 13.1 was created by James van der Keyl. This sketch has an appeal that was exceedingly difficult to capture in 3-D. The model shown in 13.2 was created by Daniel Dawson. This model has a certain appeal, but it does not quite have the appeal of the sketch. In truth, although the design did capture the original better than the other models produced during the design process, this model still had many problems.

Aesthetically, the model lacked a certain amount of realism that the sketch conveys. The details and proportions are simplified to create a cartoonish look. Technically, there were problems with the construction that would make the model hard to animate, specifically, the mouth and eyes are not in neutral positions. When a character's face is modeled, the eyes and mouth are usually modeled in a relaxed position. This position appears as a 50 percent open and 50 percent closed position. This makes the construction of face targets easier; the mouth is already halfway open, so it is simple to open it, or it can be closed just as easily.

In defense of the modeler who created this model, Daniel Dawson, the problems associated with this model were directly attributed to the direction he received, and this model represents a first pass at the final model. Daniel was given no opportunities to finesse this model.

**Figures 13.1, 13.2**
The concept and the model for the character that were originally created for the book series.

This model was chosen to proceed with the series illustration. Now that this decision was out of the way, I still needed to create a model for a tutorial. The model shown in Figure 13.2 used a polygonal construction process, and a subdivision surface smoothing pass to finish the model. Although this is a valid way to create a character model, I wanted to write a tutorial that used NURBS surfaces as a base for the subdivision polygons.

The model that eventually became the one used for the book was originally constructed as a model that used patch modeled surfaces as a basis for the final construction.

## Final Modeling Process

The character in my original sketches (Figure 13.3) did not have the edge I was looking for, so I made the jaw line more natural, and the eyes were brought forward more (Figure 13.4). Because the design I was coming up with only had to make me happy, I did not concern myself with the cute aspect of the character design. The character I was trying to build looked like the technical directors I know—edgy, burned out, but overall fairly nice people.

Upon viewing the first rendered image (Figure 13.5), I decided that this character had several advantages over the character that was originally chosen. This character had a certain appeal, but the appeal was more oriented toward adults instead of children. This character was more edgy.

The final modeling process this completed character started with a NURBS patch model. The NURBS surfaces were converted to low-resolution polygons soon after the NURBS surfaces were laid out, and finally were rendered using subdivision techniques. This workflow allowed for the quick and accurate fabrication of a model that could be edited efficiently and repeatedly.

This process is efficient for several other reasons that extend beyond the task of modeling.

1. The UVs created on the low-resolution model are transferred to the subdivided model during the subdivision process, making texture mapping very fast.
2. Animation setup is done on the low-resolution model. The controls, vertex weighting, and bindings created in animation setup are all maintained during the subdivision process.

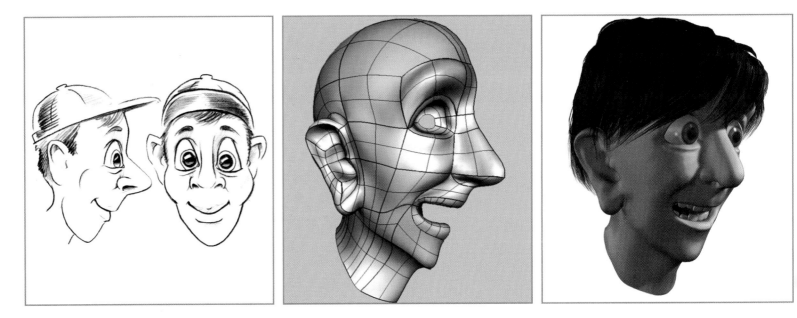

**Figures 13.3–13.5**
These diagrams illustrate the design direction taken for the final character.

3. Animation can be done on the low-resolution model, which allows for the fast manipulation of the low-resolution deformable model. The intersections and excessive wrinkling that can occur during the animation process can be prevented by increasing the resolution of the low-resolution model after animating it, and previewing the results. This gives animators instant feedback for their animation.

4. The actual subdivision can be a control that is set right before rendering the model. This makes the entire pipeline faster.

During the process that was used to get this character from concept to cover art, the ability to change the model, sometimes dramatically, was essential. This workflow put the right amount of detail in the right location. This allowed the model to change many times without distorting into a ghastly creature, like the previous attempts. This also allowed the changes to happen without changing the original design intent while the character was in development.

## NURBS Patch Modeling

The process used to create the final model started with a NURBS model based loosely on the original sketches (Figure 13.3). Throughout the course of the project, this character took on a larger role, and the NURBS patch modeling was never completed to a finished level. The models shown in Figures 13.4 and 13.5 are fairly preliminary and are useful in looking at the way the character "feels." These models have a long way to go.

The construction of the patch model started with rough splines sketched in the modeling window. The rough splines were filled in with loose patches until there was a low-resolution network of surfaces.

### Surfacing Strategies

In this example, the correlation between the muscles of the human face (Figure 13.6) and the patch layout (Figure 13.7) can be seen. There is a radial layout of surfaces around the eyes, ears, and mouth, and the surfaces of the cheek and eyebrow follow the contour of the skin.

The original NURBS ear is shown in Figure 13.8. The surface layout of the ear is similar to the surfacing layout used at the mouth and eye. Using a single surface to describe the center of the ear and having the detailed areas of the ear radiate out from the center are efficient ways to get the required detail of the ear and have this complex area transition to the smooth area of the cheek. Figure 13.9 shows a diagram of the surfaces.

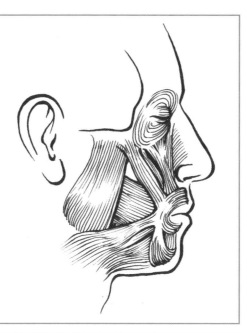

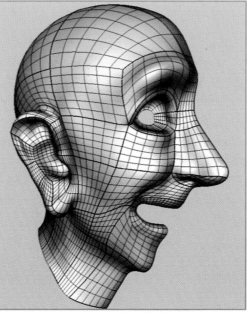

**Figures 13.6, 13.7**
The shapes of the muscles of the face correspond to the surface layout used in the NURBS patch modeling layout.

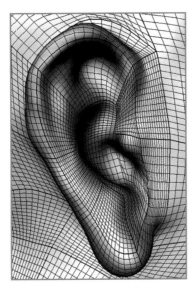

**Figures 13.8, 13.9**
The patch surface layout of the ear.

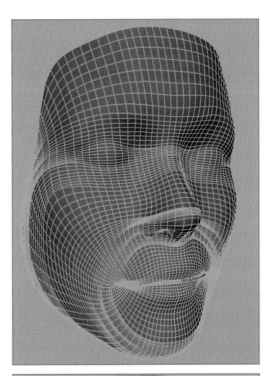

### Why a NURBS Patch Model First?

In earlier chapters, the subject of creating a model that has parameterization that follows the flow of the geometry is mentioned. Modelers can use other modeling paradigms for building a character's face, but no method handles the issues related to building a character's head as well as the patch modeling method. Other modeling techniques, such as the single-surface head, do not cover all of the issues related to surface layout as well as the patch modeling method.

First of all, the flow of the geometry does not match the musculature beneath the skin as well. And the single-surface head (Figure 13.10) has to overcompensate for the detail in the nose and eyes by adding isoparms. The patch model (Figure 13.11) can use less geometry and include just as much, if not more, detail. Most important, the extreme stretching that occurs at the back of the face and around the chin on the single surface head does not occur at all on the patch model.

Overall, a patch model has a more even distribution of geometry in the proper location, which makes this a great starting point for building the rest of the model.

### *Convert to Polygons*

The NURBS surfaces are converted to polygonal meshes. The settings used to convert the NURBS surfaces to polygonal meshes vary depending on the density of polygonal mesh that the model needs to be. In Figure 13.12, the correlation

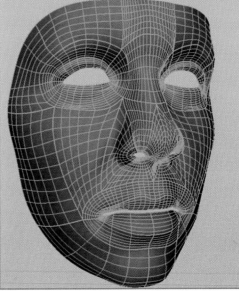

**Figures 13.10, 13.11**
The patch model has several advantages to the single-surface modeling paradigm.

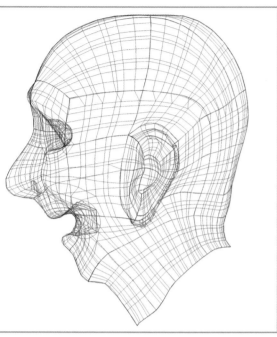

**Figure 13.12**
This shows how the NURBS surfaces convert to polygons to create the framework for the polygonal model.

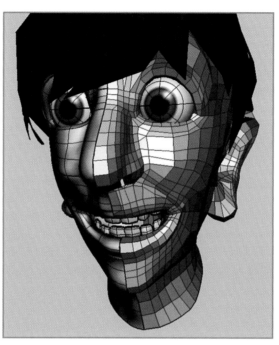

**Figure 13.13**
The model is shown after some preliminary editing.

between the conversion of the polygonal mesh and the NURBS surfaces can easily be seen. The NURBS surfaces and the polygonal mesh are superimposed on top of each other.

Initially, the distribution of the polygons is too heavy in some places and not dense enough in other places. The polygonal model has to be adjusted by hand in order to get the detail distributed in the right places. The polygonal model shown in Figure 13.13 was converted directly from the NURBS surfaces. This model has to be edited before it can be used.

## Optimization

When a NURBS mesh is converted to polygons, the problem of badly distributed geometry must be addressed before the model can be used. The first problem that is normally taken care of is the problem of too much detail in the wrong areas. Some places on the head maintain a generally smooth topology. Places like this are the top of the head, the back of the head, and the cheeks.

During the creation of a NURBS patch model, some additional isoparms are added to certain areas just to get the parameterization of these areas to line up with other parts of the model. For example, the top of the head will often get additional geometry that has been generated in the nose area because the top of the head rests directly in line with the nose. This is one of the complications that must be dealt with when working with NURBS surfaces.

Now that the model has been converted to polygons, this is no longer an issue. Now the high-resolution geometry on the top of the head can be decreased. This can be done by eliminating edges, snapping vertices to a common point (creating polygons with zero surface area), or by deleting vertices. Decreasing the resolution achieves two goals:

1. This reduces the geometric complexity of the area, which helps reduce the possibility of creating wrinkles and unwanted flashing in that area.
2. By reducing the number of polygons, the area will appear smoother when subdivision surfaces are applied to those polygons. (Figure 13.14)

**Figure 13.14**
Places like the top of the head are ideal locations for polygon optimization.

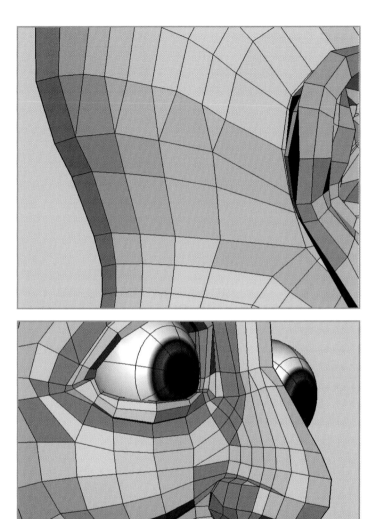

Two guidelines should be adhered to when optimizing polygonal models:

1. Try to avoid triangles. Sometimes reducing geometric complexity in a particular region will cause a transition to another, more detailed area. In cases like this, the low-resolution rows of polygons will run into higher-resolution rows of polygons. The transition has to be a series of triangles that get the two areas to smoothly flow into each other (Figures 13.15 and 13.16). This is an unavoidable circumstance, unless the polygonal model is not optimized at all after converting the model from NURBS surfaces. Certain problems will arise, however, if the model has too many triangles. Models that are all triangles are almost unusable for subdivision modeling techniques. Although triangles are sometimes a necessary evil, they should be avoided.

2. Try to maintain an even distribution of geometry if possible. There will be areas that will require fine detail, but the quadrangles on the cheek should maintain relatively the same size as the quadrangles on the top of the head. This will allow the textures to map more evenly to the geometry and will facilitate the use of subdivision modeling much easier than if there is a dramatic change in size between the polygons in different areas of the model.

**Figures 13.15, 13.16**
When areas that have different geometric complexity run into each other, a transition will occur. These areas will require triangles to get the transition to work.

## Subdivision Modeling Techniques

Subdivision modeling techniques are used to take a low-resolution polygonal object and increase the resolution using a smoothing algorithm to create a high-resolution model. Several methods work quite well to accomplish this task.

Polygon smoothing is conceptually the simplest type of subdivision modeling. The original polygonal model (Figure 13.17) is defined as the low-resolution cage, and the higher-resolution geometry is created directly from it (Figure 13.18). You can use subdivision steps to determine the final resolution of the resultant model. As a rule, the resolution should begin with one single subdivision and increase from there based on the need of the model. The entire model can be subdivided, or selected faces can be subdivided.

The advantages of using this technique are as follows:

1. As long as the history is maintained, the model can be returned to the original state by selecting the smooth node and dialing the subdivision number back to 0. Editing the high-resolution mesh, however, will cause unpredictable results if the subdivisions are set back to 0.

2. The resultant geometry type is polygons. Maya has few problems dealing with polygons and will behave in a stable way when using them.

3. UVs are maintained in a predictable manner.

Some disadvantages include the following:

1. Some artifacts can appear at the edges of models because the polygonal density is not high enough. This artifact, called *nickeling*, can be fixed by increasing the density of the polygons at the edge of the model, or by increasing the number of subdivisions in the smoothing operation.

2. The ability to interactively work on a low-resolution polygonal model while previewing a high-resolution view of the smoothed model is not available in Maya. This can be done, however, using a plug-in called connectPolyShape, which is available at www.highend3d.com. This plug-in can change the way a modeler works and is definitely worth checking out.

Subdivision surfaces use an internal interpretation of the polygonal mesh into another entity type. This entity type behaves similarly to NURBS surfaces. The easiest way to understand this process is to look at Pixar's RenderMan, which creates subdivision surfaces.

Within a low-resolution cage are quadrangles and triangles. In RenderMan, these entity types are treated differently. A quadrangle is assigned a NURBS surface. Every

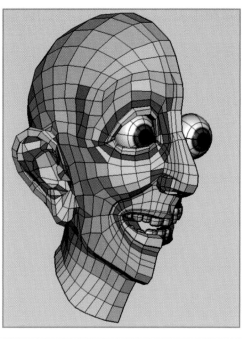

**Figures 13.17, 13.18**
Polygon smoothing is a predictable and easy way to create a high-resolution model from a low-resolution model.

quadrangle in a polygonal mesh has an infinitely smooth surface that is tangent to the adjacent surfaces. At render time, these surfaces are tessellated adaptively at a pixel level. This unique tessellation method allows for unbelievable detail when rendering displacement maps on relatively simple surfaces.

Triangles, however, are not defined as NURBS surfaces. They are defined as subdivided triangles, in a similar way that smoothed polygons behave. The ability to tessellate adaptively is reduced.

Maya behaves differently than RenderMan. The geometry can still displace better than any smoothed polygon model, and the areas where quads transition into triangles are treated differently.

These points can be seen as advantages that subdivision surfaces in Maya have over smoothed polygonal models.

Other advantages include the following:

1. Interactive editing of low-resolution polygonal cage while previewing high-resolution geometry without using plug-ins.
2. Many tools that allow quick editing, mirroring, and conversion of subdivision surfaces.

In short, Maya has developed many tools that make subdivision surfaces look attractive. But it must be noted that this entity type is notoriously unstable. Before using this entity type on a production, test it carefully and often. Results attributed to using subdivision surfaces include these:

1. Loss of UV information, especially across mirrored axes.
2. Maya has an invisible node called the *shape node* associated with every piece of geometry in the scene. Maya uses these shape nodes in the dependency graph for many important functions. Using subdivision surfaces can cause geometry shape nodes to simply disappear. Digging through the hypergraph can get the geometry back, but only after a heart attack or two.

### Detail

Detailing in polygonal modeling has to be done in combination with a way to preview the results, which is why the smoothing discussion was introduced before the discussion on creating detail. If the resultant model is going to be smoothed using subdivision modeling techniques, then the results of this additional process should be checked whenever a significant amount of work is to be done. When the lips are detailed, check them, when the ear is detailed, check it, and so forth.

Detailing usually requires the model to be split along the areas where the model has a topological change. For example, the edge of the lip is not exactly a hard edge. But if the edge of the lip is compared to the side of the cheek, it is significantly sharper.

Creating detail in regions like this requires the process of adding additional rows of polygons along these areas. To create the ridge at the edge of the lip, a row of polygons is created at the edge of the lip; when this single row is subdivided, it becomes two or more rows, adding more definition.

When applying additional rows to create detail, it is important to understand how these rows will affect the final model. Some simple rules can come in handy when these conditions arise. In the examples in Figures 13.19–13.26, different examples of polygonal smoothing are shown.

1. Sharp corners will smooth out if there are no additional rows of polygons inserted (Figures 13.19 and 13.20). Additional rows of polygons at the edges and corners help control the way the geometry is smoothed. These additional rows of polygons are used to create areas of detail in the final model.
2. In Figure 13.21, the shading artifact that blends through the single row all the way to the corner is called *flashing*. A single row of polygons will not stop flashing along the face of the square. In Figure 13.22, the corner where the rows come together was not controlled by adding an additional polygon, so the corner was smoothed unpredictably. A single row of polygons works better than no rows at all but will not provide adequate control for detailed areas.

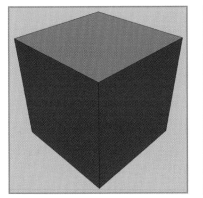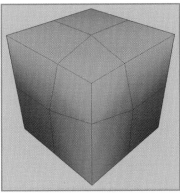

**Figures 13.19, 13.20**
A model with no rows of controlling polygons.

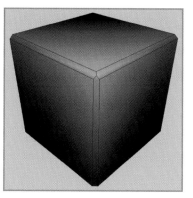
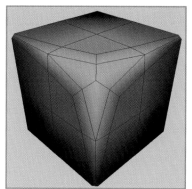

**Figures 13.21, 13.22**
A single row of control polygons.

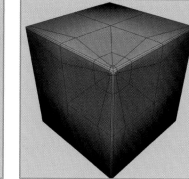

**Figures 13.25, 13.26**
A model with two rows of controlling polygons.

3. In Figure 13.23, additional polygons were added at the corner. This allowed the smoothing operation to behave more predictably in Figure 13.24.

4. In Figure 13.25, additional rows of polygons were added along the edges. Notice how the highlights on the edges are confined to the two rows. In order to control flashing, a large face on a polygonal model that transitions into a smaller face must be separated by two rows of polygons. Figure 13.26 shows how the additional rows give the smoothing operation more control.

The areas of the face that normally require additional work are the ears (Figures 13.27 and 13.28), eyes (Figures 13.29 and 13.30), nose (Figures 13.31 and 13.32), and mouth (Figures 13.31 and 13.32). The details range from major reconstruction to the simple addition of a polygon row to sharpen the area just a small amount.

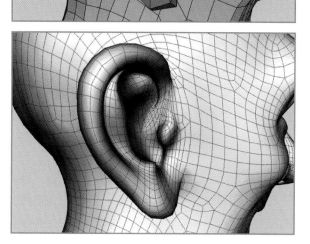

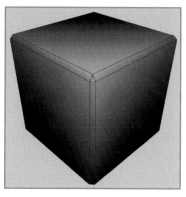
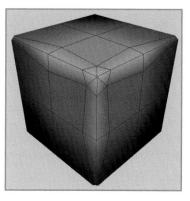

**Figures 13.23, 13.24**
Additional geometry added at the corner.

**Figures 13.27, 13.28**
The low-resolution ear (top), and the high-resolution ear (bottom).

**13. Constructing the *Inspired* Character**

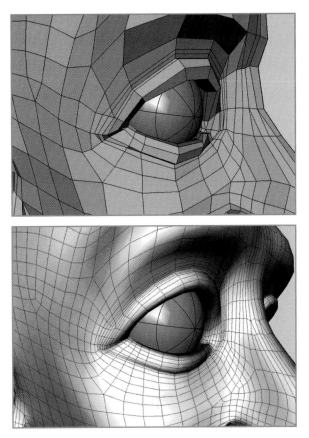

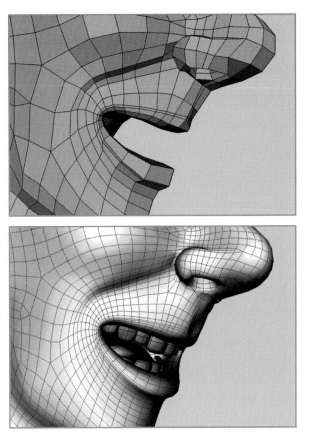

**Figures 13.29, 13.30**
The low-resolution eye (top), and the high-resolution eye (bottom).

**Figures 13.31, 13.32**
The low-resolution nose and mouth (top), and the high-resolution nose and mouth (bottom).

### Cleanup

Once the polygons have been split, sculpted, merged, deleted, and manipulated into the model that is going to be smoothed, certain cleanup tools should be used. In truth, these tools must be used every time the model is going to be previewed using the subdivision method required for the model. These first tools that should be used are *merge vertices* and *merge multiple edges*. These will simplify the unseen entities that may be creating problems.

To do a final check on the model, you can use the polygon cleanup tool. You must use this tool carefully. Be sure that the model is inspected carefully before the results of this tool are accepted; this tool can cause major problems to otherwise usable models.

### *Hair*

The original sketch had a baseball cap on the head of the character. This was an attempt to avoid what became a difficult process of making many layers of NURBS surfaces into hair. Many computer-generated characters use layers of NURBS surfaces to create hair. This character was supposed to be a young guy who did not pay careful attention to hair care, so the hairstyle would have to be loose.

The real story here is the difference between the hair that was originally proposed and what finally appeared on the character.

Figures 13.33 and 13.34 show some of the progression from long hair to the relatively clean-cut look.

## Eyes

The eyes were built from three NURBS spheres nested inside each other:

1. **A clear outer later (the cornea).** This layer is simply a clear reflective ball that surrounds the rest of the eye

2. **A colored interior layer (the iris).** This layer has a recessed, or concave, area around the color of the iris that reacts to light. When light is directed above the eye, the iris will have additional reflection that occurs beneath the pupil. This anatomy is physiologically incorrect, but this lighting has become an accepted way that eyes appear in computer-generated characters. The characters in the Pixar films and the PDI films have their eyes constructed in a similar manner. The opening for the pupil is simply a hole that has a cluster that controls the diameter of the hole. This allows for animation of the size of the pupil.

3. **A black inner layer (the pupil).** This layer is adapted to fit the iris. The shader on this layer is a black surface shader that emits no light whatsoever.

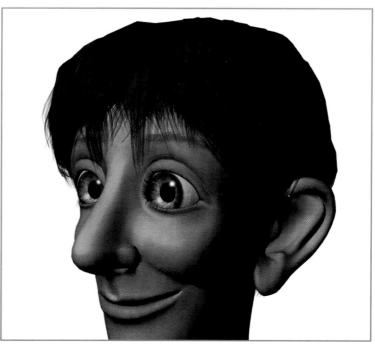

**Figure 13.35**
A close-up of the eye reveals some of the way the eye was built.

13. Constructing the Inspired Character

211

### Teeth, Gums, and Tongue

These were simple models. The teeth are simple NURBS spheres that have been flattened to resemble teeth, and the gums are surfaces that have been sculpted to accept the simple teeth.

The tongue is a half sphere that has been modified to resemble a tongue. All of these items are NURBS construction because this type of model is relatively easy to create, map, and animate. Even though these parts are important, the focus of this chapter does not need to cover this material.

### Facial Animation and Blend Shapes

In the production of an animated character, the character can have the face animated in two basic ways. One way is to have animation setup control the face using various setup techniques. This requires expertise on the part of the setup technical directors. In a large production facility, the efficiency of scale can make difficult jobs like this commonplace. Many characters have already been set up that can be taken apart and reused. In a small production, the process of creating facial controls can be time consuming. This is especially true because no other similar characters can have their controls "recycled" for the new character.

On this production, despite my best efforts to avoid this, the production decided early on that the facial animation would be controlled using blend shapes. Blend shapes are 3-D morph targets that have the exact topology as the face they are controlling.

### Full Face Shapes versus Local Face Shapes

In the creation of face shapes for an animated character, there are two basic schools of thought regarding the way the face should be animated using blend shapes. One method is to use the entire face as a specific target. If the character is going to frown, then the entire face is sculpted into a frown shape. The eyebrows are sculpted into a furrowed appearance, and the entire mouth is sculpted into a real scowl.

Face targets like this are normally sculpted to the maximum range, which can be used as the production dictates. If the shape is a 100 percent frown, then the production can use this shape in increments of 20 percent, 40 percent, and so on, to create frowns of less intensity.

Local face shapes are broken down into specific regions. These regions are separated into left, right, and center regions. If there was a smile to be modeled, the blend shape would be a left smile, a right smile, and a center smile. This gives the animator a lot of control as to what part of the face will be affected by the blend shape.

For this project, the local blend shapes were a necessity. But because I know that the vast majority of animation time using blend shapes was spent trying to get multiple blend shapes to animate as a single channel, I also added some blend shapes that took up an entire region. I modeled a left smile and a right smile, and I also modeled an overall smile as well. I modeled a left furrowed brow and a right furrowed brow, and I modeled an overall furrowed brow.

The jaw was to be animated using a skeletal setup. The jaw position is not animated using blend shapes. The modeling of the blend shapes had to be coordinated with the animation of the jaw. Figures 13.36 through 13.47 show the jaw in various stages of being opened or shut along with the blend shapes being shown. This helped visualize how the blend shapes would behave during the modeling process.

I was careful to try to keep the mouth blend shapes from affecting any other regions, and the eye blend shapes localized to the eye region. In this way, these particular shapes were hybrid global/local blend shapes. They affected an entire area, but only the area intended to animate, not the entire face.

When I was creating the localized blend shapes, the areas that were affected stayed on one side of the face. There were many shapes not shown here that broke each part of the face into even smaller regions. These regions were isolated to areas like one eye (Figures 13.42 and 13.43), one eyebrow (Figure 13.45), or one corner of the mouth (Figure 13.46).

Most blend shapes are modeled about 20 percent past the most extreme point where the animator is expected to use them. This allows for more elastic animation and gives greater flexibility when combining blend shapes.

### Shapes and Phonemes

The decision of which shapes to build came from two primary sources. First, Rick Grandy, the technical editor for this book, came up with a preliminary list, and then the animator, Kyle Clark, came up with some items that he needed to get this project done. Overall there were 66 targets built for this animation, and there will probably be some more that need to be built as more animation is done. Some

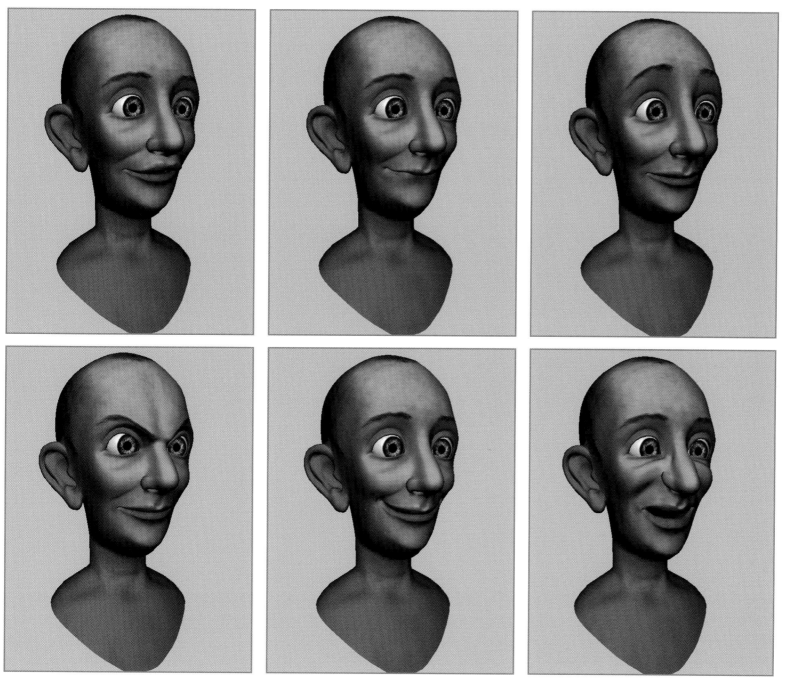

**Figures 13.36–13.41**
Blend shapes that affected larger, less localized areas of the face.

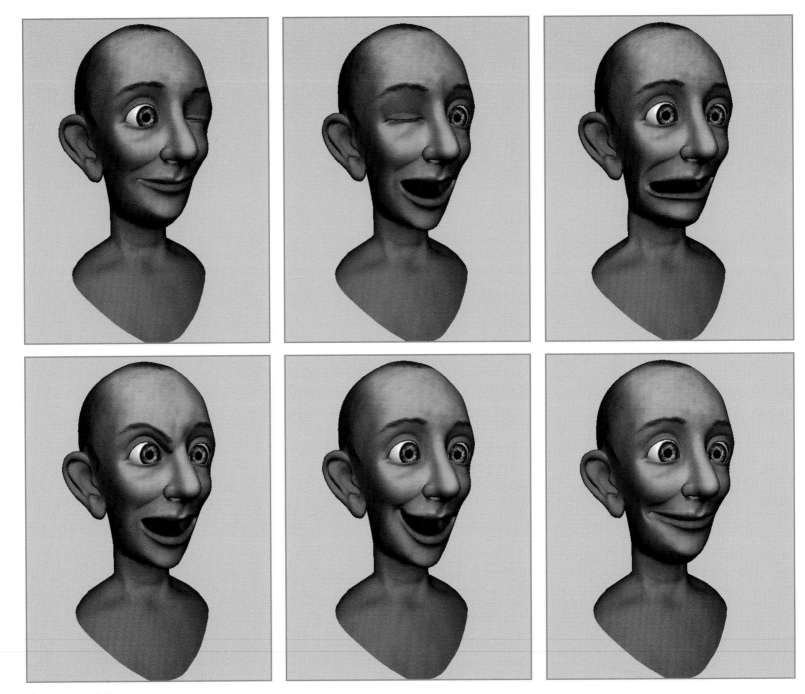

**Figures 13.42–13.47**
Localized blend shapes.

**13. Constructing the *Inspired* Character**

models used for production have more than 200 blend shapes modeled. The face shapes were broken down by region:

1. **Eyebrows, left, center, and right.** The shapes created for this region allowed the eyebrows to animate up and down, slide inward toward the center or out away from the center, and bow in the middle upward and downward. Shapes for the brow animate the eyebrows into even smaller regions: the left, right, and center for the left brow, and the left, right and center for the right brow.

2. **Eyelids, left and right.** The shapes made for the eyelids allowed for the eye to close, by pulling the upper lid down, and allowed the eye to squint, by pulling the upper and lower lids to meet in the center.

3. **Face (for broad shapes), left and right.** The face groups had shapes that animated the cheeks up and down, moved the cheeks in and out, and puffed the cheeks out and sucked them in. There was also some cheek deformation on broad mouth shapes, such as the dread, sneer, smirk, and grin.

4. **Mouth (the largest group), left, center, and right.** These shapes created simple as well as complex mouth movement. The simple movement includes moving the each lip up, down, curl in, curl out, corner up, corner down, corner side movement inward, corner side movement outward, and shapes that smoothed out the corners of the mouth.

   The complex shapes required the modeling of the frown, smile, furrowing, puckering, pouting, yawning, and kissing.

5. **Overall face shapes, localized by region.** These shapes simply used large areas of the face to accomplish a single task. This kind of approach is preferable when there is a specific target that the animator may want to hit with a single blend shape.

   These shapes include mouth smirk, mouth sneer, mouth dread, mouth wince, eye furrow, eye squint, and mouth smile.

   The mouth regions were extended to include the cheeks, and the eye regions were extended to include the forehead and eyebrows.

*Phonemes* are face shapes directly related to speech. Different theories exist as to which phonemes are required for animation of speech. Thirteen accepted shapes are recognized as *vismemes*, which are used in the creation of English speech. These shapes are as follows:

1. Closed mouth: P in pie, B in book, M in mother.
2. Pursed lips: W in wicked, OO in root.

3. Rounded lips, corners of the mouth slightly puckered: R at the beginning of a word, OO in book.
4. Lower lip drawn to upper teeth: V in victory, F in French.
5. Tongue between teeth with gaps on the side of the tongue: TH in think.
6. Tongue behind teeth with gaps on each side of tongue: L in look.
7. Relaxed mouth, mostly closed teeth, tongue visible behind the teeth: D in dog, T in tag, Z in zebra, S in sit, R in car, N in nothing.
8. Slightly open mouth, mostly closed teeth, corners of the lips slightly tightened: CHI in chime, JI in jive, SH in shy, VI in vision.
9. Slightly open mouth, mostly closed teeth: Y yawn, G in get, K in kitchen.
10. Wide mouth, slightly open lips: EA in meat, I in rip.
11. Neutral mouth, teeth slightly parted, jaw dropped slightly: E in bet, U in but, AI in bait.
12. Round lips, jaw dropped slightly: OA in toad, O in rope.
13. Open mouth, jaw dropped: A in math, O in shop.

For the list of shapes that would be modeled for this model, the phonemes were reduced to eight basic shapes:

1. Wide, slightly open lips: E in evening.
2. Round lips, jaw slightly open: O in oh, O in toast.
3. Round lips, corners of the mouth puckered: OO in book.
4. Closed mouth: P in pie, B in book.
5. Lower lip drawn to upper teeth: F in fine, V in vase.
6. Lips pursed: W in work.
7. Mouth open, tongue visible from inside mouth: T in tank, D in dog.
8. Relaxed mouth, mostly closed teeth, tongue visible behind the teeth: S in sit.

## Wire Deformer Rig for Face Shape Creation

For the purposes of creating a fast way to create blend shapes, I created a wire deformer rig. The wire deformer makes the creation of expressions very quick. By manipulating the points on the curves, I was able to move the surface of the skin in a very elastic, natural way.

Another thing that was working in my favor, in a big way, was that the model being manipulated was a low-resolution cage. This version of the model was very fast to edit, and the smoothed results always looked better than if the model had been edited in high-resolution.

**Figure 13.48**
Figure 13.48 indicates where the curves were drawn to create the wire deformers used to edit the model for blend shapes.

During the process of modeling blend shapes, the animation rig that had the jaw rotation skeleton was used to ensure that the rotation used for the blend shape jaw matched the rotation used by the jaw on the actual animation rig.

### Cleanup and Testing

The modeler needs to test and clean up blend shapes after making them. Testing blend shapes is a critical part of the modeling process. Many things can go wrong during the creation of blend shapes. Any time the model is exported from Maya in another format (like .obj) will scramble the order of the polygons in the model. Anything that affects polygon ordering will create many problems.

When testing the model, the modeler should be looking for technical problems as well as aesthetic problems. The technical problems will become evident quickly and require no additional discussion.

The aesthetic problems include the following:

1. Does the shape look natural? Does it look like a shape that would normally occur on the face?

2. Does the shape cause undesirable stretching and twisting? Most expressions on a real face do not cause too much stretching of the skin, but on a cartoon character, this is not the case. In extreme poses, there will be some stretching that needs to be dealt with, so the modeler needs to determine whether the stretching is acceptable or not.

3. Are the polygons distributed as evenly as possible for the blend shape? Uneven distribution of the polygonal topology will cause the geometry and textures to deform unnaturally. The skin in a character is an elastic sheet that covers the bones and muscles, so the modeler has to determine if that sheet is getting stretched too much in one place.

4. Test the final blend shapes with the hair, eyes and teeth in place. Are there any intersections of the skin surface with the hair, eyes, and teeth?

### UVs

In order to get the character rendered, the modeler needs to apply UV coordinates to the character. The process of editing UVs has a fairly straightforward goal: Will the texture artist be able to paint textures on this character that will not twist or deform unnaturally?

There are many methods for applying UVs. For this section, the basic application types will not be discussed. In order to texture this model, there were two primary methods employed in the application of UV coordinates. One method was used solely on the head, and the other method was used on the rest of the character.

When unfolding UVs on a model, several things need to be accomplished:

1. The spaces between the UV coordinates should have roughly the same size proportions as the polygons that the UVs are associated with. If the polygons in the eyelid area of a character are tightly packed together compared to the polygons on the side of the head, then the UV spaces in the eyelids should not be spread out either. Uniform application of texture coordinates depends on a uniform distribution of points relative to the original polygonal model.

2. UV coordinates have a tendency to get tangled up. The mesh of UV coordinates should be organized on the final model in such a way that it is clear that no tangled UVs are on the model.

3. UV coordinates should not overlap with other UV coordinates. When an orthographic texture-mapping scheme is used, the UVs on the front of a model will overlap with the UVs on the back of the model. If the texture that was being applied was a bullet hole that shot directly through the object, this would be fine. Otherwise, organic models should not have UV coordinates that overlap. Overlapping UVs duplicate texture in two or more areas of the

model. A common place that this occurs is the ear. The front of the ear will get a map that shows the detail of the ear, but the detail of the ear will often appear behind the ear as well if the coordinates are not taken care of.

4. The UV space of the UV coordinates should fall between the UV space ranging from 0 to 1. Many texture mapping programs allow for the distribution of texture space to fall well outside of these coordinates, and if the texture mapper knows what he or she is doing, this rule can be broken to increase efficiency. However, because paint programs paint maps that fall within the actual map and not outside the map's own parameterization, then using the parameterization of 0 to 1 will ensure that the map that is being painted will fit correctly.

## UV Editing Using Texture Maps

The best way to check to see if the UVs are working correctly is to preview the UV work using a texture map on the model. Different maps accomplish different things while unmeshing the UVs on a production model. These maps can be used in progression to work out the UV mapping issues one step at a time. The most common test maps, shown in progression, are:

1. **A Color and number grid.** These maps are useful in the initial unwrapping of UVs on a model. Several maps of this type are commonly available. The map shown in Figure 13.49 is a map I made in Photoshop in about 15 minutes. Maps like these are designed so no numeral (or letter, depending on the map) will fall in the same colored square twice throughout the map. This map has 10 numerals used 10 times each. The placement of the numerals in rows helps establish orientation while viewing the map on the model. The colors are more random but at the same time are somewhat organized diagonally, also helping to establish orientation.

   These maps are useful during the initial unwrapping stage because the unique pattern helps establish which areas are overlapping, are being repeated, or are twisted. Because each numeral or color combination only appears once, checking for repeating numeral or color blocks can help eliminate overlapping and tiling.

2. **Checkerboards or grids.** These maps are useful in getting the excessive twisting and deformation out of the UV set in a model. The colored grid can be distracting to view and can hide many problems associated with UV work. By using a less distracting pattern that has evenly spaced partitions, the modeler can check for twisting and stretching much more easily.

3. **Organic noise patterns.** The noise map is the acid test for fine-tuning the UVs so there is no stretching. By the time the noise map is applied, there should be no overlapping UVs or twisted UVs; the noise map will not be able to help identify those problems. The noise map does one thing, but it does it well. The noise map shows stretching.

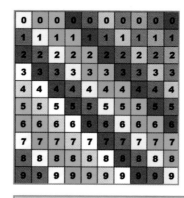

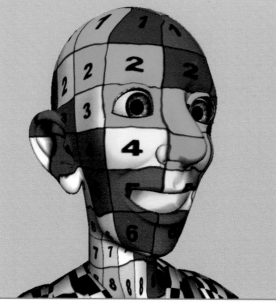

**Figures 13.49, 13.50**
The colored grid map used for unwrapping the UVs on an organic shape (top). The same map applied to the model (bottom).

In the example shown in Figure 13.54, the noise map is applied to the model. This map in Figure 13.54 was generated in Photoshop using the texturizer filter in about a minute. In previous tests, the mapping seemed fine, and the stretching was minimal. After the noise map is used, the stretching in the ear and across the nose is easily apparent (Figure 13.55).

The stretching inside the mouth is really out of control, but that is an area that will not be seen, so it will normally not have to be as accurately mapped and modeled as the rest of the head.

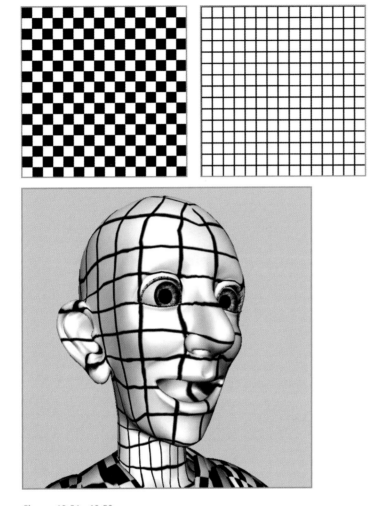

**Figures 13.51– 13.53**
Easy-to-read black-and-white maps used for unwrapping the UVs on an organic shape (top left, center). The grid map applied to the model (bottom).

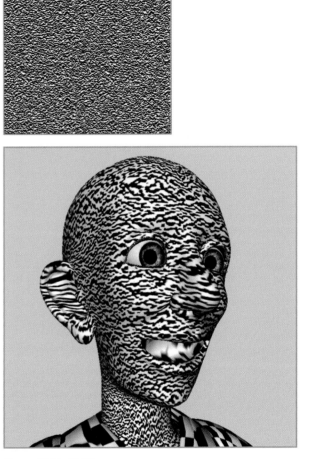

**Figures 13.54, 13.55**
A typical noise map (top). The noise map applied to the model (bottom).

It will be helpful to view these textures in real time so rendering is only used for a final test. Real-time texture viewing will speed up the UV editing process dramatically. Unfortunately, procedural textures do not update in real time; they can only be viewed using a software render. Most graphics cards are optimized to accept bitmapped or file-based textures. A file that has a grid or checkerboard in it can be assigned to the model, and the file-based texture will update in real time if the modeler is on a machine with a decent graphics card.

## Face: Relax

The face was done simply by starting with a cylindrical texture coordinate system. This provided a basis for unfolding the texture that allowed the small polygons in the eye area to remain small, and the large polygons on the side of the head to remain large.

From this starting point, the individual vertices were pulled manually within the UV texture editing window along the texture edges to line up with the UV borders, ensuring that the exterior vertices did not go beyond the 0 to 1 boundaries.

From that point, it was important to ensure that the overlapping areas within the ear, mouth, nose, and eye sockets were all flat and clean. This was done by pulling some of the points in these problem areas to the hidden interiors of these areas. The places in the eye socket, mouth, nostrils, and ear inner are safe places to hide a lot of things. The overlapping UVs in the eye socket were pulled to the center of the eye, the mouth interior was pulled to the interior of the mouth, and so forth.

The UVs inside the eye socket were selected in the 3-D modeling window (finding them in the texture editing window is too confusing). When the relax function was applied the these UVs, the UVs averaged themselves evenly within these safe zones. The head was split at the top because the hair would cover the top of the head, and I did not need to worry about matching the UVs in that area.

Other UVs that needed relaxing were also carefully selected in the modeling window and relaxed in the texture editing window. The fastest way to do a job like this is to simply grab all the UVs and relax them all at once. The problem with this method is that all the UV spaces are averaged out to be the same size. There will be excessive detail in areas that have smaller polygons and not enough detail where the polygons are spread out.

## Body Parts: UV by Hand

The body was a much simpler model in many ways. The problem with getting UVs on simple geometry like this is that there are no default methods for applying UVs to these polygonal shapes that will make the textures wrap onto them as easily at

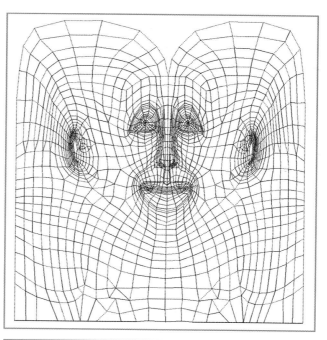

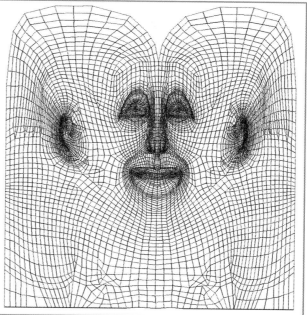

**Figures 13.56, 13.57**
UV coordinates for the low-resolution head (top). Subdivided polygons allowed the UVs to be transferred to the high-resolution head without any additional work (bottom).

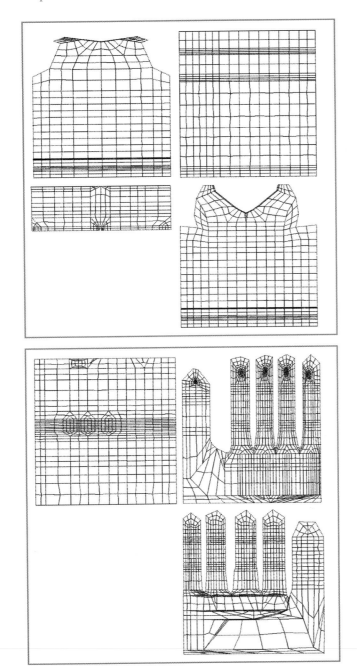

they would if there were NURBS shapes. It doesn't take long to texture map simple tubes if they are NURBS surfaces, because the parameterization is inherent in the surface itself. Using polygons to create these parts of the body posed an additional challenge of getting these parts to map smoothly.

For the most part, the application of UVs using a texture mapping tool was simply a formality. The texture coordinates for these body parts had to be completely modeled in the UV texture window to achieve uniform parameterization. Manually adjusting the UVs into this uniform configuration was a tedious task and took about as much time to do as the modeling of these simple body parts.

The completed UV work is shown in Figure 13.60. The checkerboard texture lines up evenly across the body, the legs, and the arms.

**Figure 13.60**
The completed work on the UVs.

**Figures 13.58, 13.59**
The UV coordinates for the shirt. Note the uniform parameterization along the front and back (top). The UV coordinates of the arms and hands (bottom).

## The Eyes

The eyes were mapped using a single map for the iris. The interesting part of this part of the character is the way the specularity had to be handled. I was trying to achieve a specific look, and using an anisotropic shader provided me the kind of specular sheen I was in search of. The problem with this was that the specularity spread all over the eyeball, causing it to look really glowy and weird. I used a specularity map to keep the shininess only in the iris—that was the end of the weird glowing eyeballs.

Every character model presents different challenges. When the production pipeline differs than the example shown here, different techniques should be employed for some of the steps illustrated here. The methods used in this tutorial to create blend shapes and texture UVs are very universal and are useful for all character models. The final model shown in Figure 13.62, shows the texture maps created by Lopsie Schwartz, the animation set up created by Michael Ford and Alan Lehman, the animation pose created by Kyle Clark, and the model and lighting that I created for the cover of the book.

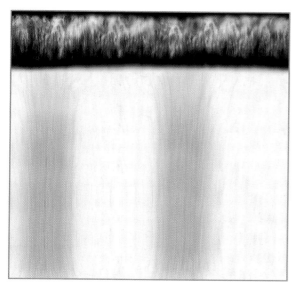

**Figure 13.61**
The texture map used for the iris.

**Figure 13.62**
The final model.

13. Constructing the *Inspired* Character

221

# Glossary

The following terms are defined with respect to their use in this book. More comprehensive glossaries of lighting and effects terms can be found in *Visual Effects in a Digital World*, by Karen Goulekas, and in *CG101*, by Terrence Masson.

## Symbols

**2D**. *See Two-Dimensional*.

**3D**. *See Three-Dimensional*.

## A

**Aim Vector**. The direction in which a constrained object is pointing toward the object it is constrained to.

**Algorithm**. A step-by-step procedure for solving a problem or accomplishing some end, especially by a computer.

**Animate**. Change or motion from frame to frame; to give life to.

**Animation Curve**. *See Function Curve*.

**Animation Supervisor**. The person who oversees the animation for a project.

**Anticipation**. An action that prepares the audience for a bigger motion in the opposite direction.

**Arc**. The curved path an object takes when moving between two points.

**Aspect Ratio**. The ratio of width/height of a an image plane.

**Attribute**. A parameter of an object that can be modified or animated.

**Axis**. A straight line passing through the origin that indicates direction in the coordinate space.

## B

**Background**. The part of the scene furthest away from the viewer.

**Bind Pose**. The pose that a skeleton is in when you create a rigid or smooth bind.

**Binding Skin (Skinning)**. Attaching surfaces (or lattices that control surfaces) to joints so that the skeleton will deform the object(s).

**Biped**. A creature that walks on two legs (humans, kangaroos, monsters, robots, and so on).

**Bones**. A visual extension of joints when joints are in a hierarchy.

**Bounding Box**. A box that just contains the object with which it is associated. Used to represent the object's spatial limits.

## C

**Camera**. Object that determines what is captured in an image, and through which action is viewed.

**Cartesian Coordinate System**. A system in which a point is located in space by a set of three coordinates representing the distance along three mutually perpendicular axes usually labeled X, Y, and Z.

**CG Supervisor**. *See Computer Graphics Supervisor.*

**Chain**. A series of joints in a hierarchy.

**Channels**. The animatable attributes of an object. Animation is created when one or more channel values change over time.

**Character Rig**. The internal skeleton and controls that allow you to manipulate and animate a character.

**Cheat**. A technique used to sell an action or object in which obvious flaws are hidden from the camera view.

**Child**. An object in a hierarchy that is connected beneath another and inherits the information of the object above it.

**Cluster Deformer**. A cluster deformer is a node that allows you to control an object's points (CVs, vertices, or lattice points), enabling you to have animation channels on an object at the component level.

**Component**. The individual pieces that create the geometry in the shape nodes, including vertices, edges, hulls, faces, edit points.

**Computer Graphics Supervisor**. The person responsible for the quality and efficiency of the 3D work on a project.

**Constraint**. Generally a direct connection of attributes on one object to the corresponding attributes on another object.

**Construction History**. The information concerning all of the operations performed on an object, including how it was created and deformed.

**Continuity**. Seamless assembly and natural flow of scenes with respect to time, space, color and direction.

**Contrast**. The ratio of bright to dark values in an image.

**Control Vertice**. A NURBS control point that allows you to alter the shape of the surface.

**Coordinate Space**. The location in 3D space as defined by the X, Y, and Z axis.

**Counter Animation**. Altering a section of a character or object in response to its influence from an object above it in the hierarchy.

**Curve**. *See Function Curve.*

**CV**. *See Control Vertice.*

**Cycle**. An animation that can seamlessly repeat an infinite number of times.

# D

**DAG**. Directed Acyclic Graph, the contents of scene hierarchy in Maya.

**Dailies**. The daily screening of the previous day's work for review by directors and supervisors.

**Default Pose**. A neutral position for a character that serves as a starting point to begin rigging.

**Deformable Object**. Any type of object that has control points.

**Deformation Order**. When placing deformers on a surface, the deformation order determines which deformers will be evaluated first by the software. This becomes critical when using multiple deformers, such as a blend shape with a skinned surface.

**Deformer**. An object that deforms or change other objects.

**Dependency Loop**. A feedback error expressed by Maya when evaluating a connection. The dependency arises in that an attribute cannot be controlled by an attribute that it is controlling.

**Depth of Field**. The range of distances in front of a camera in which objects will remain in focus.

**DG**. Dependency Graph. A visual connection of an object's attributes to other nodes in the scene as represented in the Hypergraph.

**Digital Effects Supervisor**. The person who is responsible for all of the digital effects on a production.

**Digitize**. The encoding of 2D or 3D data from a physical model or drawing to create an accurate representation in the computer.

**Direct Skinning Deformers**. Deformers which use skeletons to control any type of object that has control points.

**Director**. Person responsible for creating the final realization of the production.

**Director of Photography (Cinematographer).** The person responsible for all lighting and photography on a production.

**Displacement Map.** An image mapped to an object in which the color channel values in a given pixel are used to represent a direction and amplitude in which to transform that point on the object.

**Dopesheet.** An animation editor in which keyframes are represented by individual bars that can be moved and scaled in time.

**Double Transformations.** When a point is subjected to a deformer's action twice. An example would be if you skinned an object to a joint and then put a lattice on the same object and parented that lattice directly under the same joint chain. The object would translate once from the skinning operation, and then a second time because of the lattice.

**D.P.** *See Director of Photography.*

# E

**Ease In.** The gradual speeding up of an object as it begins moving from a resting state.

**Ease Out.** The gradual slowing of an object as it begins moving toward a resting state.

**Edge.** A straight line between two vertices on a polygonal object.

**Element.** An individual part of a scene, character, or image that is combined with others.

**Envelope.** Specifies the weight value of the deformer's influence, from 0 to 1.

**Euler Rotation.** Rotations around three axes, X, Y, and Z, which are evaluated in a determined order (XYZ, YZX, ZXY, and so on).

**Exposure Sheet.** *See X-sheet.*

**Expression.** A mathematical formula, given to an object or attribute, that automatically performs an operation.

# F

**Falloff.** A gradual tapering of an effect from stronger to weaker or vice versa.

**Field of View.** The horizontal or vertical angle viewed through the camera lens.

**Final.** A shot that has been approved as complete by the director.

**FK.** *See Forward Kinematics.*

**Focal Distance.** The distance from the camera image/film plane at which there is sharpest focus.

**Focus.** 1) The emphasis of the scene or image. 2) The adjustment on a camera to set the distance that appears sharpest in view.

**Forward Kinematics.** Method of animating skeletons in which each bone is individually rotated.

**Frame.** A single image in a sequence.

**Frame Range.** The set of contiguous frames. A start frame and end frame.

**Frame Rate.** The rate at which frames are played back to produce moving pictures; for example, 24 frames per second for 35mm film.

**Function Curve.** A graphical representation of the computer's interpolation between key frames; often referred to as simply a *curve*.

**Function Curve Editor.** *See Graph Editor.*

# G

**Geometry.** Either a NURBS surface, a NURBS curve, or a polygonal surface.

**Gesture.** The positioning of a character to express an emotion or thought.

**Gimbal Lock.** The convergence of true rotation axes of an object.

**Global.** Manipulates an object with an axis of the same orientation as the world, regardless of the hierarchy.

**Graph Editor.** Animation editor in which motion and time are manipulated through modification of spline curves.

**Ground Plane.** The reference surface in a scene indicating the floor. Often used to receive shadows.

**GUI.** *See (UI) User Interface.*

## H

**Handles.** The control points that modify the tangents in the Function Curve Editor.

**Hardware Render.** A rendering process that uses the computer hardware's graphics card to quickly create shaded images or frames.

**Hierarchy.** A series of nodes that are connected to each other in a parent-child relationship.

**High-res.** High resolution. Often used to describe the resolution of a character's geometry.

**Hotkeys.** User-defined shortcuts assigned to keys on the keyboard that are used to automate frequently used tasks and increase workflow.

## I

**Icon.** A small image used to represent a file, window, command, or program.

**Iconic Controllers.** Curves used to control a character rig.

**IK.** *See Inverse Kinematics.*

**Image Plane.** The planar area in the camera onto which the image is focused by the lens.

**In-Between.** A pose created between two extreme or "key" poses in a scene. Used to control timing and arcs as a character transitions from key frame to key frame.

**Interest.** The focus or target of the viewer or camera.

**Interpolation.** Calculation of intermediate values between two or more previously determined values.

**Inverse Kinematics.** Method of animating skeletons in which the computer solves the bending of a joint, such as an elbow or knee, based on the position of one object, usually an IK Handle.

## J

**Joint.** The building block of a skeleton that determines the pivot point of a bone.

## K

**Keyframe.** A frame at which important position, rotation, scaling, intensity, blur size, and so on are saved to preserve and define the movement or performance of an animated object or character.

**Key Light.** The primary light source illuminating a scene.

**Kinematics.** The mechanics of motion.

## L

**Lattice.** A structure of points for carrying out free-form deformations on any deformable object.

**Local Rotation Axis.** The direction an object will rotate when rotated in local mode.

**Local Space.** An alignment of the transform axis to the parent of the object.

**Looping.** Playing an animation repeatedly.

**Low-res.** Low resolution. Often used to describe the resolution of a character's geometry.

## M

**Manipulator.** A control handle used to alter objects' transforms in 3D space.

**Maquette.** A small-scale practical model used as a 3D reference for character design.

**Marquee Select.** To click and drag over an object(s) in order to select the object(s).

**Match.** *See Matchmove.*

**Matchmove.** The process of extracting the frame-by-frame camera and/or object motion from a live action plate by hand/eye so that computer-generated elements appear to move properly in the scene.

**MEL.** Maya Embedded Language, the scripting language of Maya.

**Membership Set.** Generally a collection of points in a deformer set, such as all of the points on a surface controlled by one cluster.

**Motion Blur.** The smearing of an object in an image based on its motion relative to the camera. As the shutter exposes the film for a specific period of time, any motion occurring during that period is captured in a single frame.

# N

**Node.** A representation of an object or set of objects in which all information for that object(s) is referenced.

**Normal.** *See Surface Normal.*

**Normalize.** To linearly convert values to a range between zero and one.

**Null Node.** A transform node that contains no surface or object.

**NURBS (Non Uniform Rational B-Spline).** A surface or curve controlled by CVs.

# O

**Object.** Any entity in a scene.

**Object Space.** The result of an object's transform in addition to the hierarchy above it.

**Origin.** The center of world space; the point at which all world space coordinates are at zero.

# P

**Pan.** Rotation of the camera around its vertical axis.

**Parallax.** The apparent difference in position of an object seen by each individual eye.

**Parent.** 1) To attach a node above another in a hierarchy. 2) The node directly above another in a hierarchy.

**Parse.** To execute part or a segment of a script. Parsing is valuable when you're creating or debugging a script because it allows you to track down errors by limiting the amount of code that is executed.

**Path.** A line used to control an object's direction and speed of movement.

**Pick Walk.** Method of selecting objects in a hierarchy or control points in order by using the arrow keys on a keyboard.

**Pipeline.** A sequence of steps defining the workflow of a show or series of shots from conception to final output.

**Pivot Point.** The location from which an object will rotate.

**Pixel.** The smallest discrete unit in a digital image.

**Plate.** Selected film footage scanned into the computer for use in digital compositing.

**Plug-in.** An additional piece of software which can be integrated to existing software to enhance capabilities and features.

**Pole Vector.** An element of a rotation plane IK handle that enables one to change the joint chains orientation.

**Pose.** The gesture or posture of a character at a given time.

**Prefix.** Organizational words or characters placed at the beginning of file or element names. For example: `Scene1_anim_v1`.

**Prop.** An object in a scene that remains static or with which a character interacts.

**Proxy.** A low-resolution stand–in image or object used to increase interactivity.

# Q

**Quaternion.** A rotation value derived through a mathematical equation that uses four numbers. A rotation system that uses quaternion values will avoid gimbal lock but cannot be represented on a graph with X, Y, and Z function curves.

# R

**Real Time.** Relating to actual time, where 24 frames will play in one second on your computer.

**Rendering.** The process of calculating an image from all scene information (cameras, objects, materials, lights, and so on).

**Resolution.** The horizontal and vertical number of pixels used to define an image.

**Reverse Hierarchy.** Reversing the hierarchical order of control on a chain of objects.

**Rig.** Any geometrical architecture designed to place and control nodes.

**Right-Handed Coordinate System.** The coordinate system most often used in computer graphics, where the positive X-axis points east, the positive Y axis points upward, and the Z axis points south. So named because, with the right hand opened and thumb extended, the index finger points down X, the palm faces Y, and the thumb points in Z.

**Rigid Bind.** A direct skin deformer, similar to clusters in that a single control point is assigned and controlled by a single joint.

**Roll.** Rotation of the camera along its viewing axis.

**Root Joint.** The highest joint in a chain's hierarchy. There can be only one root joint in a chain.

**Rotation.** Changing an object's rotation in world space.

**Rotation Order.** Specifies which axis rotates first, second, and last when an object's rotation occurs one axis at a time.

**Rotoscope.** The process of creating mattes or animation for each frame of a sequence of images by tracing the object by hand.

# S

**Scene.** The contents of a file that contain all of the data that is created in a software package.

**Scrubbing/Scrub.** The process of viewing animation by clicking the left mouse button and dragging the time slider at the desired rate.

**Sequence.** A series of related shots and scenes.

**Sequence Supervisor.** The person responsible for quality and continuity of work created for a particular sequence.

**Serpentine.** A curved line that crosses an imaginary straight line more than twice.

**Set.** *See Membership Set.*

**Settings.** Information about the working environment, such as any units of measurement, playback speed, frame range, and so on.

**SGI.** 1) A computer manufactured by Silicon Graphics, Inc. 2) An 8-bit RGBA image storage format (.sgi extension).

**Shape Node.** The child of a transform node; this is where the geometry information is stored.

**Shot.** A single camera view of action without interruption.

**Sibling.** An object that shares the same parent.

**Skinning.** The process of attaching geometry to bones, allowing the geometry to deform based on the movements of the joints.

**Smooth Bind.** A direct skin deformer that allows several joints to influence the same deformable object points.

**Space.** *See Coordinate Space.*

**Spline.** A curve using control vertices (not necessarily on the curve) to define its shape. Types of splines include Bezier, B-spline (generalized Bezier-spline), non-periodic B-spline, uniform B-spline, NURBS (non-uniform rational B-spline), and Hermite-spline.

**Squash and Stretch.** The modification of an object to indicate impact or acceleration.

**Storyboard.** A series of drawings illustrating the key moments in a scene, sequence, or film.

**Subject.** The person or object being photographed.

**Suffix.** Words or characters placed at the end of object or file names.

**Surface Normal.** A vector defined at each point on a surface and oriented in the direction furthest away from that point.

# T

**Take.** The filming of a scene. Each time a scene is re-shot is a new take.

**TD.** *See Technical Director.*

**Technical Director.** The person in charge of rendering and combining the elements of a computer graphics shot. The definition of this term varies among different studios from a pure graphics programmer to a pure 2D artist.

**Texture Map.** An image mapped to an object to define its color and opacity.

**Three-Dimensional (3D).** Having dimensions in width, height, and depth. A 3D object can be rendered from different viewing angles.

**Tilt**. Rotation of the camera around its lateral axis.

**Timing**. How long an object or character takes to perform an action.

**Top Node**. The highest node in a hierarchy.

**Torso**. The portion of a character above the waist, excluding the arms, neck and head.

**Track**. *See Tracking*.

**Tracking**. Recording the position (2D or 3D) of a particular feature for every frame of a shot. 2D tracking results in the pixel positions per frame. 3D tracking results in the camera and object positions and camera settings per frame.

**Transformations**. The operations of translating, rotating, or scaling.

**Translation**. Changing an object's position in world space.

**Turntable**. A render test of a CG object rotated in front of the camera and used to evaluate modeling and textures.

**Tweak**. 1) To adjust. 2) An adjustment.

**Two-Dimensional**. Constrained to a plane having dimensions in only width and height; can only be viewed orthogonally.

# U

**UI** (User Interface). Either Graphical or Command Line environment in which commands are executed.

**UNIX**. A computer operating system developed by AT&T/Bell Laboratories.

# V

**Vector**. A magnitude with direction usually defined by an X, Y and Z value. The magnitude is the distance from the location (X, Y, Z) from the origin (0,0,0). The direction is the direction from the origin to the location.

**Vertex**. A point in 3D space used to define an edge or curve.

**Visual Effects Supervisor**. The person responsible for all visual effects utilizing any technique required to best realize the director's vision.

# W

**Wireframe**. The basic representation of an object in a 3D environment excluding all shading, lighting, and texture information.

# X

**X-sheet**. Used to plan animation. Contains columns to record dialogue, scene notes, frame counts, and camera movement.

# Z

**Zero Out**. The process of returning all objects and attributes to their default, or "zero" positions.

# Index

Index